BUILDING

ARCHITECTURAL & INTERIOR DESIGN

MODELS *FAST!*

Written and Illustrated by

G. Matthew Buckles

Belpine Publishing Company

P.O. Box 2291 Rancho Cucamonga, CA 91729-2291

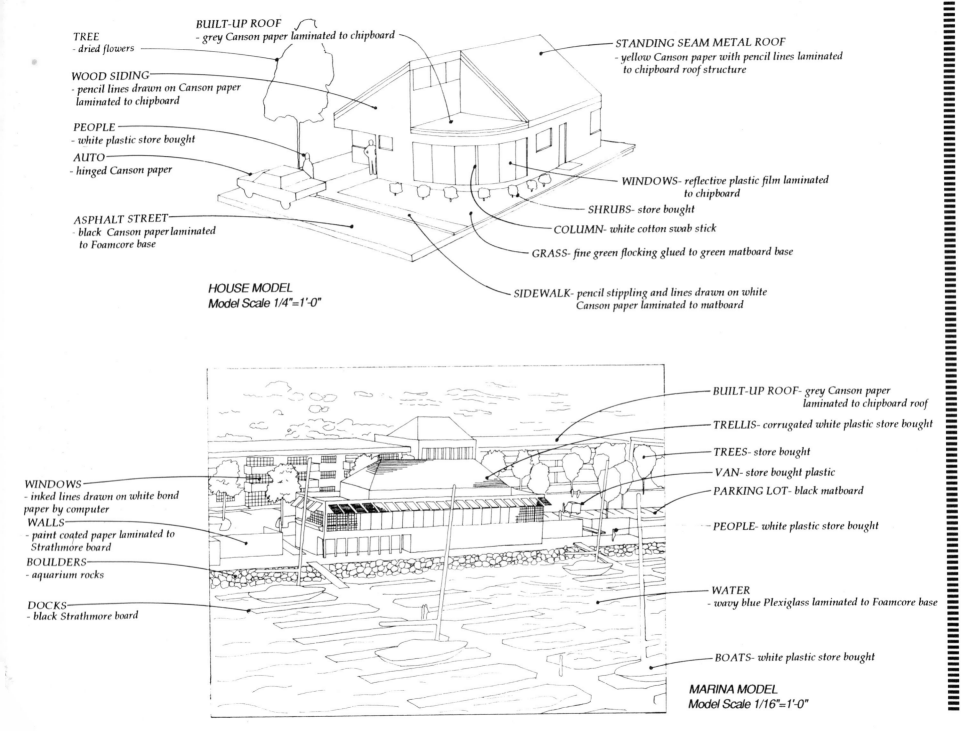

TREE
- dried flowers

BUILT-UP ROOF
- grey Canson paper laminated to chipboard

STANDING SEAM METAL ROOF
- yellow Canson paper with pencil lines laminated to chipboard roof structure

WOOD SIDING
- pencil lines drawn on Canson paper laminated to chipboard

PEOPLE
- white plastic store bought

AUTO
- hinged Canson paper

WINDOWS- reflective plastic film laminated to chipboard

SHRUBS- store bought

COLUMN- white cotton swab stick

ASPHALT STREET
- black Canson paper laminated to Foamcore base

GRASS- fine green flocking glued to green matboard base

SIDEWALK- pencil stippling and lines drawn on white Canson paper laminated to matboard

HOUSE MODEL
Model Scale 1/4"=1'-0"

BUILT-UP ROOF- grey Canson paper laminated to chipboard roof

TRELLIS- corrugated white plastic store bought

TREES- store bought

VAN- store bought plastic

PARKING LOT- black matboard

PEOPLE- white plastic store bought

WINDOWS
- inked lines drawn on white bond paper by computer

WALLS
- paint coated paper laminated to Strathmore board

BOULDERS
- aquarium rocks

WATER
- wavy blue Plexiglass laminated to Foamcore base

DOCKS
- black Strathmore board

BOATS- white plastic store bought

MARINA MODEL
Model Scale 1/16"=1'-0"

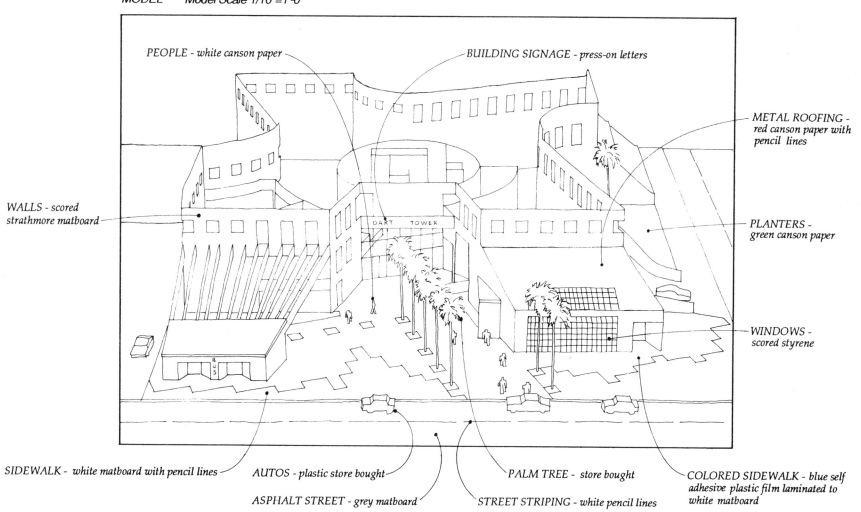

MODEL   Model Scale 1/16"=1'-0"

PEOPLE - white canson paper

BUILDING SIGNAGE - press-on letters

METAL ROOFING - red canson paper with pencil lines

WALLS - scored strathmore matboard

DART TOWER

PLANTERS - green canson paper

WINDOWS - scored styrene

SIDEWALK - white matboard with pencil lines

AUTOS - plastic store bought

PALM TREE - store bought

COLORED SIDEWALK - blue self adhesive plastic film laminated to white matboard

ASPHALT STREET - grey matboard

STREET STRIPING - white pencil lines

BUILDING ARCHITECTURAL AND INTERIOR DESIGN MODELS FAST! Copyright 1991 by G. Matthew Buckles. Printed and bound in the United States of America.

Published by Belpine Publishing Company, P.O. Box 2291, Rancho Cucamonga, California 91729 - 2291.

ISBN 0-9629294-4-1

Contents

Acknowledgments

George Bird
Dina Bruu
Delores Buckles
Gloria Buckles
Robert Buckles
Feola Deenihan Archuleta Architects
Safi Ishrati
Roger Jinks
S. Kim
Chris Larson
Christopher Mayes
Mauricio Oberfeld
Tim Spence
Lindy Zichichi

CHAPTER 6
Constructing Scaled Building Components

CHAPTER 7
Constructing Scaled Landscape Components

Introduction

This book was written to assist designers in expressing their creative concepts. Its level of communication is geared to the first time model builder whether they are a design student or working professional, who is relatively familiar with design terms and drafting tools. It describes in detail both graphically and narratively how to construct architectural and interior design models. The construction methods utilize only drafting tools; no power tools are needed. The entire model can be built at your drafting table with results equal to those of a professional model maker utilizing thick plastics and power tools.

CHAPTER ONE describes various types of models and goes on to explain their individual roles in the design process. Each is built for a specific function to correlate with the various types of drawings produced during the design process. This marriage of three dimensional forms with two dimensional graphics is the best possible means of producing a well thought-out design solution.

CHAPTER TWO describes in a narrative and graphic form the fastest means of constructing a schematic study model. Since design students have little spare time in their busy academic schedules,they can appreciate any methods for saving time. Some of the techniques may seem simple and even self-explanatory, but then no time is wasted in experimentation. In this Chapter we will go through the step-by-step process of constructing a one story house model that you can build for practice, or that you can follow while building your own design. The construction methods apply to all building types.

CHAPTER THREE deals with making revisions to your schematic study model. We will look at the fastest methods of increasing and decreasing a window opening, moving a wall, and removing a roof. Since the purpose of a schematic model is to convey your building design during the design process, you must learn how to revise it quickly and cleanly just as you would your plans and elevations.

CHAPTER FOUR describes the different model construction materials and their uses. Various types of cardboards, matboards, papers, knives, glues and plastics are discussed in a narrative and graphic form.

CHAPTER FIVE takes you away from model building techniques for a moment to discuss the theory behind model making: 'thinking to scale'. In order to produce professional results, you must visualize how the building materials can best be simulated at the scale of the model. For example, the matboard finish and thickness must be considered to properly represent your model walls. Scaled objects such as people, cars, and trees must also be considered to give the model a discernable scale. You will learn how to visualize in model form your building design so that it can best be represented in a three-dimensional manner.

CHAPTER SIX describes techniques for constructing many of the most common building components. Construction methods for various types of columns, beams, walls, floors, roofs, skylights, trellises, space frames and stairs at various scales will be described in a step-by-step graphic form. This Chapter will be very helpful to you for future model building.

CHAPTER SEVEN deals with techniques for constructing the most common outdoor landscape components. Decks, patios, trees, fences, grass, ground covers, flowers, lakes, ponds, oceans, fountains, cars, parking lots, boats, planes and people are discussed and depicted at various scales.

I recommend that you first read CHAPTERS ONE, FOUR and FIVE to get familiar with model types and materials prior to performing any procedures. You can then go directly to Chapter 2 and begin building the model. If time permits, you may want to read the entire book once all the way through to get familiar with terms and procedures before starting your model. But this is not necessary if you need to start construction immediately.

After reading and working with this book I hope that you will have more confidence in your model making abilities. I hear so often from design students that they are "no good" at model making. I believe that they feel this way because they have not built enough models to gain the self confidence necessary to enjoy model building. This book will eliminate much of the experimentation necessary for the beginning model maker and enable them to produce professional results much faster. Good luck and be persistent.

G. Matthew Buckles

CHAPTER 1
Model Types

The design model, whether intended for architectural, interior or engineering purposes, is a three-dimensional representation of your concept, and should be an integral part of the design process. The three phases of development comprising the 'design process' are: conceptual, schematic and design development. A series of models should be built in correlation with the two-dimensional drawings throughout the design process. These two are shown graphically to the right.

A models' classification depends on what purpose it is to serve, whether it is to convey a design concept to your instructor and classmates, or a finished product to a client. For our purposes of describing model building techniques, the classifications will be defined as: CONCEPTUAL, SCHEMATIC STUDY and FINAL PRESENTATION.

These three classifications of models are intertwined with each other in their purpose and, in the case of the schematic and final presentation models, can be altered to serve the purpose of another.

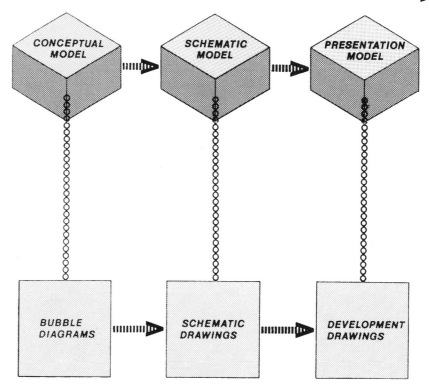

THE DESIGN PROCESS

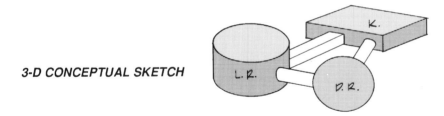

2-D BUBBLE DIAGRAM

3-D CONCEPTUAL SKETCH

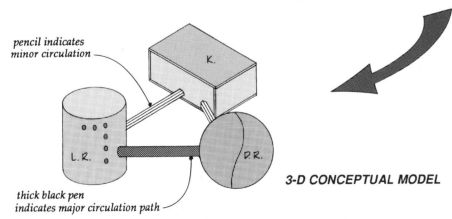

*pencil indicates
minor circulation*

3-D CONCEPTUAL MODEL

*thick black pen
indicates major circulation path*

THE 3-DIMENSIONAL DESIGN PROCESS

CONCEPTUAL MODEL

The conceptual model is a three dimensional representation of a two dimensional conceptual bubble diagram. The model can be as abstract as circulation forms penetrating nodes and focal points, or as literal as corridors leading to rooms. The model has no specific scale but must relate to the bubble diagrams in their proportioning and importance of the spaces.

Conceptual Model Purpose

The main purpose of a conceptual model is to express a design idea in a three dimensional form, and should be constructed in correlation with the two dimensional bubble diagrams. As in the bubble diagrams, the different rooms would be considered as different spaces with different functions and would therefore be expressed in dissimilar manners. For example, in our sample house design, the living room will be constructed in a larger and different manner than the dining room or kitchen.

The materials used for building a conceptual model can be anything you choose in order to express your ideas. Common items such as aerosol can caps, tennis balls, ping-pong balls, apples, oranges and plastic bottles can serve as focal points and rooms. Items such as pencils, pens, cardboard tubes and tapes can serve as circulation modes. The choice is up to you.

Conceptual Model Scale and Color

Since there is no specific scale or required shape that will put the conceptual model into literal terms, you as the sculptor are free to do anything you desire to express your ideas. But, you must keep in mind that the size proportioning of the objects representing rooms and spaces need to relate with each other in the same manner as bubbles in the bubble diagrams. The bubbles vary in size depending upon their importance. The living room may be simply a tin can with holes poked in it to simulate daylighting, while the dining room is represented by a tennis ball of smaller proportions. You have complete freedom to do anything you want.

Color on a conceptual model expresses the importance of focal points and circulation in the same manner that size proportioning does. Two spaces of equal size and shape can be differentiated by painting one of them a bright red or yellow, thus making that space more important than the other. Just as in our society where differing colors invoke different emotions and reactions, the same can be done on the model. For example, red 'demands' attention, while black invokes mystery. Listed below are some colors and the emotions they express.

RED .... Attention
YELLOW. .... Caution
BLUE .... Passive
GREY .... Neutral
BLACK .... Mysterious
WHITE .... Pristine

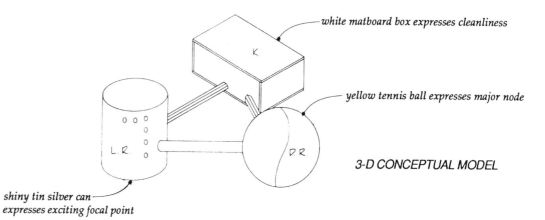

The conceptual model components should relate proportionally with the 2-D bubble diagrams.

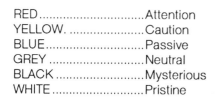

white matboard box expresses cleanliness

yellow tennis ball expresses major node

3-D CONCEPTUAL MODEL

shiny tin silver can expresses exciting focal point

Color on a conceptual model expresses the importance of nodes and focal points.

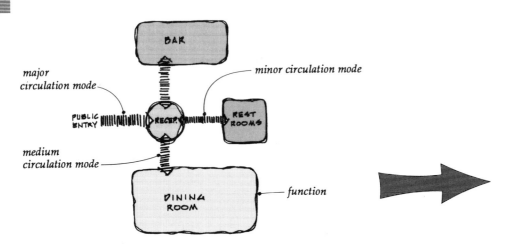

major circulation mode

minor circulation mode

PUBLIC ENTRY

RECEP.

BAR

REST ROOMS

medium circulation mode

function

DINING ROOM

BUBBLE DIAGRAM (PUBLIC)

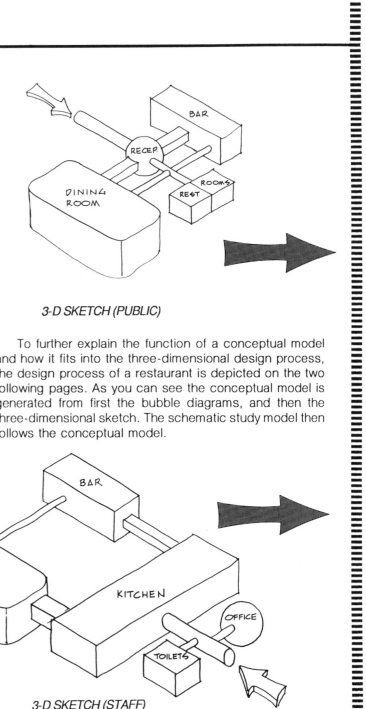

3-D SKETCH (PUBLIC)

THE 3-D DESIGN PROCESS

To further explain the function of a conceptual model and how it fits into the three-dimensional design process, the design process of a restaurant is depicted on the two following pages. As you can see the conceptual model is generated from first the bubble diagrams, and then the three-dimensional sketch. The schematic study model then follows the conceptual model.

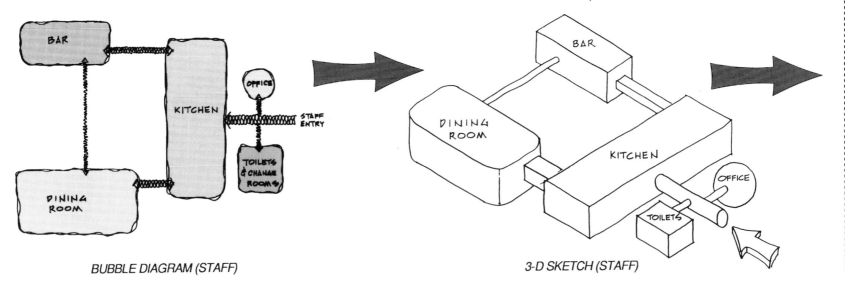

BUBBLE DIAGRAM (STAFF)

3-D SKETCH (STAFF)

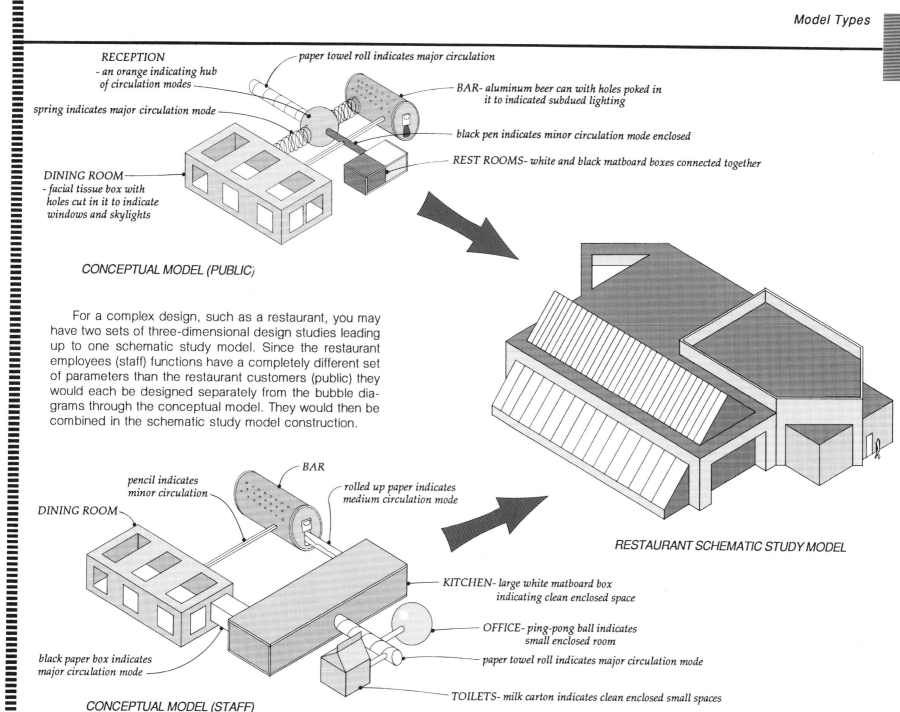

RECEPTION
- an orange indicating hub of circulation modes

paper towel roll indicates major circulation

BAR- aluminum beer can with holes poked in it to indicated subdued lighting

spring indicates major circulation mode

black pen indicates minor circulation mode enclosed

REST ROOMS- white and black matboard boxes connected together

DINING ROOM
- facial tissue box with holes cut in it to indicate windows and skylights

CONCEPTUAL MODEL (PUBLIC)

For a complex design, such as a restaurant, you may have two sets of three-dimensional design studies leading up to one schematic study model. Since the restaurant employees (staff) functions have a completely different set of parameters than the restaurant customers (public) they would each be designed separately from the bubble diagrams through the conceptual model. They would then be combined in the schematic study model construction.

RESTAURANT SCHEMATIC STUDY MODEL

pencil indicates minor circulation

BAR

rolled up paper indicates medium circulation mode

DINING ROOM

KITCHEN- large white matboard box indicating clean enclosed space

OFFICE- ping-pong ball indicates small enclosed room

black paper box indicates major circulation mode

paper towel roll indicates major circulation mode

TOILETS- milk carton indicates clean enclosed small spaces

CONCEPTUAL MODEL (STAFF)

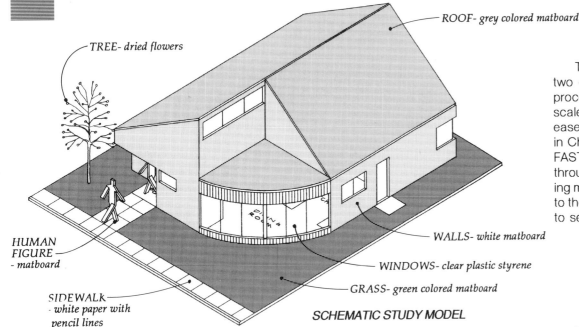

TREE- *dried flowers*

ROOF- *grey colored matboard*

HUMAN
FIGURE
- *matboard*

SIDEWALK
- *white paper with
pencil lines*

WALLS- *white matboard*

WINDOWS- *clear plastic styrene*

GRASS- *green colored matboard*

SCHEMATIC STUDY MODEL

SCHEMATIC STUDY MODEL

The schematic study model is constructed during the two dimensional schematic drawing phase of the design process. It is built to a specific architectural or engineering scale and should be the same scale as the drawings for ease of construction. This is the type of model described in Chapter 2 on "HOW TO BUILD A SCHEMATIC MODEL FAST". The study model is constructed and revised quickly throughout the design process, with window openings being made larger or smaller and walls being moved according to the design changes. The model can ultimately be revised to serve as the final presentation model.

Study Model Purpose

The purpose of a schematic study model is exactly as the name implies, a STUDY model. It is built to see the proportioning of masses and voids, and the spaces implied by them. Therefore, the walls and other components of the model should be removable for repositioning. It should be literal enough to express walls and windows at an appropriate scale, but not so literal as to express building materials.

Study Model Scale

It should be noted that the larger the scale of the model, the easier it is for the eye to see proper proportioning and details. Generally, architectural and interior design models are built at either 1/8" or 1/4"=1'-0" scale. Smaller scales are used for site models. But the most important factor to remember is that the larger the scale of the model, the longer it will take to build. A 1/4" scale model will take approximately twice as many hours to build as a 1/8" model.

SCHEMATIC FLOOR PLAN

*floor plan
print*

*green colored
matboard*

MODEL BASEBOARD

The scale of the model should be at the same scale as the schematic drawings for ease of construction.

If the model is built at the same scale as the schematic drawings much time can be saved by simply transferring the elevations and floor plans onto the selected model material (chipboard, Strathmore, matboard, etc.). Transferring involves photocopying or blueprinting your design drawings and attaching them to the selected board with spray adhesive. This procedure saves a lot of time, since the elevations and floor plans do not have to be drawn again onto the board. The walls and roof are cut out with a utility knife and the photocopy paper is removed. Small traces of glue may remain on the board, and is acceptable on a schematic study model. The thickness of the board selected for the model walls must relate to the model scale. Generally the walls of a building are approximately 6" thick, so therefore the walls on a 1/8"= 1'-0" scale model need to be 1/16" thick for an exact representation. But this thickness of matboard is very difficult and time consuming to cut. It is much faster and more appropriate to use a thinner board for schematic study models. Save the 1/16" thickness for final presentation models where exact detailing is required. (See Chapter Four for more detailed information on matboard types).

So the scale of the model is determined by: (1) the scale of your schematic drawings, (2) the amount of time available to build the model, and (3) the thickness of your model walls.

Foamcore board is recommended for walls on 1/4" scale models and larger.

The thickness of the model walls must be considered when selecting the scale.

Study Model Workmanship

The workmanship of a study model is usually rough and messy by the time the final design has been decided upon, since it has been revised several times. Window openings and walls are relocated to ultimately achieve the proper proportioning of masses and voids. (See Chapter 3 for making model revisions). Neatness is not the main objective of a study model, a well thought out expression of your design concept is.

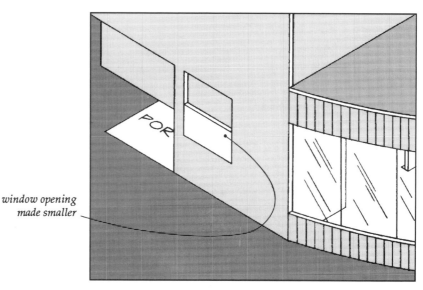

window opening made smaller

The schematic study model is usually rough and messy due to the revisions, yet it expresses your design concept.

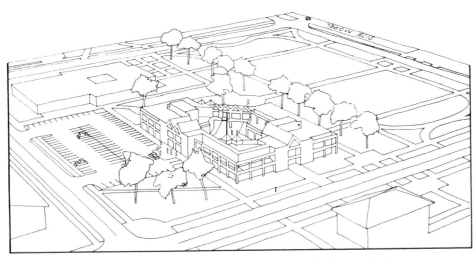

white matboard walls

colored matboard base

The model 'reads' better if the intersecting planes are of different colors or shades.

Study Model Color

Color and material indications are not usually applied to a schematic study model, with the exception of the baseboard and roof. While useful on conceptual or final presentation models, color becomes distracting on a study model where the main objective is to express the design intent. It is recommended that the entire model be constructed using only two colors or shades. The visual definition between two intersecting planes, such as a wall and floor, is much easier to 'read' if they are of differing shades. An all white model constructed of only white Strathmore board, or an all grey model of chipboard, lacks the differing light values necessary for 'reading' the model. A combination of two or more shades is most desirable, making all vertical planes (walls) one color and all horizontal planes (floors and roofs) another.

FINAL PRESENTATION MODEL

The final presentation model is built at the end of the design process, after the design development drawings are complete. All design decisions should be worked out by this time in order to avoid unsightly and time-consuming mistakes. Therefore it is best to finish the presentation drawings first so that any last minute design changes can be made on paper instead of the model.

The final presentation model is presented to the client along with the final presentation design drawings. The model generally has color, building material indications, and scale figures to simulate the actual proposed building as realistically as possible. The scale should be the same as the schematic drawings.

The final presentation model is built to accompany the design development drawings and is usually as literal as possible.

Transforming a Study Model into a Final Presentation Model

A schematic study model can also be altered to serve as a final presentation model. If care is taken while constructing and revising the model, color and material patterns can be applied to the walls and floor to bring it up to the standards of a final presentation model. You simply apply realistic features such as building material indications and figures to make the model 'read' in more literal terms. Much time can be saved by transforming a schematic study model into a final presentation model.

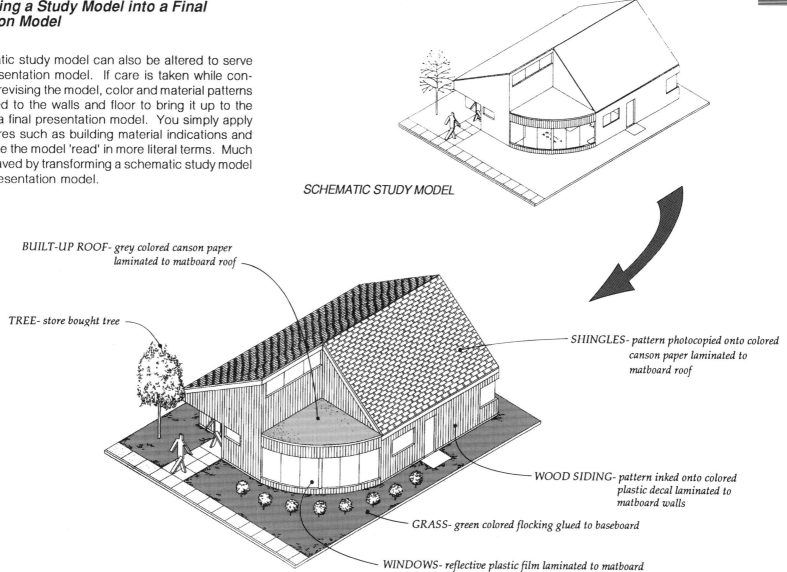

SCHEMATIC STUDY MODEL

BUILT-UP ROOF- grey colored canson paper laminated to matboard roof

TREE- store bought tree

SHINGLES- pattern photocopied onto colored canson paper laminated to matboard roof

WOOD SIDING- pattern inked onto colored plastic decal laminated to matboard walls

GRASS- green colored flocking glued to baseboard

WINDOWS- reflective plastic film laminated to matboard

FINAL PRESENTATION MODEL

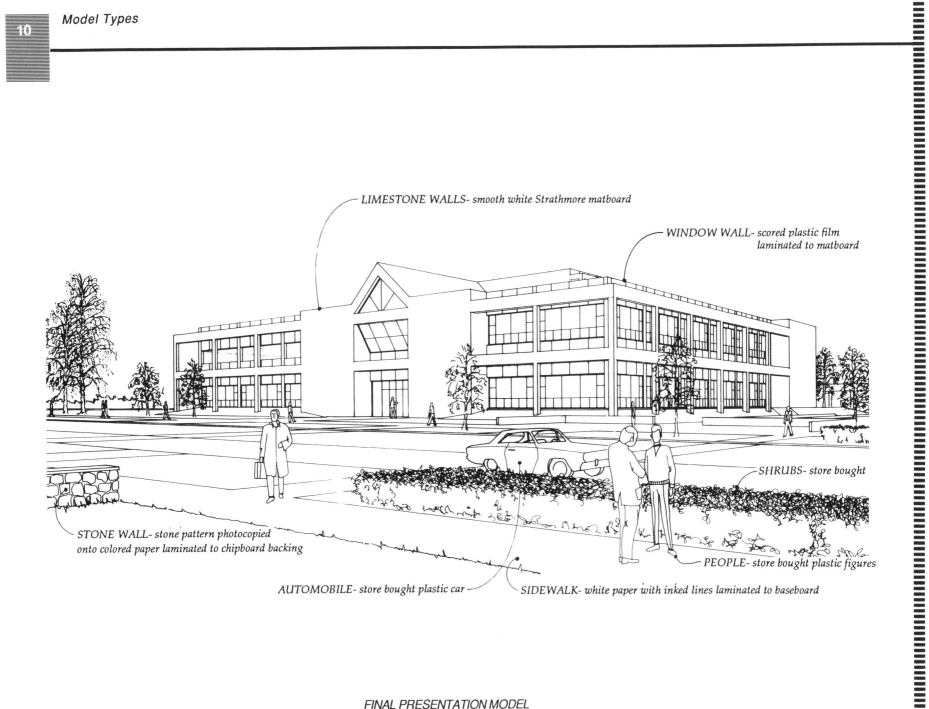

LIMESTONE WALLS- *smooth white Strathmore matboard*

WINDOW WALL- *scored plastic film laminated to matboard*

SHRUBS- *store bought*

STONE WALL- *stone pattern photocopied onto colored paper laminated to chipboard backing*

PEOPLE- *store bought plastic figures*

AUTOMOBILE- *store bought plastic car*

SIDEWALK- *white paper with inked lines laminated to baseboard*

FINAL PRESENTATION MODEL

CHAPTER 2

Building a Schematic Model FAST

Does this sound like your situation? Your design instructor informed your class three weeks ago that everyone must build a model of their design for the final presentation. And now you have only three days to learn how to construct a three dimensional representation of your design. Well first off, relax! In this chapter we will go through a step-by-step process of model making procedures resulting in a presentable three dimensional model of your design. We will look at: the drawings needed for constructing a model, the necessary materials, construction of the model base, transferring your design drawings to the selected matboard, construction of the walls, construction of the windows, roof construction, sidewalk construction, and finally the construction of scaled objects, such as people and trees.

In order to explain the procedure in a realistic manner we will illustrate in a step-by-step process the construction of a typical house model. It will be identical to the type of model which first and second year architecture students are required to build in their design studios.

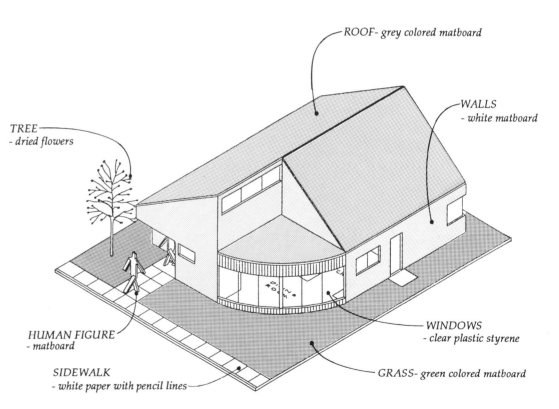

ROOF- *grey colored matboard*

WALLS
- *white matboard*

TREE
- *dried flowers*

WINDOWS
- *clear plastic styrene*

HUMAN FIGURE
- *matboard*

SIDEWALK
- *white paper with pencil lines*

GRASS- *green colored matboard*

SCHEMATIC STUDY MODEL

CONSTRUCTION OF SCHEMATIC STUDY MODEL

The house will be one story with two bedrooms, a kitchen, a living room, a dining room, and one bathroom. The site is flat with one tree in the front yard. The roof will be a combination flat and gable type in order for you to see the two typical types of roof construction. The model will be built at 1/4"=1'-0" scale and the drawings should therefore be at the same scale. On the following pages are the required drawings necessary to build the model. (The drawings on these pages are at 3/32"=1'-0" scale if you would like to photocopy them and build the model as we describe each step).

Complete All Design Drawings

The first step to building your model is to have your design drawings complete, and when I say complete I mean totally complete. All dimensions, slopes, and sizes of every component (windows, walls, roofs) must be decided upon and drawn to scale before beginning construction of the model. This will eliminate time consuming errors during construction.

SCHEMATIC FLOOR PLAN

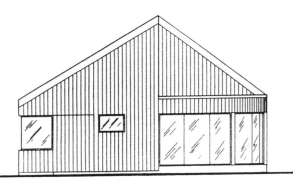

SCHEMATIC SOUTH ELEVATION

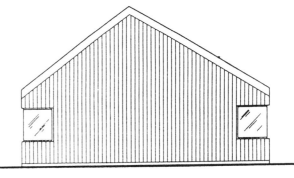

SCHEMATIC NORTH ELEVATION

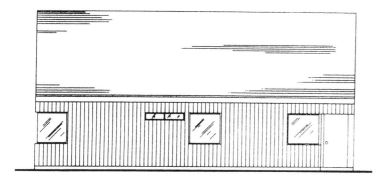

SCHEMATIC WEST ELEVATION

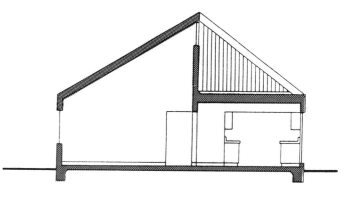

SCHEMATIC CROSS SECTION

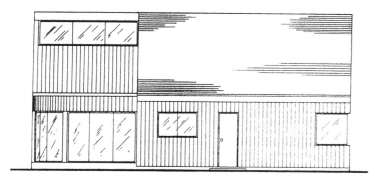

SCHEMATIC EAST ELEVATION

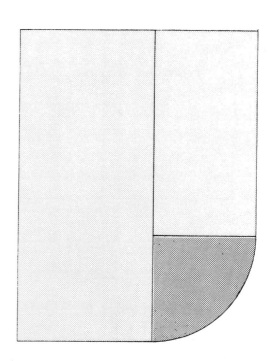

SCHEMATIC ROOF PLAN

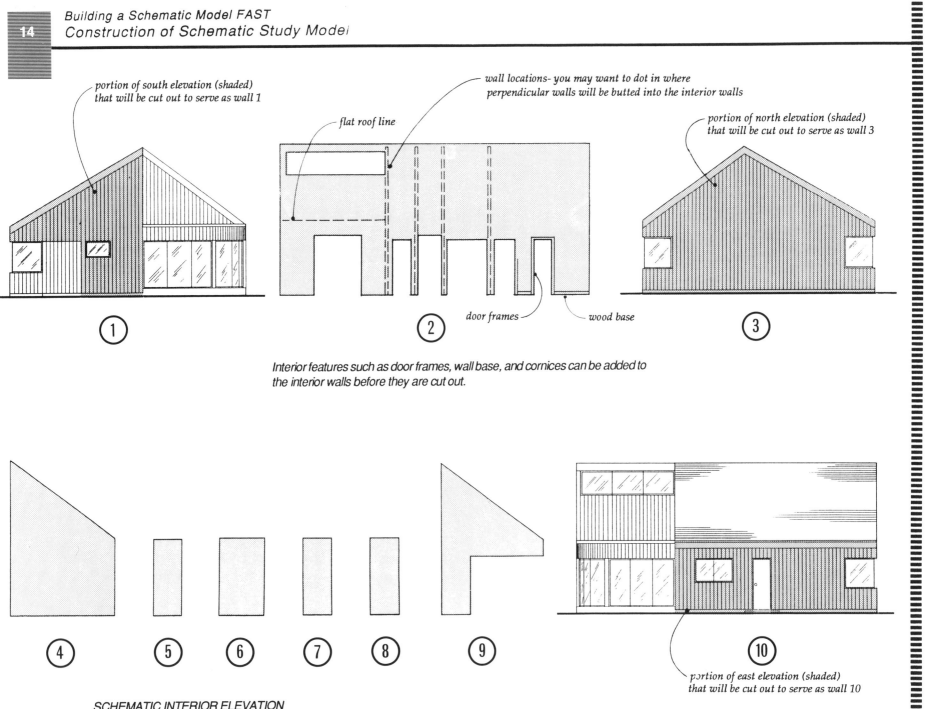

portion of south elevation (shaded)
that will be cut out to serve as wall 1

wall locations- you may want to dot in where
perpendicular walls will be butted into the interior walls

flat roof line

portion of north elevation (shaded)
that will be cut out to serve as wall 3

door frames

wood base

① ② ③

Interior features such as door frames, wall base, and cornices can be added to
the interior walls before they are cut out.

④ ⑤ ⑥ ⑦ ⑧ ⑨ ⑩

portion of east elevation (shaded)
that will be cut out to serve as wall 10

SCHEMATIC INTERIOR ELEVATION

SCHEMATIC INTERIOR ELEVATION

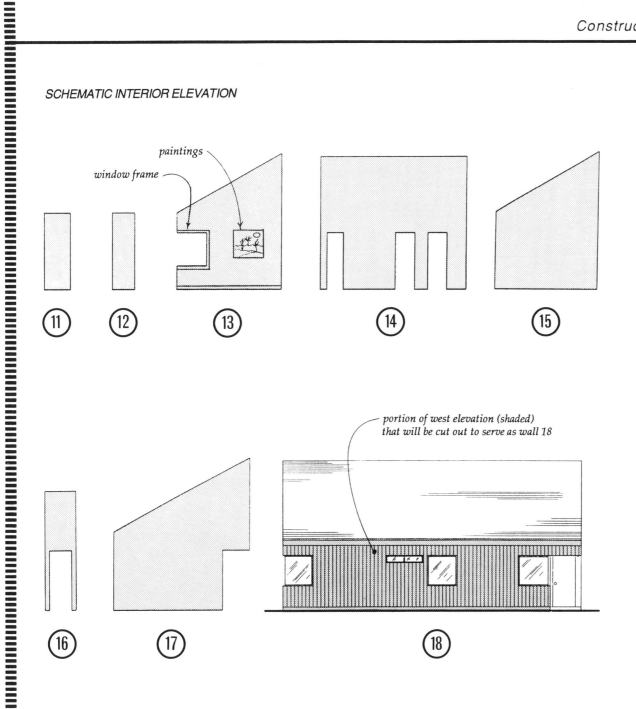

paintings
window frame

⑪ ⑫ ⑬ ⑭ ⑮

portion of west elevation (shaded)
that will be cut out to serve as wall 18

⑯ ⑰ ⑱

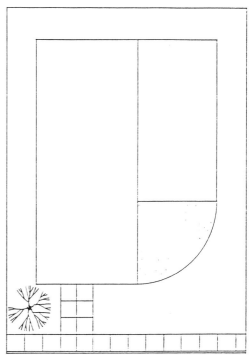

SCHEMATIC SITE PLAN

Before beginning construction you must draw on your floor plan print where all of the model walls will be placed on the plan. You must decide how the walls will relate to each other at intersections, and how they will relate to the walls drawn on the plan.

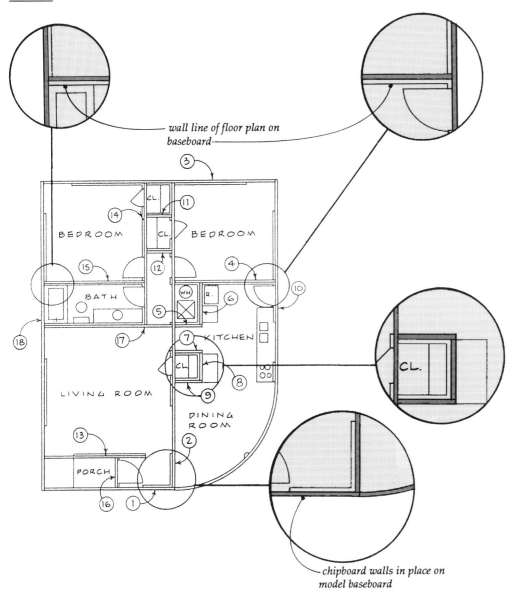

wall line of floor plan on baseboard

chipboard walls in place on model baseboard

As you can see in the illustrated floor plan to the left every wall will be connected to another wall in either a T-intersection or at a right angle. You must decide which walls should butt into others and which should be continuous. Generally the exterior perimeter walls and longest interior walls are continuous, with the shorter interior walls butting into them.

Also indicated in the illustrated floor plan is how the thin matboard walls relate to the 1/8" thick walls drawn in plan. Since the chipboard walls will be a little less than 1/16" thick you must decide where they will be placed in relation to the walls in plan. Generally, the model's exterior perimeter walls are placed at the outside line of the plan while the interior walls are located wherever you wish.

The location of the walls will be discussed further and explained in more detail when we construct them, but for now try to understand the concept of how the actual chipboard walls will relate to one another at intersections and on the floor plan.

Each wall on the model is numbered and should be drawn at the selected scale prior to starting construction. The walls will be constructed in the sequence as numbered.

MATERIALS FOR CONSTRUCTION

Once your design drawings are complete you are ready to begin constructing the model. Below is listed all the materials that will be needed to build the model:

- One sheet of dark green matboard (24"x36")
- Stapler
- White glue (preferably Elmers)
- Xacto knife
- Utility knife
- Metal ruler
- Artists Adhesive spray glue
- Super spray glue
- Three sheets of chipboard (30"x40")
- Drafting equipment
    - pencils
    - triangles
    - erasers
    - scale
    - circle template
    - erasing shield
    - compass
    - T-square or parallel bar

See Chapter 4 for a description of the materials listed above.

compass

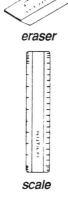

scale

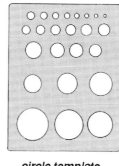

circle template

pencil

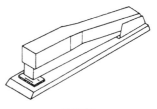

stapler

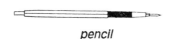

Xacto knife

t-square or parallel bar

utility knife

triangles   *spray glue*   *white glue*

metal ruler

erasing shield

CONSTRUCTING THE MODEL BASE

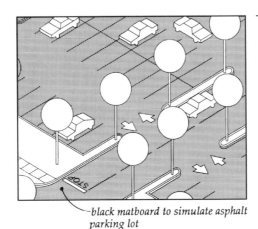

green matboard to
simulate grass

black matboard to simulate asphalt
parking lot

The matboard selected for the baseboard can be any color you desire to simulate the ground material.

We will begin building the model by first constructing the model base. For small bases such as ours (15" square or smaller), one layer of chipboard or matboard is rigid enough to serve as the baseboard. For our baseboard we will use a dark green colored matboard to simulate the sites' ground cover. You could also use a black matboard to simulate asphalt or light grey to simulate concrete. The first step is to cut the matboard down to its required size of 10"x14".

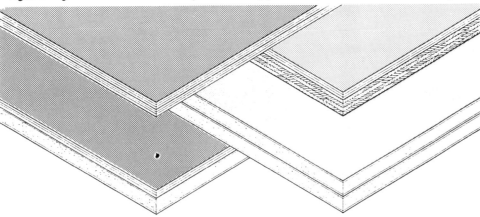

Two layers of matboard laminated together is good for bases 12" to 18" square.

One layer of matboard laminated to a sheet of plywood is good for bases 24" to 36" square.

One layer of matboard laminated to Foamcore is good for bases 12" to 24" square.

Two layers of Foamcore laminated together is good for baseboards 18" to 36" square.

BASEBOARD LAMINATION TECHNIQUES

Cutting Matboard

Cutting matboard is the most common procedure performed in the model making process and should be done with the utmost care. This is where almost all accidents occur. You must think about a cut before performing it. The main consideration to keep in mind when cutting matboard is to have your matboard and straightedge secure under pressure before starting the cutting stroke. This is achieved by securing the matboard to your drafting board with staples or tape, and by exerting enough pressure on your straightedge to keep it from moving during the cutting strokes. Let's take a look at this procedure:

(I recommend that you first read through all of the steps of a procedure before starting with Step 1. Knowing the desired end result will make the process easier to follow).

NOTE: For ease of reading these instructions while working on your model components, the type will be enlarged so that the book can be read while sitting next to your drafting board.

Step 1   Secure the cutting chipboard.

First, secure a sheet of chipboard on top of your drawing board with staples or drafting tape (preferably staples). This board will protect your drawing board while you are cutting your model components.

Step 2 Secure the model baseboard to cutting board.

Next, secure your model base matboard on top of the cutting board with staples or tape as illustrated, making sure that the bottom edge of the matboard is parallel with your T-square or parallel bar. If you don't want staple holes in the matboard, use drafting tape to secure it down, but I have found that staples hold it more firmly in place. If you choose tape, use only the drafting type since other tapes (transparent, masking, plastic, etc.) will pull some of the paper off your finished matboard.

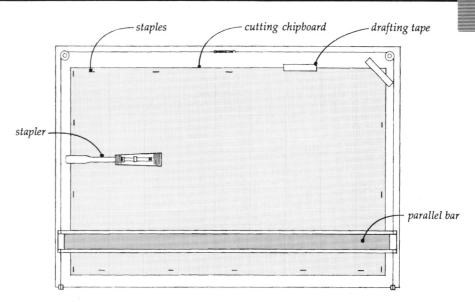

1 Secure the cutting chipboard to the drafting board with either staples or drafting tape.

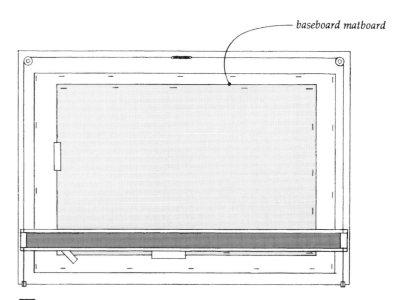

2 Secure the model base matboard to the cutting chipboard with staples.

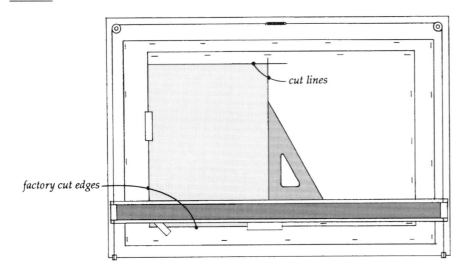

3 Draw the baseboard cut lines onto the matboard.

Step 3 Draw the baseboard cut lines.

Now measure and draw the horizontal and vertical cut lines with your drafting tools (pencils, scale, T-square, triangles). A light line is sufficient and can be easily erased with a white eraser if necessary. Lay out your baseboard at one of the lower corners of the matboard to utilize the factory cut edges. Now you are ready to cut the board.

Step 4 Perform the horizontal cut.

It is usually better to perform your horizontal cuts first and then the vertical cuts. Move your T-square or parallel bar up to the line and lay a metal ruler on top of it as illustrated. The ruler will be your cutting straightedge, or you can use the parallel bar edge if it is metal. I do not recommend using the plastic bar edge until you have more experience in cutting. (Il. 4a)

Before performing any cut, think about where the knife is going to end up if it slips off the cutting edge. Always pull your cutting strokes in a sideways direction away from your body, and stop for a moment to visualize the path of the knife before making the cut. Make sure that you do not have any fingertips in the path of the blade. The split second it takes to think safety is a calming moment that is necessary before performing any dangerous task. (Il. 4b)

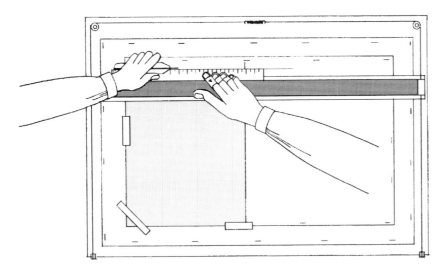

4a Perform the horizontal cut.

Now, hold the utility knife in your drawing hand in the same manner as you would a kitchen knife, and press down with your other hand on the parallel bar and ruler in the same manner as if you were drawing a line. You will have to press very hard to keep the ruler from moving during the cutting stroke. If the ruler moves, you will not have a straight cut. The thicker the board is, the harder you will have to press down on the ruler and the more strokes you will have to make. Do not try to cut all the way through the board on your first cutting stroke. It will take at least two or three strokes. On the first stroke, cut only half way through the board and move the knife slowly. Don't be in a rush. Remember to keep the blade at a 90 degree angle to the board during the strokes in order to obtain square edges.

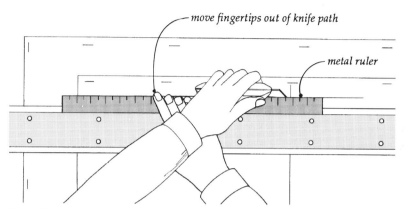

4b *Always stop for a moment before each cut to visualize the path of the knife. Make sure no fingertips are in the way.*

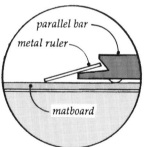

4c *When pressing down on the metal ruler, make sure it is wedged tight in the groove of the parallel bar.*

During the time between the strokes you must keep the straightedge in place. Continue holding it in its position and let up on the pressure to rest your arm. Now perform your second stroke, but apply a little more pressure on the knife to see if you can cut all the way through the board. If it looks like you are going to have to exert a lot of pressure to go all the way through, let up and cut only three fourths of the way through the board. Now you should be able to safely cut through on the third stroke.

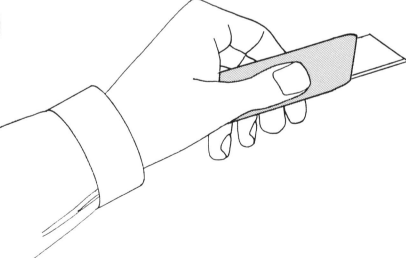

Hold the knife in your drawing hand in the same manner as you would a kitchen knife.

Step 5 *Perform the vertical cut.*

The next step is to perform the vertical cut. The best method to perform vertical cuts is to position a triangle with its bottom edge against your parallel bar so you can get an exact 90 degree cut. It will be very important in the wall and roof construction to have exact 90 degree angles in order to obtain corners and joints that properly meet.

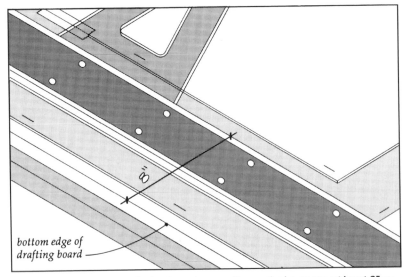

— *metal or plastic triangle*

5a *Perform the vertical cut.*

Place your triangle (metal if you have one, or an old plastic one that you will not need for drafting) at the desired cut line in the same manner as if you were drawing a vertical line. Hold your utility knife in your drawing hand and press down hard on the triangle with your other hand so that it does not move during the cutting stroke. Cut through the board in the same manner as you did with the horizontal cuts, performing two or three strokes to go all the way through. (II. 5a)

bottom edge of drafting board —

8"

5b *When performing vertical cuts make sure the vertical cuts are at least 8" up from the bottom of the drafting board.*

Again, think safety before every stroke, because now the blade is coming down toward your body instead of away from it. Make sure the stroke is at least 8" up from the bottom of your drafting board and thus a safe distance from your torso. Keep your fingers that are holding the triangle safely out of the path of the knife. (II. 5b)

Hold the triangle in the same position for all three strokes, and do not move your fingers away from the triangle between strokes if possible. Cut all the way through the entire length of the cut. Do not pull the piece away from the remaining board until it is completely cut through. Ripping the last 1/4" or so of uncut board will leave a distracting uneven edge that could create problems later on in the construction. (Il. 5c)

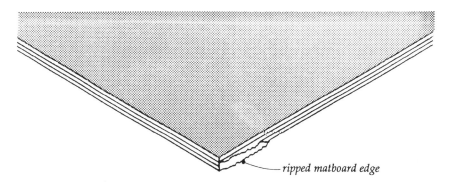

ripped matboard edge

5c *Cut all the way through the matboard before trying to separate the pieces.*

Now you have the basic principles of cutting matboard and the baseboard for your model. One last tip before we move on to construction procedures is to flatten out the cut edges of your matboard.

Step 6   *Flatten the flared edges.*

If you look closely at the board you just cut, you will see that the edges are now 'flaired up' due to the cutting procedure. Flatten the edge by running your fingernail across the entire length of board. This will give the board a crisp professional appearance. The sharper the edges, the better the appearance of the finished model.

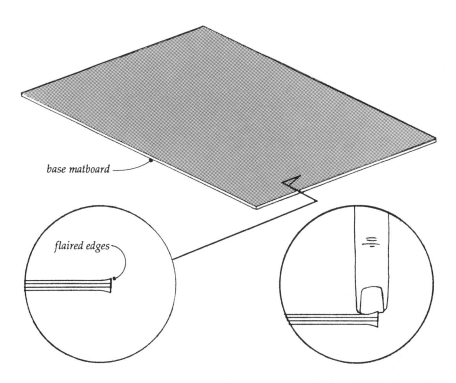

base matboard

flaired edges

6 *Flatten the flared cut edge with your fingernail the entire length of the board to obtain sharp edges.*

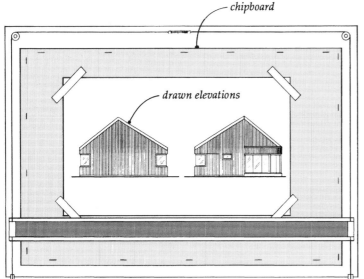

chipboard

drawn elevations

METHOD #1   Redraw the design drawings onto matboard.

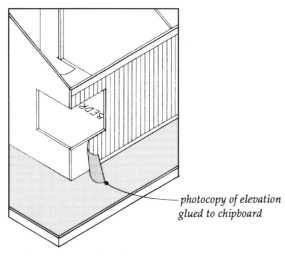

*photocopy of elevation
glued to chipboard*

*METHOD #2   The fastest method for transferring your design drawings
onto chipboard is to photocopy the drawings and attach them to the chipboard with spray adhesive.*

TRANSFERRING YOUR DESIGN DRAWINGS ONTO MATBOARD

The next step in constructing your model is to transfer your design drawings onto the chipboard you will be using for your building components (walls, roof and floor). This can be achieved by one of two methods: redraw the design drawings onto the chipboard; or attach photocopies of the drawings to the chipboard.

Method #1   Redraw the design drawings.

One method is to redraw the plans and elevations directly onto the chipboard in pencil or ink. This is the cleanest and most professional method, but also the most time consuming.

Method #2   Attach photocopies to matboard.

The fastest method of transfer is to photocopy or blue-print your design drawings and apply the print to the chipboard with spray adhesive. This is an excellent method for schematic models which are meant to be built and revised quickly. Lets look at this transfer process more closely.

Step 1   Copy design drawings.

First, take your design drawings to a blueprint company to get them printed, or have them photocopied on a copying machine. If they are drawn on vellum or sketch paper, you can get them reproduced in blue, black or brownline at the blueprint company. The cost can vary depending on the type selected. If they are drawn on non-reproducable paper such as bond, then your only choice is a blackline photocopy on thin bond paper. This is not as desirable as the thicker print paper (available from the blueprinter) when the spray adhesive is applied.Whatever type of paper is used it is a good idea to get two or three copies of each drawing in case of mistakes.

blueprint thickness

blackline thickness

blackline or brownline illustration paper thickness

photocopy thickness

1 *Brownline and blackline can be printed on a thicker stock illustration paper than blueline paper and attaches to the chipboard better.*

Step 2   Separate the drawings.

Next, separate the copied drawings (elevations, plans and sections) from each other, leaving approximately 2" of paper around the perimeter of each drawing. The cuts can be performed with scissors or an Xacto knife and they do not have to be straight cuts. The objective is to merely separate the drawings from each other.

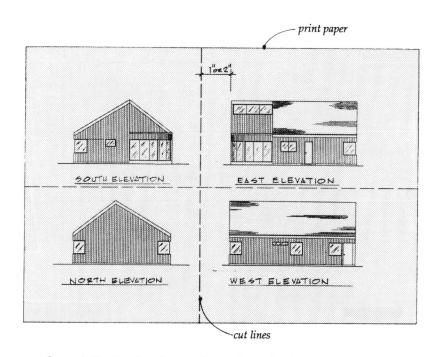

print paper

SOUTH ELEVATION   EAST ELEVATION

NORTH ELEVATION   WEST ELEVATION

cut lines

2 *Separate the drawings from each other by cutting the print paper, leaving approximately 2" around each elevation.*

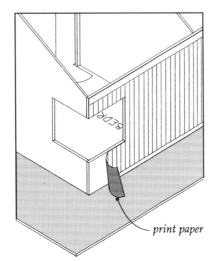

3b *If you want to leave the print paper on the chipboard use Super spray glue.*

3a *If you want to be able to remove the paper use Artists Adhesive spray glue.*

print paper

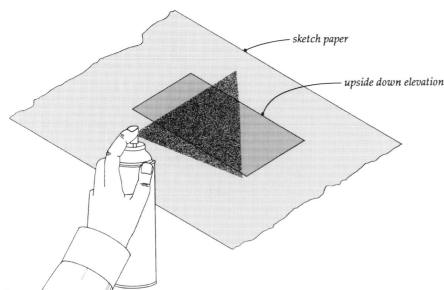

sketch paper

upside down elevation

3c *Apply only a light coat of spray glue to the paper, do not saturate.*

Step 3   Apply spray adhesive to elevations.

The next step is to apply spray adhesive to the back of the prints. Spray the elevations only; do not spray the back of the floor plan yet. Lay the prints upside-down on sketch paper spread out in a wide area on the floor.

Now select the type of spray glue to be used. If you want to be able to remove the print paper from the chipboard after the piece is cut out, use Artists Adhesive spray glue. This is a less tacky glue that allows the user to remove and relocate artwork once it has been set in place. For design studio models you can save the time of removing the print paper by using a Super spray glue, and leave the paper on. Whichever type of glue you decide to use, follow the manufacturers' instructions and apply a light coat. Do not saturate the paper, only a small amount of glue is necessary.(II. 3c)

Step 4   Attach chipboard to cutting board.

Next, attach the chipboard that will be used for your elevations to your cutting board. Line up the bottom edge with the parallel bar and secure the chipboard to your cutting board with drafting tape.

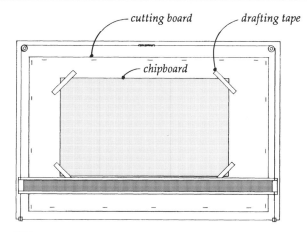

cutting board — *drafting tape*

chipboard

4 *Attach the chipboard to your cutting board.*

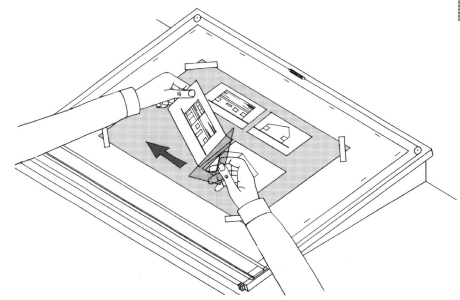

5a *Hold one end of the elevation sheet up in the air while smoothing the sheet out with a straightedge from the other end.*

Step 5 Attach elevations to chipboard.

To attach your elevations to the chipboard, first set one end down on the chipboard while holding the other end in the air. With the use of a triangle or any straightedge, press the paper in a sliding motion onto the matboard and continue holding the other end in the air until the straightedge meets that end. As long as the strips of print paper are not wider than your straightedge, approximately 12", the paper should smooth out without any bubbles or creases. (Il. 5a)

Lay a sheet of sketch paper over the elevations and smooth out the paper with your hands, pressing down very hard to achieve a strong bond. Set the elevation boards aside and move on to the next step. (Il. 5b)

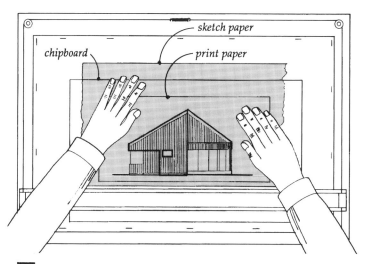

sketch paper

chipboard — *print paper*

5b *Smooth out the elevations with your hands.*

Step 6   Attach floor plan to baseboard.

It is time to attach your floor plan print to your model baseboard. First, tape down your floor plan on top of your cutting board. Using your Xacto knife, metal ruler and triangle, cut out the floor plan at the outside line of your exterior walls. The Xacto knife is held in your drawing hand and used in the same manner as a drafting pencil. You should be able to cut completely through in one stroke.(Il. 6a)

Before applying glue, set the plan on your baseboard and make a pencil mark on the matboard at each corner of where it is going to be placed. (Il. 6b)

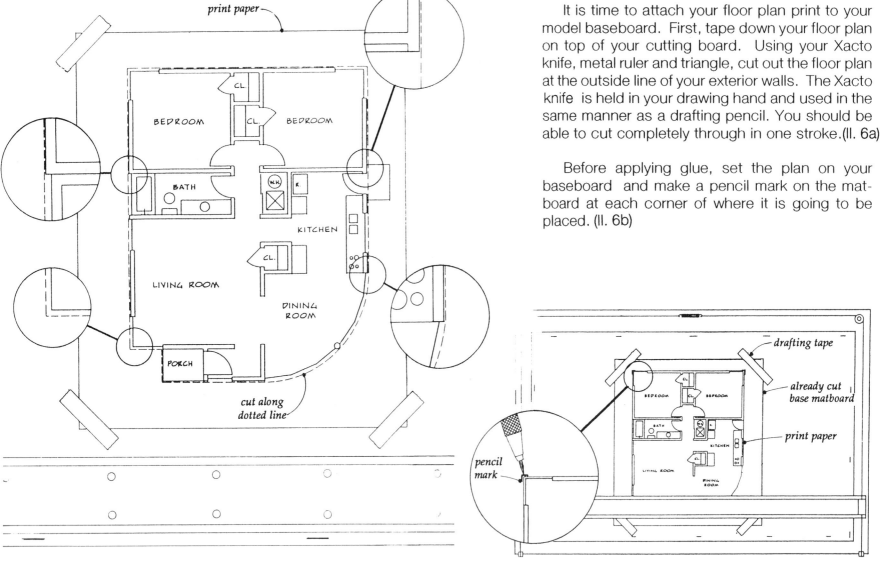

6a Cut out floor plan at perimeter wall line.

6b Set the floor plan down on the baseboard and make a pencil mark on the matboard at each corner.

Spray the back of the plan with Super spray glue, making sure to cover the edges evenly. Do not use Artists Adhesive since the floor plan sheet is the bonding element between your walls and baseboard. (ll. 6c)

Set one end of the plan down on the baseboard at the pencil marks and hold the other end up in the air. Smooth it down with a straightedge in the same manner as with the elevations. (ll. 6d)

Lay a sheet of sketch paper over the plan and smooth it out with your hands, pressing down very hard at the perimeter of the plan to make sure you have a good bond. It is important to have a good bond at the perimeter since this is where your walls are going to be attached to the baseboard. (ll. 6e)

Remove the sketch paper and you are now ready to begin constructing the walls.

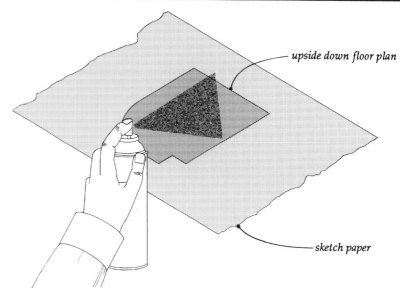

upside down floor plan

sketch paper

6c *Apply Super Spray adhesive to the back of the floor plan.*

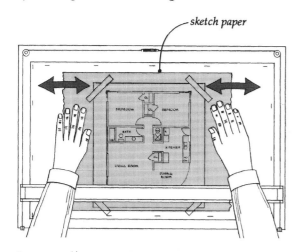

sketch paper

6e *Lay a sheet of sketch paper over the plan and smooth it out with your hands.*

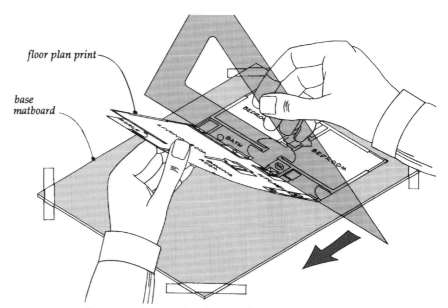

floor plan print

base matboard

6d *Set one end of the plan down and hold the other end up in the air while smoothing it out with a straightedge.*

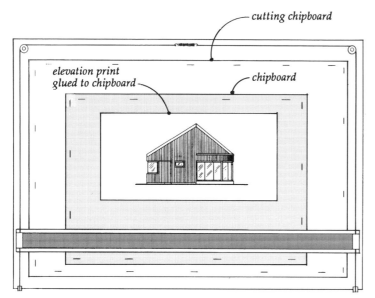

cutting chipboard

elevation print
glued to chipboard

chipboard

1 Line up the elevation with your parallel bar and staple it to the cutting chipboard.

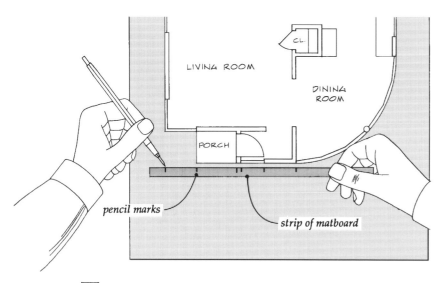

LIVING ROOM

CL.

DINING ROOM

PORCH

pencil marks

strip of matboard

2a Verify the wall lengths of your plan with the elevation.

CONSTRUCTING THE WALLS

Now that you have transferred your design drawings to the chipboard, you are ready to begin cutting out and attaching the walls to the baseboard. Let's look at this procedure more closely.

Step 1 Attach south elevation to cutting board.

Begin by laying your south elevation on top of your cutting board, lining up the horizontal lines with your parallel bar. Now staple the chipboard down to your cutting board as illustrated. Wall 1 will be cut out of your south elevation.

Step 2 Verify wall dimensions.

To verify that the length of wall 1 on the baseboard is the same length as that on the south elevation, lay a thin strip of matboard or paper below the wall line on the plan, and make pencil marks of the exact dimensions, as illustrated. (II. 2a) Now set the strip of matboard below the elevation and verify that the dimensions are the same. (II. 2b) This measuring technique will be used extensively throughout the model making process, since it gives a faster and more accurate measurement than using a scale. Once you have adjusted the wall lengths on your elevation, you are ready to cut out the wall.

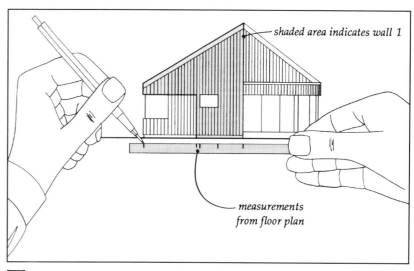

2b *Verify the wall lengths of your elevation.*

Step 3   Cut out wall 1.

Using your utility knife, metal ruler, parallel bar and triangle cut out wall 1 in the same manner as you did the baseboard. Perform your horizontal cuts first and then your verticals, saving the longer cuts for last. You will see that shorter cuts take more strokes of the knife, so be patient. If there are any window or door openings in the wall, cut them out first. Short cut lengths necessary for windows are more difficult to perform once the wall has been cut and removed from the stapled-down chipboard.

After all cuts have been performed, smooth down the flaired edges with your fingernail. To avoid ripping the last portion of board always make sure all cuts are complete.

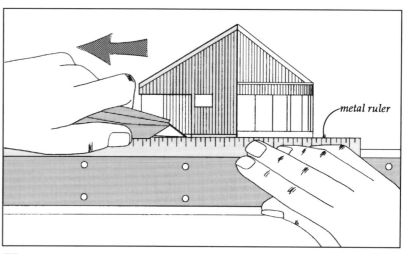

3 *Cut out wall 1 from the chipboard.*

Step 4   Set wall 1 on the floor plan.

Set your first wall on the floor plan where it is to be located not yet applying any glue. Hold it up at the outside edge of the plan and take note of how wall 2 will have to be cut short to compensate for the wall matboard thickness of wall 1. This must be considered before any further cutting of walls. Go all the way around the perimeter of your plan and take note of where walls will be butted up to one another and will therefore have to be cut shorter.

BEDROOM   CL.   CL.   BEDROOM

BATH

KITCHEN

LIVING ROOM

DINING ROOM

CL.

PORCH

chipboard walls

CL.

line of floor plan below

4b As noted on page 16 mark on your floor plan baseboard where all of the walls will be butted up against each other. The walls will be constructed in the numbered sequence.

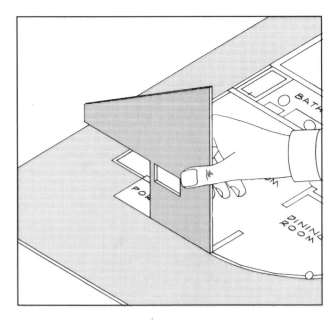

4a Set wall 1 in place on the floor plan and take note of its relationship to wall 2.

Step 5 *Measure and cut out wall 2.*

Using the 'thin strip of matboard' method of measuring, verify the elevation dimensions of wall 2 with the floor plan and adjust the elevation to match the plan if necessary. You need to cut out your second wall before gluing down wall 1 so that they have each other to stand up. (ll. 5a & 5b)

Once you have verified the wall length dimensions, cut out the wall and smooth down the flaired edges with your fingernail. Now set it in place on the plan butted perpendicular to your first wall making sure they are both the same height. Now you are ready to glue the walls together and to the baseboard. (ll. 5c)

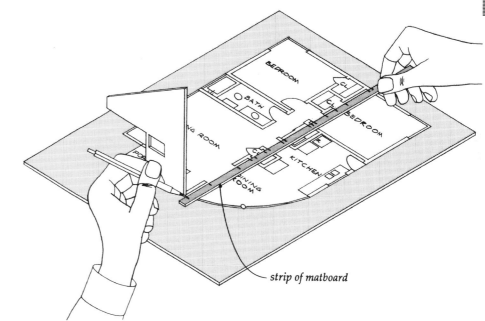

strip of matboard

5a Check the dimensions of wall 2 on the floor plan with the elevation as you did with wall 1.

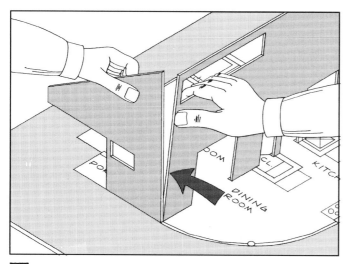

5c Set both walls up without any glue to verify that they are the same height.

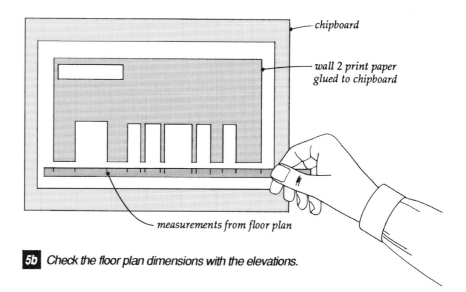

chipboard

wall 2 print paper glued to chipboard

measurements from floor plan

5b Check the floor plan dimensions with the elevations.

Step 6   *Apply glue to wall 1.*

To attach the walls together and to the base-board, a thin layer of white glue must be applied to the wall edges. The fastest method of applying glue to a board edge is as follows:

First, squeeze out a thick line of glue at least as long as the board edge onto a spare piece of chipboard. (Il. 6a)

Push the board edge at a 45 degree angle into the glue until the entire edge is covered. Do not push so far that the glue gets onto any other surface except the edge. (Il. 6b)

Now, because of the thickness of the glue, there is too much on the edge. Remove some of the glue by simply touching the edge down onto the spare piece of chipboard as illustrated. (Il. 6c)

piece of matboard

glue

6a *Squeeze out a line of glue as long as the wall.*

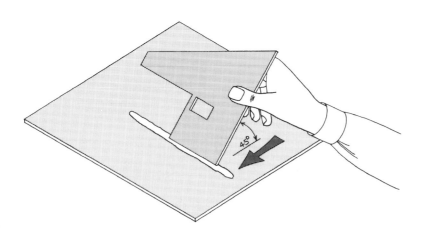

6b *Push the board edge into the glue until the edge is covered.*

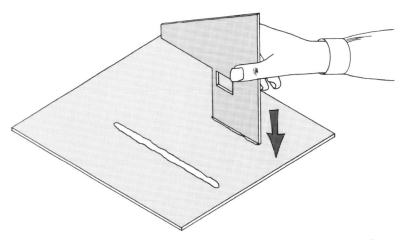

6c *Remove some of the excess glue by touching the edge down on a spare piece of cardboard.*

NOTE: In order to keep your model neat and clean during construction, the glue should be applied with care. Apply only small amounts of glue to components, and try to keep your hands and fingertips as clean as possible. After wiping glue off the model always remove the excess glue from your fingertips before touching any other parts. Excessive glue will give your model a messy appearance and detract attention from your design intent.

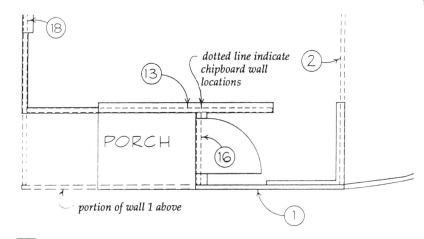

7a Set wall 1 down on the baseboard in its proper location.

Step 7 Attach wall 1 to the baseboard.

With a thin layer of glue on the bottom edge, set wall 1 on the floor plan at the perimeter of the wall line. (Il. 7a) Press down and hold it for about 30 seconds. If it does not stand up by itself, a long piece of drafting tape can be applied to it and the baseboard to hold it in an upright position while you apply the glue to wall 2. Do not use masking tape or plastic tape because they will pull the outer layer of paper from the matboard when removed. (Il. 7b)

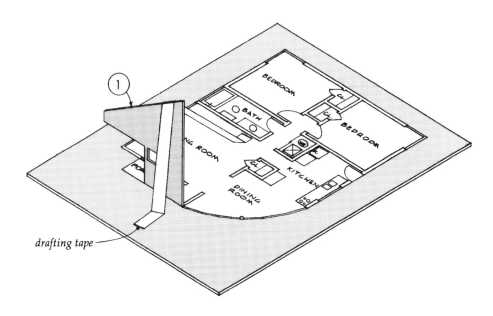

7b Attach wall 1 to the baseboard.

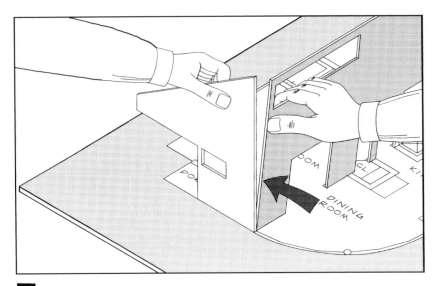

8a *Attach wall 2 to the baseboard.*

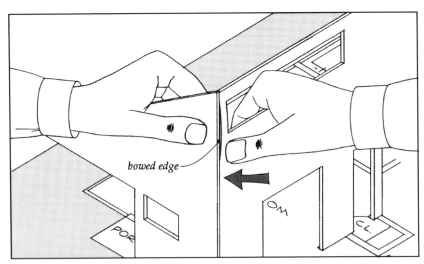

8b *Hold each wall between your forefinger and thumb and adjust the joint to properly align the edges to a 90 degree corner.*

bowed edge

Step 8 *Attach wall 2 to the baseboard.*

Apply a line of glue to the bottom and side edge of wall 2 in the same manner as you did with wall 1. Set the bottom edge down first on the plan and tilt wall 1 back a few degrees. Now push wall 1 up against wall 2 so that you have their edges butted together at a 90 degree angle. (ll. 8a)

Adjust any portion of the joint that does not properly meet by holding wall 1 between your forefinger and thumb, while pushing on wall 2 with your other thumb. (ll. 8b)

Wipe any excess glue from the edge with your fingertip in one fast swipe. Going over it twice will leave a messy residue. (ll. 8c)

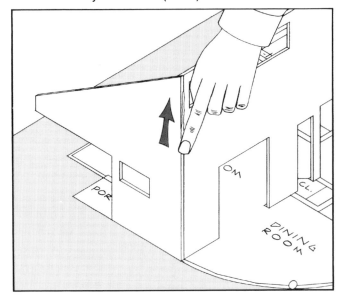

8c *Wipe any excess glue from the joint with your finger in one swipe.*

Step 9 *Apply drafting tape across joint.*

The two walls should stand together without falling, but you could apply a strip of drafting tape across the top to hold them together while you build the rest of the model.

Step 10 *Apply glue to inside of joint.*

It is also a good idea to reinforce the interior of the joint with a continuous line of glue as illustrated. Remove some of the excess glue by running your finger upward in one swipe.

Let the walls set for about a half an hour while you cut out walls 3, 4, and 5. Once the glue has dried hard enough that the walls do not move when lightly pushed on, the tape can be removed. Now the rest of your walls can be built against walls 1 and 2.

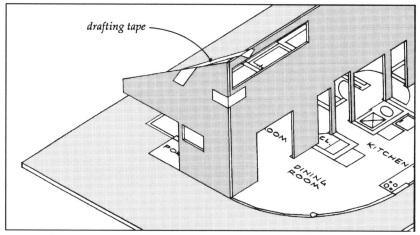

9 *Apply a strip of drafting tape across the two walls to hold them in place while building the rest of the model.*

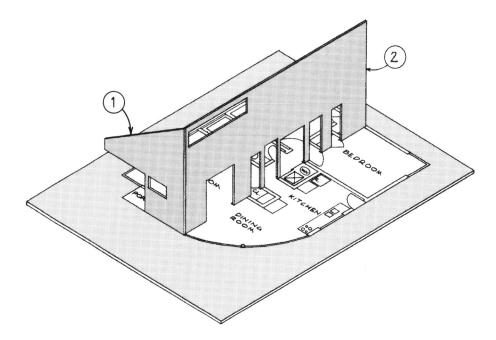

Walls 1 and 2 in place.

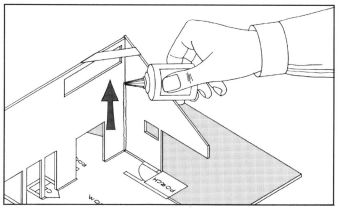

10 *Reinforce the interior of the joints with a line of glue.*

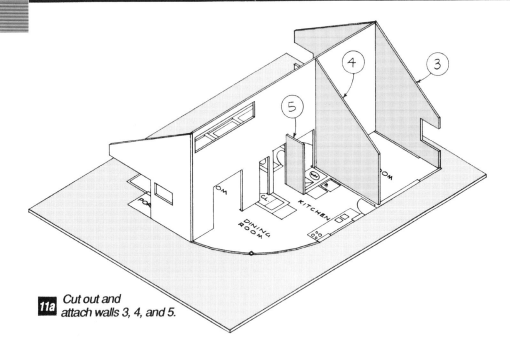

11a Cut out and attach walls 3, 4, and 5.

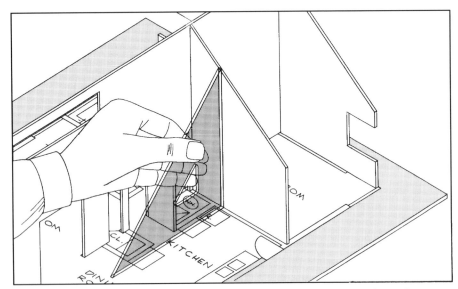

11b Check the vertical angle of the wall with a small triangle to make sure it stands at a 90 degree angle to the base.

Step 11 *Construct walls 3, 4, and 5.*

The next step is to construct walls 3, 4, and 5 against walls 1 and 2. Follow the same procedures as previously described for constructing walls 1 and 2:

- Verify wall dimensions on your plan and elevations referring to the floor plan for wall lengths and butted joints;

- Cut out the walls with a utility knife and triangle to get sharp 90 degree corners;

- Flatten flaired edges;

- Push wall edges through the line of glue and tap on chipboard to remove excess glue;

- Set the bottom edge down first on the plan and push it against the other wall;

- Check the vertical angle of the wall with a small triangle; (ll. 11b)

- Apply drafting tape across the top edges. (ll. 11c)

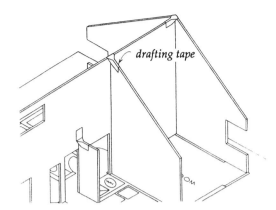

11c *Apply strips of drafting tape across the joints until the glue is dry.*

Step 12 *Construct walls 6, 7, and 8.*

Next, attach walls 6, 7, and 8 to the model. Short length walls such as these can be quickly applied by setting each wall in place in the numbered sequence, and holding each joint for about ten seconds while gently blowing on it. If only a small amount of glue is applied, the joint will hold tight while adjacent walls are built against it, and drafting tape is not needed to hold it in place while it dries. Be sure your fingers are completely clean before erecting each wall. It is a good idea to have a wet cloth at your drafting table to frequently clean the glue from your fingers.

Step 13 *Construct wall 9.*

Cut out and attach wall 9 in the same fashion. Make sure the length and slope of wall 9 is the same as wall 4.

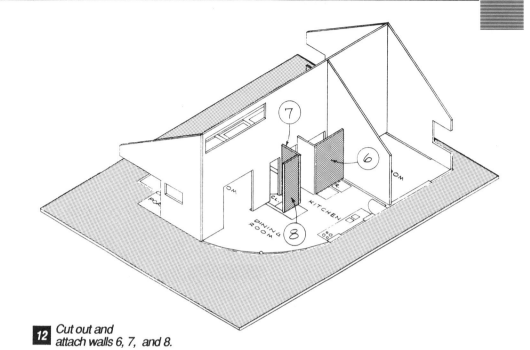

12 *Cut out and attach walls 6, 7, and 8.*

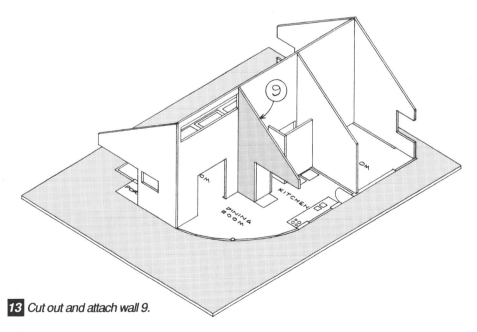

13 *Cut out and attach wall 9.*

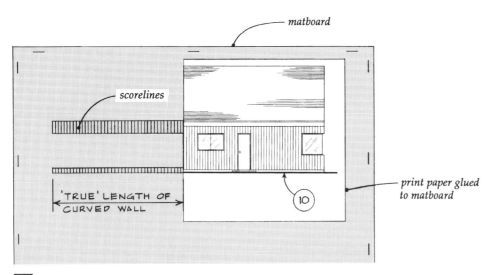

14a *Measure the 'true' length of the curved wall.*

flexible plastic architectural scale

matboard

scorelines

'TRUE' LENGTH OF CURVED WALL

print paper glued to matboard

10

14b *Cut vertical scorelines along the portion of the wall that will be curved.*

Step 14 Construct wall 10.

The next step is to cut out and attach the curved exterior wall 10. Follow the typical procedures for constructing walls, but for the curved portion you must first determine the 'true' radiused length and then score it. Let's look at these procedures:

- First, with the use of a thin strip of matboard or flexible architectural scale measure the 'true' length of the curved wall by bending it next to the wall on your floor plan. (Il. 14a)

- With this measurement draw the true length on the chipboard adjacent to your laminated print of wall 10. (Il. 14b)

- Now, with the use of your utility knife and triangle cut vertical scorelines at approximately 1/8" on center along the portion of the wall that will be curved as illustrated. Be careful not to cut all the way through the board, but if you do, transparent tape can be applied to the back to mend the cut. Perform the score cuts first before any other cuts.

Once you have the piece cut out smooth down the flaired edges and attach it to the baseboard.

To attach the vertical edges of wall 10 to the edge of wall 1:

- First, utilizing the 'thin strip of matboard' method mark on wall 1 where the top of wall 10 will be attached (II. 14c)

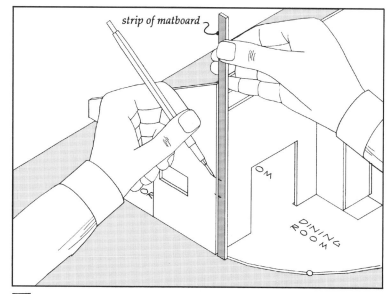

14c *Mark on the edge of wall 1 where the top of wall 10 will be attached.*

- Next, apply a thin layer of white glue to the edge of wall 10 and attach it to wall 1.

- Hold it in place for a few minutes and apply a piece of drafting tape to the joint as illustrated, to hold it place until the glue is dry. Remove the tape after a couple of hours. (II. 14d)

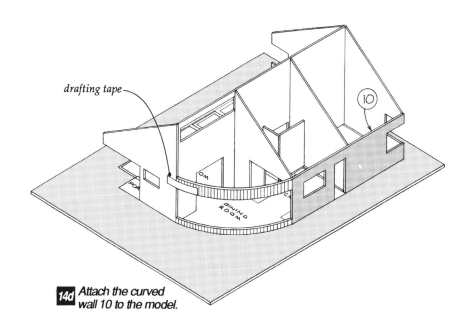

14d *Attach the curved wall 10 to the model.*

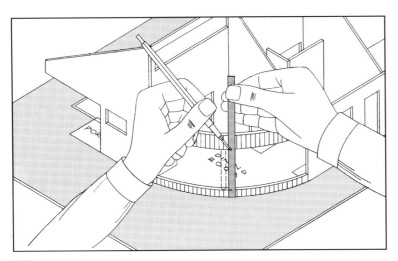

15a Measure the required length of the column.

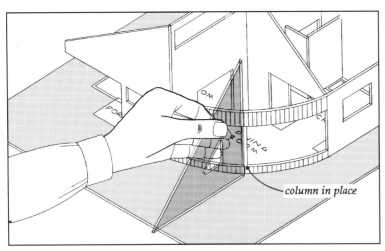

└── column in place

15c Set the column in place with glue on each end and check its verticality with a
small triangle.

Step 15 *Attach round column to wall 10.*

Cut out and attach a round column into wall 10. Since a round paper cotton swab is 1/8" in diameter it will serve as a 6" diameter column on our 1/4" scale model.

- First measure the required length of the column with a thin strip of matboard and mark the length of the column on a cotton swab stick. (Il. 15a)

15b Cut the paper stick by rolling an Xacto knife blade over it.

- Next, cut the stick at the marks by rolling an Xacto knife blade over it on top of your cutting board . Remove the cotton tips first so the stick rolls easier. Cut through in a rolling motion until the blade goes through. You will find that this technique gives you the cleanest and sharpest cut. (Il. 15b)

- Now apply a small dab of white glue to both ends of the column and set it in its proper place between the top and bottom portions of wall 10. Check its verticality by placing a small triangle next to it as illustrated, and adjust it if necessary. (Il. 15c)

Step 16 *Construct walls 11, 12, and 13.*

Cut out and attach walls 11, 12, and 13 in the same manner as you did with the previous walls. Be sure to check that the vertical angle of the walls is 90 degrees. Wall 13 will have to be held in a vertical position with a strip of drafting tape across wall 1 until an adjacent wall can be built against it.

Step 17 *Construct wall 14.*

When setting wall 14 down on the plan correct any misaligned portions of the wall by pushing on it with a straightedge into its proper position. (ll. 17b)

Apply a layer of glue on the vertical edges of walls 11 and 12 with your fingertip and rotate wall 14 up to them. Hold the joint for about 10 seconds and it should stay in place.

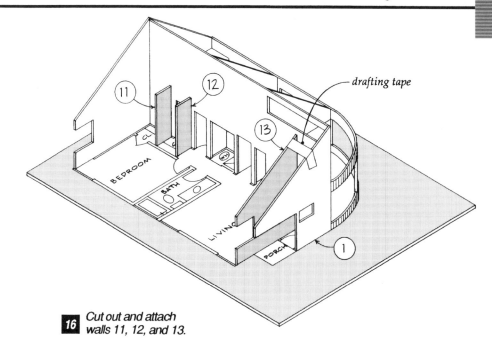

drafting tape

16 *Cut out and attach walls 11, 12, and 13.*

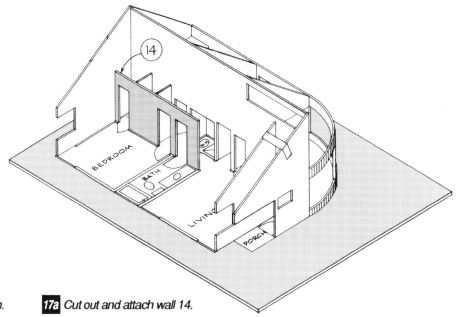

17a *Cut out and attach wall 14.*

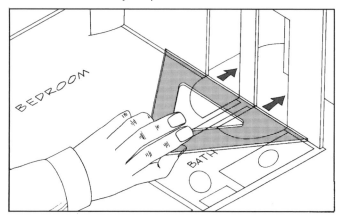

17b *With the use of a triangle push the base of the wall into its desired position.*

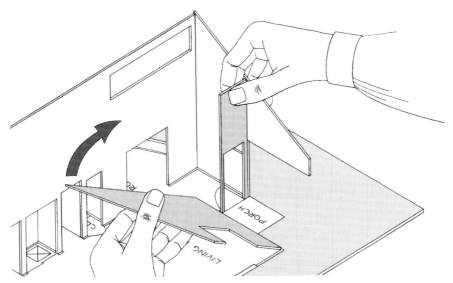

drafting tape

18a *Cut out and attach walls 15 and 16.*

18b *Attach wall 16 by rotating wall 13 down, and attach wall 16 to wall 1 first.*

Step 18 *Construct walls 15 and 16.*

Cut out and attach wall 15 to the base by applying a line of glue to the bottom edge and attaching it to the floor plan at its proper location.

- Attach wall 15 to wall 14 by applying a line of glue to the inside vertical joint. Check the vertical angle of the wall with a small triangle and apply a strip of drafting tape across the joint to hold them together. (Il. 18a)

- Wall 16 is a difficult piece to cut out and attach to the model. The thin vertical members must be cut out cleanly with 90 degree edges and attached to the adjacent walls with care.

- Rotate wall 13 down and out of the way while you attach wall 16 to wall 1. Then apply a thin layer of glue to the left edge of wall 16 and rotate wall 13 up into position. Check the vertical angles with a small triangle. Apply a strip of drafting tape across the walls to hold them together until the glue dries.

Step 19 *Construct wall 17.*

Set wall 17 in place and check its verticality with a rectangular piece of chipboard, since there is not enough room for a small triangle. The piece of chipboard should have 90 degree cuts and a base of at least 1".

Step 20 *Attach wall 18.*

The last wall to attach is wall 18. Apply a thin layer of glue to the bottom edge and attach it to the baseboard. Then, apply a thin layer of glue to the vertical edges of walls 1, 3, 13, 15 and 17 with your fingertip and rotate wall 18 up into its vertical position. Align the vertical edges and apply drafting tape at the corners if necessary.

Now, with all of the walls in place you can either add plastic windows into the openings or begin constructing the roof. If your model is a quick study model, window glazing may not be necessary; ask your instructor. Nevertheless, we will first look at adding glazing to the window openings and then construction of the roof.

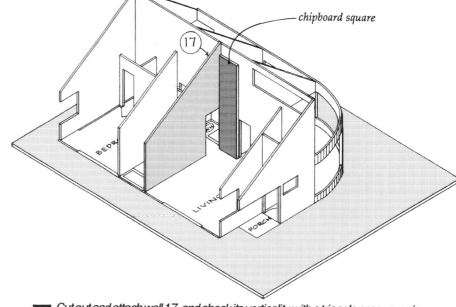

chipboard square

19 *Cut out and attach wall 17, and check its verticality with a triangle or square piece of chipboard.*

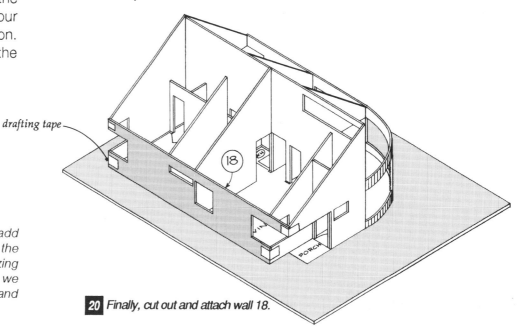

drafting tape

20 *Finally, cut out and attach wall 18.*

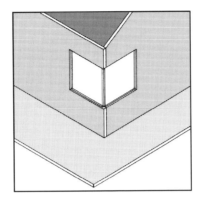

SURFACE MOUNTED WINDOW

transparent tape

styrene

INSET WINDOW GLAZING

CONSTRUCTING THE WINDOWS

Once all the walls are in place the window glazing can be set in the openings. The best glazing material for openings of this size and scale is clear plastic styrene available at hobby stores in 8"x10" sheets 1/32" thick. (Refer to chapter 4 for more information on styrene). The plastic can be cut to fit exactly within the matboard opening, or cut oversized and attached to the inside wall surface with plastic transparent tape. Lets look at the procedures for the inset window glazing.

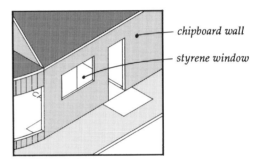

chipboard wall

styrene window

Step 1   *Secure styrene to cutting board.*

First, secure the styrene sheet to your cutting board with drafting tape at the corners and edges as illustrated. (Il. 3a)

Step 2   *Measure window opening size.*

Next, with the use of a thin strip of matboard measure the exact dimensions of the opening. (Il. 2) Mark the size on the styrene with an Xacto knife. (Il. 3b)

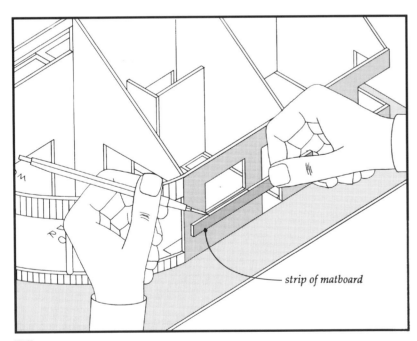

strip of matboard

2 *Measure the window opening.*

Step 3   *Etch the cut lines into the sheet.*

With the use of an Xacto knife and triangle etch the cut and scorelines into the plastic as if you were drawing them with a pencil. Pencil lines drawn onto the plastic are not dark enough to see for guidelines. Continue etching the lines until you have scored half-way through the sheet along the scorelines. (ll. 3b)

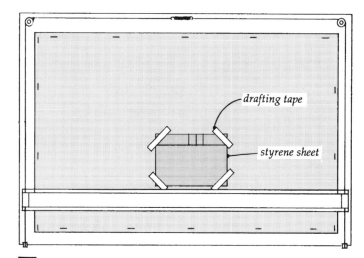

3a *Etch the cut and score lines into the plastic.*

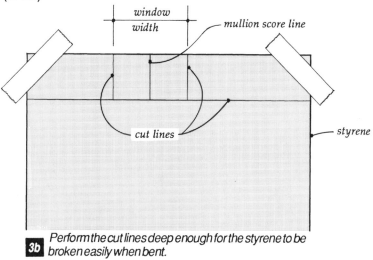

3b *Perform the cut lines deep enough for the styrene to be broken easily when bent.*

Step 4   *Break the sheet at the score lines.*

After you have scored all the cut lines remove the sheet from the cutting board and bend the sheet at the cut lines until it breaks. It may be necessary to cut all the way through the plastic at the horizontal cuts in order to break the plastic at the vertical cut lines. Once the window is separated from the sheet it is ready to be placed in the opening.

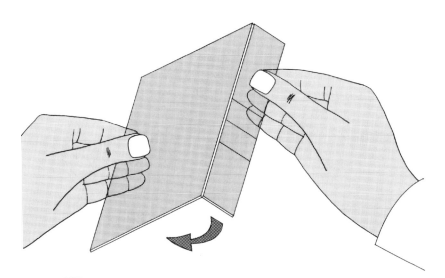

4 *Bend the sheet at the score line until it breaks.*

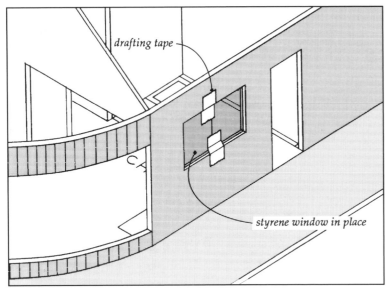

5 Set the glazing in the opening and apply drafting tape to hold it in place.

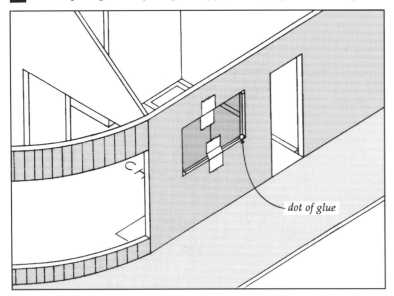

6 Place a small dot of glue at each corner.

Step 5   Set the glazing in place.

Hopefully it will be a tight enough fit that the plastic stays in place on its own. If not, apply a strip of drafting tape at the top and bottom to hold it in place while you apply glue to the corners.

Step 6   Apply glue to the corners.

Place a small dot of white glue at each corner of the glazing and matboard, being careful not to apply too much glue. All that is needed is a small bond between the plastic and matboard.

Let the glue dry for a couple hours and then remove the drafting tape. The window is now complete and gives a very realistic simulation of a full scale window. Repeat this construction technique for all of the windows.

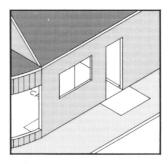

FINISHED STYRENE WINDOW

Let's now look at the procedures for constructing the segmented window in the curved portion of wall 10.

Constructing a Segmented Window

The fastest and easiest method for constructing the hinged segmented window in wall 10 as well as the corner windows is as follows:

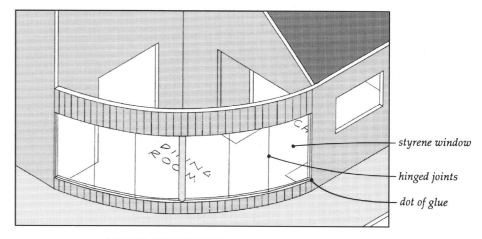

HINGED SEGMENTED WINDOW

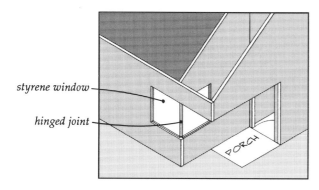

HINGED CORNER WINDOW

Step 1 Measure the window dimensions.

First, utilizing the 'thin strip of matboard' method measure the dimension of each segment from the floor plan as illustrated.

Step 2 Etch the guidelines and mullions.

Mark the window and mullion locations on the styrene and etch the guidelines. Score half-way through the plastic at the mullion and cutlines.

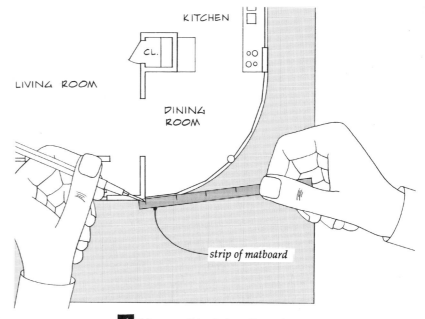

1 *Measure the window dimensions.*

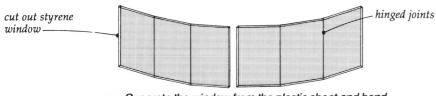

2 Etch the window score lines onto the sheet of styrene with an Xacto knife.

score lines
drafting tape
styrene sheet
cut lines (darker)

cut out styrene window
hinged joints

3 Separate the window from the plastic sheet and bend it at the mullions.

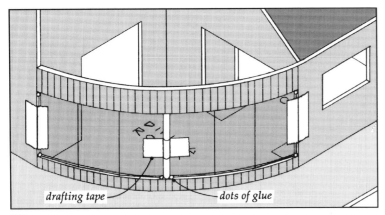

drafting tape
dots of glue

4 Set the window in place and apply glue at the corners to hold it in place.

Step 3   Detach window and bend at mullions.

Now, detach the window from the sheet and bend it at the mullion scorelines. If scored deep enough the joint will stay in the bent position.

Step 4   Attach glazing to opening.

Set the glazing in place and apply drafting tape to the edges to hold it while you apply glue. Apply small dots of white glue to the corners and allow two hours for it to dry before removing the tape.

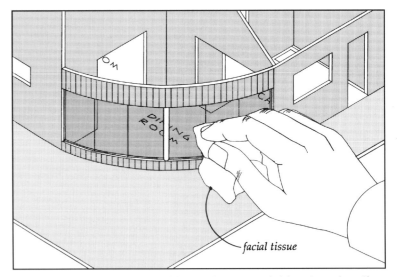

facial tissue

After the glue has dried it is a good idea to wipe the fingerprints off the window with a facial tissue being careful not to push the window out of place.

CONSTRUCTING THE ROOF

Once you have constructed all of the walls you are ready to begin constructing the roof. As indicated in the design drawings our house has a combination gable and flat roof. We will build the flat roof first.

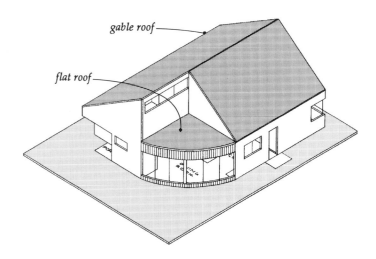

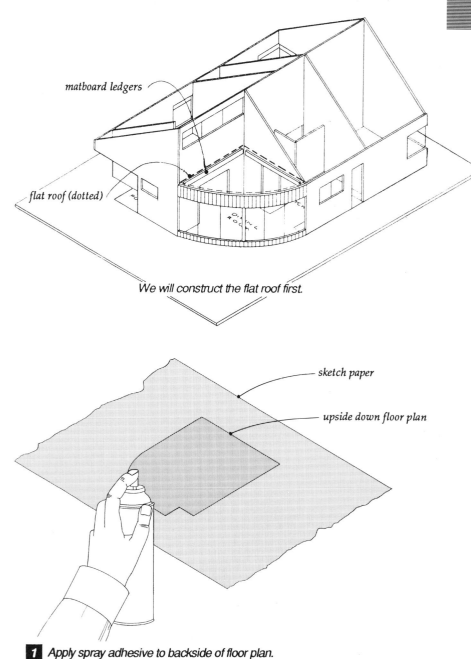

We will construct the flat roof first.

Constructing The Flat Roof

Step 1   Apply adhesive to floor plan.

To make the flat roof fit properly on top of the exterior walls, an additional copy of your floor plan must be used. First, spray the back of the floor plan blueprint that you set aside at the beginning of the model making process with a light coat of Artists Adhesive spray glue. Do not use Super spray glue unless you plan on leaving the paper on the roof.

1 *Apply spray adhesive to backside of floor plan.*

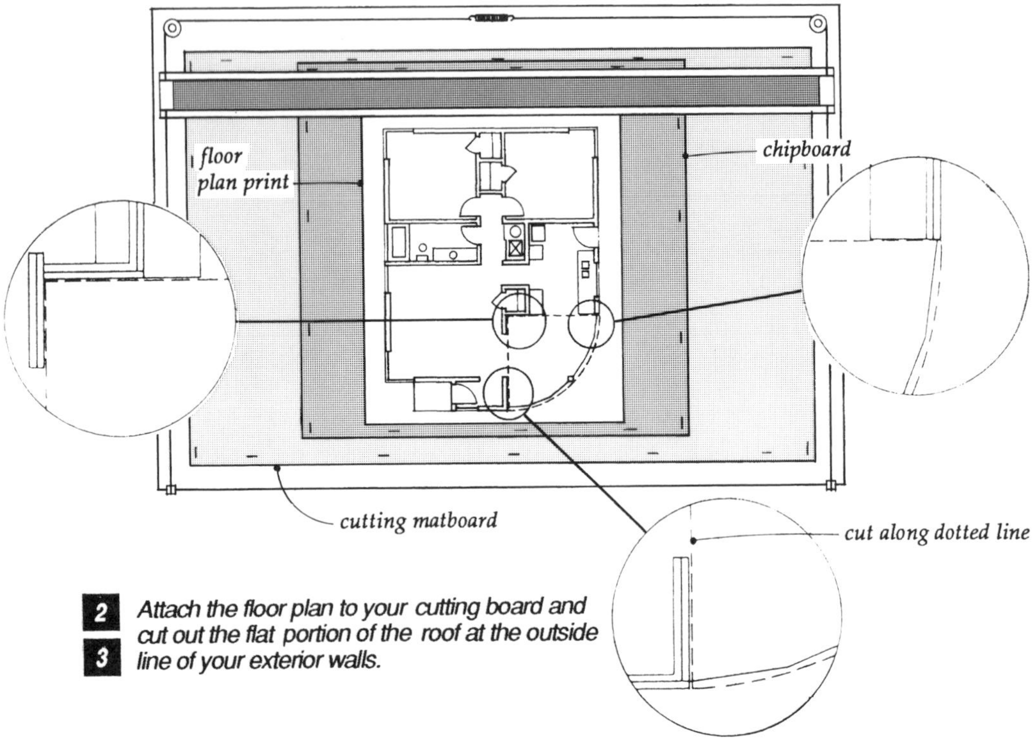

floor
plan print

chipboard

cutting matboard

cut along dotted line

2 Attach the floor plan to your cutting board and
3 cut out the flat portion of the roof at the outside
line of your exterior walls.

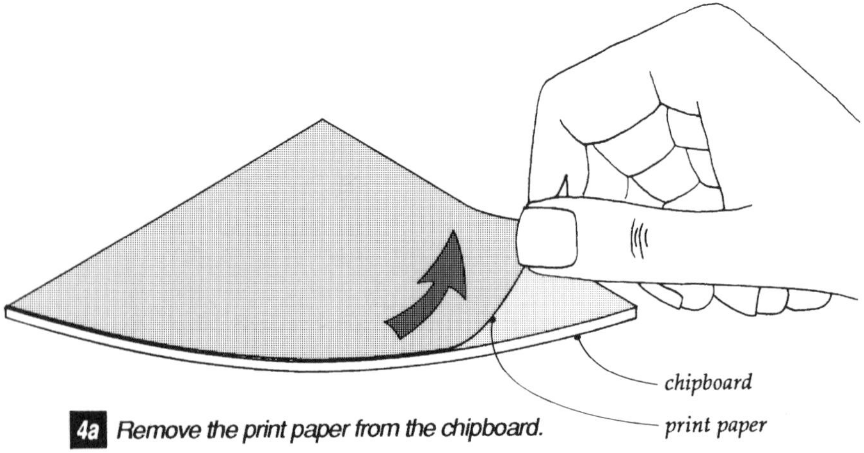

Step 2 Attach floor plan to sheet of chipboard.

Now, set the plan down on a sheet of chipboard
stapled to your cutting board and smooth it out with
your hands. Don't forget to place a sheet of sketch
paper over the plan before smoothing it out.

Step 3 Cut out the flat roof.

Cut out the flat portion of the roof from the floor
plan with a utility knife along the outside line of the
exterior walls, where your currently constructed
walls are sitting on the baseboard. If any of the
walls were not built in the same place as indicated
on the floor plan adjust your cutline accordingly.

Step 4 Remove print paper.

Now that you have your roof cut out remove the
print paper from it. The paper should lift up easily if
Artists Adhesive was used. If the paper does not
come off easily and sticks to the roof, it can be
covered up by adhering a sheet of grey paper on
top of it to simulate built-up roofing. This procedure
is as follows:

First, spray the top side of the cut out roof with
Super spray glue and set it down on a sheet of grey
paper. Canson paper has the best texture for
simulating grey roofing.

chipboard

print paper

4a *Remove the print paper from the chipboard.*

Next, simply cut through the paper with an Xacto knife along the edge of the matboard and smooth down the flaired edges with your fingernail. (Il. 4b)

The roof is now ready to be placed on top of the exterior walls. But, as you can see, the roof is not supported at the back since there are no short walls to support it. Therefore, ledgers must be attached to the back walls for the roof to set on top of.

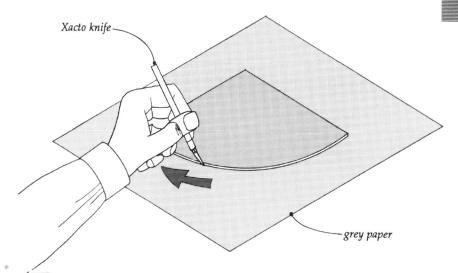

4b Set the roof on top of a sheet of grey paper and cut along the edge.

Step 5   Cut out and attach ledgers.

Set the roof aside and cut out two thin strips of chipboard approximately 1/8" x 3" to serve as ledgers.

Next, utilizing the 'thin strip of matboard' method of measuring, measure the height of your exterior bearing walls as illustrated.

With this measurement make two marks on the back walls to locate where the ledgers will be attached. Now apply a small line of glue to the back of your ledgers and attach them to the walls at the two marks you made. Make sure they are level with the tops of the bearing walls before allowing the glue to dry. Let the ledgers dry for about 10 minutes before setting the roof on top of them.

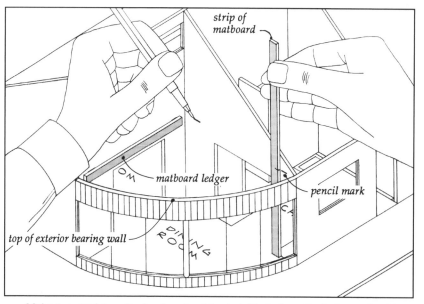

5 Make two marks on the back walls at the height of where the ledgers should be located.

6 *Set the roof on top of the walls and ledgers and trim any overlapping edges.*

overlapping edge

DINING ROOM

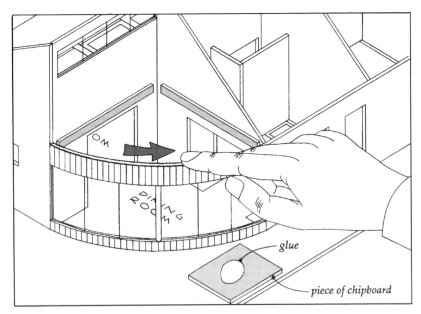

7 *Apply a thin layer of white glue to the top of the walls and ledgers.*

glue

piece of chipboard

DINING ROOM

Step 6 *Trim any overhanging edges.*

With the ledgers in place, set the roof on top of the walls to make sure it fits properly. Trim any roof edges that may be overhanging the walls by setting the roof on your cutting board and cutting them with a utility knife. The roof can now be glued to the top of the walls if so desired.

Step 7 *Apply glue to the top of the walls.*

The glue should be applied carefully so that it does not run down the sides of the walls, and is best done by applying the glue with your fingertip, as follows:

- First, squeeze out a small dab of white glue (about the size of a quarter) onto a spare piece of chipboard.

- Next, dip the tip of your index finger into the glue and run your finger along the top of the wall as illustrated. There is now too much glue on the edge even though you may not think there is, so wipe off your finger and remove some of the glue by running your finger along the edge. Do this a number of times until there is only a thin layer of glue on the edge, not a crowned bead.

- You must move quickly when applying glue to the top of walls, since it will dry on one side of the model while you are still applying it on the other side.

Step 8 *Attach roof to top of walls.*

Now, set the roof on top of the walls. Push down on it and remove any excess glue that oozes out at the edges with only one swipe of your index finger. If the wall is buckled inward or outward and does not line up with the edge of the roof, push on the wall with your finger from the inside or outside to align the two.

Next, apply small pieces of drafting tape across the roof and wall wherever necessary to hold the joint together until the glue dries. After the glue has dried carefully remove the tape and your flat roof is finished.

We will now build the gabled portion of our roof.

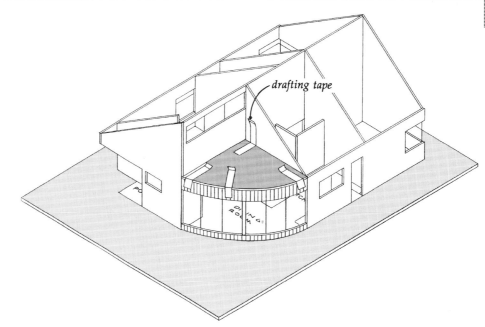

drafting tape

8 *Apply drafting tape to the joints until the glue is dry.*

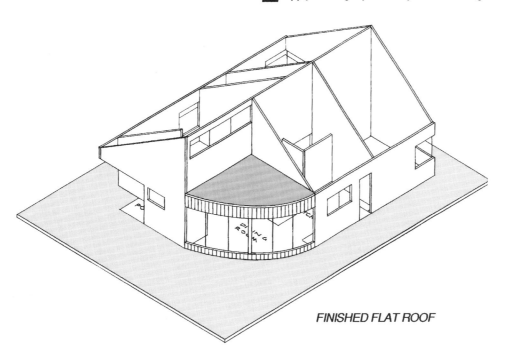

FINISHED FLAT ROOF

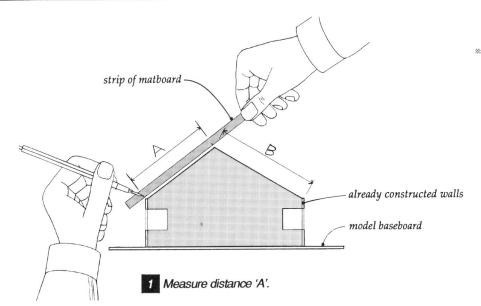

strip of matboard

A

B

already constructed walls

model baseboard

1 *Measure distance 'A'.*

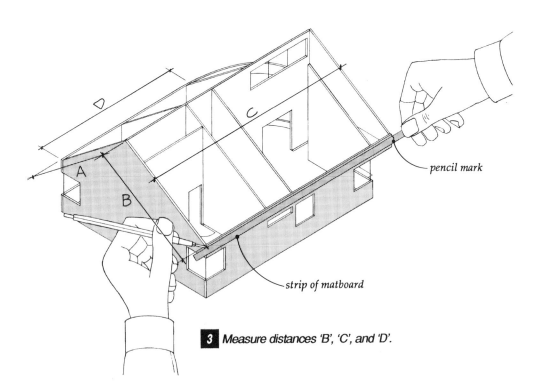

D

C

A

B

pencil mark

strip of matboard

3 *Measure distances 'B', 'C', and 'D'.*

Constructing The Gable Roof

Step 1 *Measure distance 'A'.*

First, measure the length of the sloping wall 'A' with a thin strip of matboard as illustrated. (Il. 3)

Step 2 *Draw two parallel lines distance 'A'.*

Staple a sheet of chipboard to your cutting board and draw two lines distance 'A' apart as illustrated on the following page. (Il. 3)

Step 3 *Measure distances 'B', 'C', and 'D'.*

Now, measure the length of your other sloping wall 'B' and draw a line this distance on the chipboard as illustrated. (Il. 3)

Then, measure the length of the roof perpendicular to the sloping walls and draw the two lines making two adjacent rectangles. This is your model roof plan with corrected dimensions. (Il. 3)

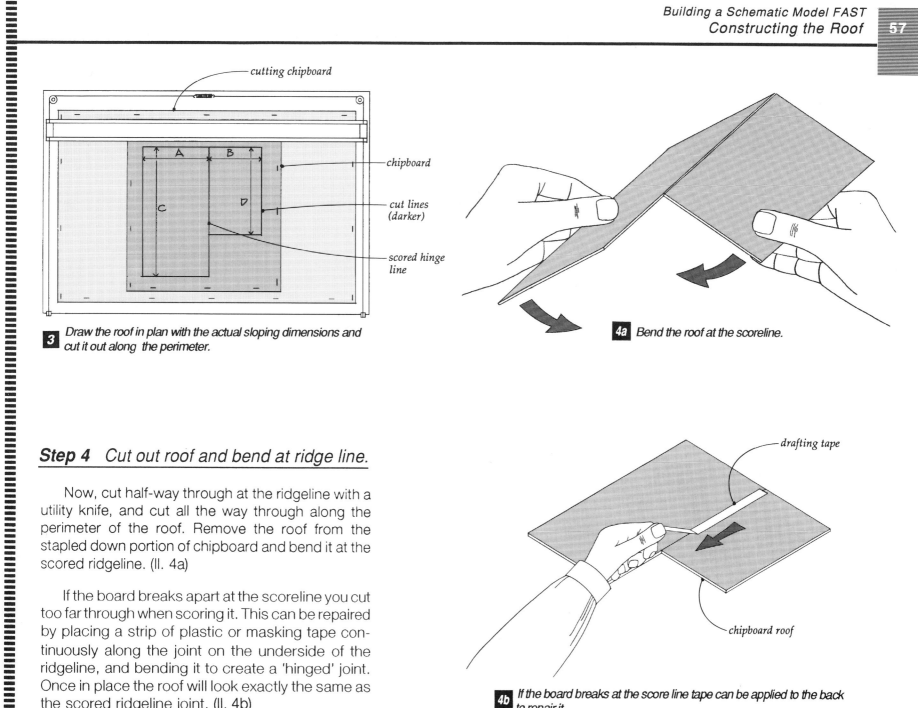

cutting chipboard

chipboard

cut lines (darker)

scored hinge line

3 Draw the roof in plan with the actual sloping dimensions and cut it out along the perimeter.

4a Bend the roof at the scoreline.

Step 4 Cut out roof and bend at ridge line.

Now, cut half-way through at the ridgeline with a utility knife, and cut all the way through along the perimeter of the roof. Remove the roof from the stapled down portion of chipboard and bend it at the scored ridgeline. (Il. 4a)

If the board breaks apart at the scoreline you cut too far through when scoring it. This can be repaired by placing a strip of plastic or masking tape continuously along the joint on the underside of the ridgeline, and bending it to create a 'hinged' joint. Once in place the roof will look exactly the same as the scored ridgeline joint. (Il. 4b)

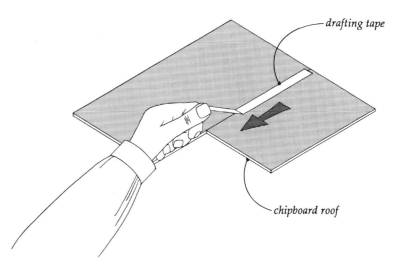

drafting tape

chipboard roof

4b If the board breaks at the score line tape can be applied to the back to repair it.

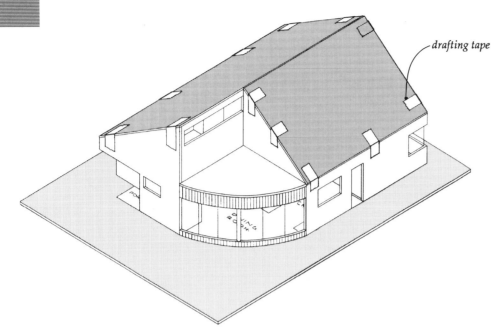

drafting tape

5 *Set the roof on top of the walls and apply strips of drafting tape along the joints until the glue is dry.*

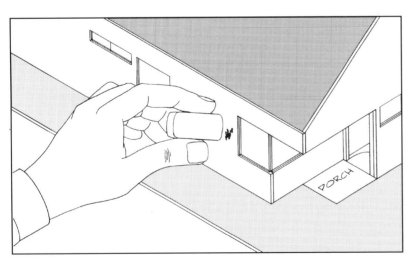

Clean off marks and fingerprints with a white plastic eraser.

Step 5   Set the roof in place.

Now you have the roof ready to be placed on top of the exterior walls. As with the flat roof you have the option of glueing the roof down or having it removable. To glue it down follow the same procedures as described for the flat roof:

- Apply a thin layer of white glue to the top of the walls removing excess glue with your fingertip.

- Set the roof on top of the walls and apply drafting tape at the edges to hold it down.

- Carefully remove the tape once the glue has dried.

FINISHED GABLE ROOF

After the roof is attached, your house is complete. Check all joints to make sure they are secure and apply more glue if necessary. Clean off any dirt or pencil marks with a white plastic eraser.

The next step to completing the model is to attach the sidewalk and porch.

CONSTRUCTING THE PORCH & SIDEWALK

Constructing the porch and sidewalk is a simple process of drawing scorelines onto a piece of white paper and attaching it to the model base. Let's look at the process:

Step 1   Attach paper to your cutting board.

First, tape down a sheet of white bond paper to your cutting board with the bottom edge lined up with your parallel bar.

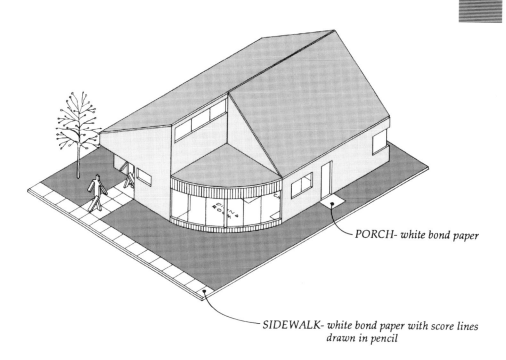

PORCH- *white bond paper*

SIDEWALK- *white bond paper with score lines drawn in pencil*

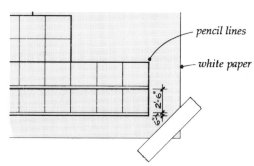

pencil lines

white paper

2'-6"

2b Residential sidewalks are generally 2'-6" wide with scorelines spaced 2'-6" apart.

Step 2   Draw the outline and score lines.

Draw in pencil or ink the outline of the concrete and the joint lines. Generally sidewalk scorelines are 2'-6" apart. Measure the back porch dimensions from your floor plan.

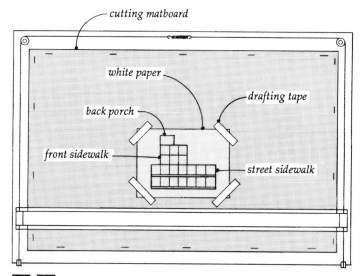

cutting matboard

white paper

drafting tape

back porch

front sidewalk

street sidewalk

1 **2a** Draw the outlines and scorelines of the sidewalk and porch.

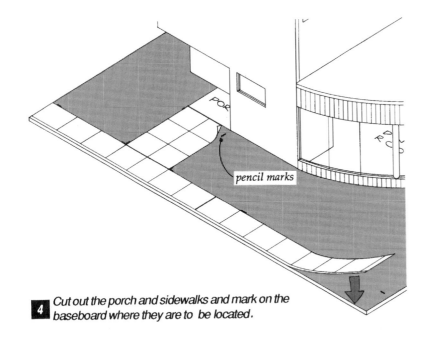

pencil marks

4 Cut out the porch and sidewalks and mark on the baseboard where they are to be located.

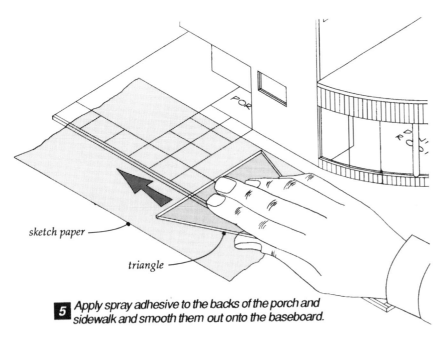

sketch paper

triangle

5 Apply spray adhesive to the backs of the porch and sidewalk and smooth them out onto the baseboard.

Step 3 *Cut out the porch and sidewalk.*

With the use of an Xacto knife and triangle, cut out the porch and sidewalk at their edges.

Step 4 *Mark location of sidewalk on baseboard.*

Make marks on the baseboard with a pencil where the sidewalk will be placed. Three or four marks along the distance of the walk will be sufficient.

Step 5 *Apply spray adhesive.*

Now, apply Super spray adhesive to the backs of the sidewalk and porch and attach them to the baseboard. Lay a sheet of sketch paper over them and smooth it out by sliding a triangle across it. Your sidewalk and porch are now complete.

Now, with the sidewalk and porch in place we will look at adding scaled objects to the model.

ADDING SCALED OBJECTS

The next step is to add some scaled objects (human figures, trees, cars, etc.) to the model that will give the house a discernable human scale. For our study model one or two human figures and a tree will be sufficient. If you would like to add some cars to the model refer to Chapter 7. Let's look at a technique for constructing chipboard human figures.

Constructing Human Figures

Step 1   Draw human figures on matboard.

First, staple a sheet of chipboard to your cutting board. Draw two or three people in elevation at the model scale onto the chipboard. (The figures on this page are drawn at 1/4" scale if you would like to trace or photocopy them).

Step 2   Cut out figures.

Begin cutting out the figures along the lines with a utility knife and straightedge in the numbered sequence indicated in the illustration. Some of the cuts will be so short that the only way to penetrate through the chipboard is to push down hard on the knife until it goes through it and into the cutting board. Remove the figures from the chipboard and smooth down their edges with your fingernail.

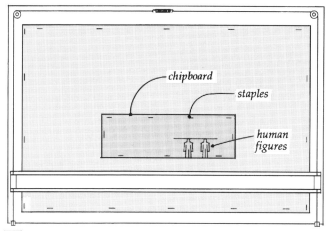

1 Draw human figures in elevation on the matboard.

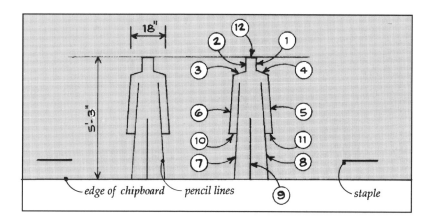

2 Cut out each figure with a utility knife in the series indicated beginning with 1.

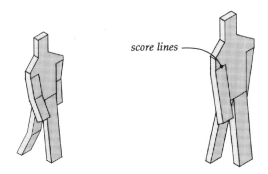

score lines

3 Move the arms and legs in opposite directions. The arms and legs can also be scored and bent at the knees and elbows.

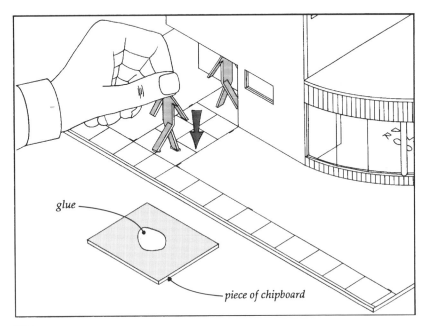

glue

piece of chipboard

4 Attach the figures to the model base.

Step 3   Move the arms and legs.

Bend the arms and legs in opposite directions at the shoulders and hips so that the figure will stand up by itself when glued to the baseboard. You may have to score one side of the matboard to move them.

The arms and legs can also be scored at the elbow and knee joints if desired.

Step 4   Attach the figures to the model.

To attach the figures, dip the bottom of both legs into a dab of white glue and place the figures on the model base somewhere next to the building. The most natural locations are on the porch or sidewalk.Let the figures set undisturbed for at least one hour.

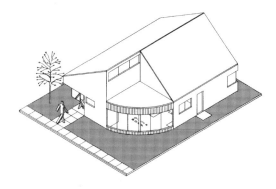

With the figures attached to the model, let's now look at constructing scaled trees.

Constructing Trees

Scaled trees on a schematic model can be constructed in many different ways; Styrofoam balls on sticks, frayed wires, or dried flowers for example. We will use dried flowers on our model. (See Chapter 7 for more tree types).

Dried wild flowers can be bought at craft stores and are available in various sizes and colors. For student schematic models, flower buds approximately 1/16" in diameter or smaller look most appropriate. Remember to 'think to scale' when selecting the flowers. Ask yourself, "Will this bundle look like a tree at my model scale?"

Let's look at the procedures for attaching a dried flower tree to our model:

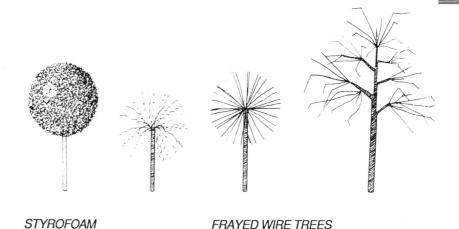

STYROFOAM
BALL TREE

FRAYED WIRE TREES

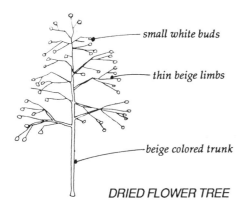

— *small white buds*

— *thin beige limbs*

— *beige colored trunk*

DRIED FLOWER TREE

Step 1 *Shape the tree into its proper form.*

Separate one or two branches from the bundle of flowers to use as your model tree. Shape the branches into a tree form that is approximately 15' in diameter and 30' high at the model scale.

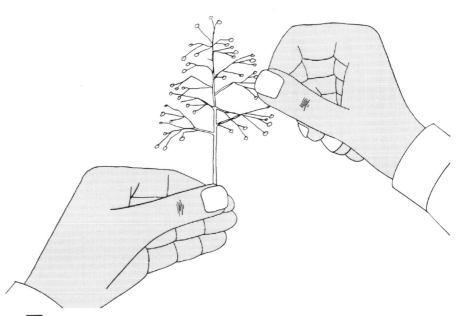

1 *Shape the tree by breaking off limbs until you have the desired form.*

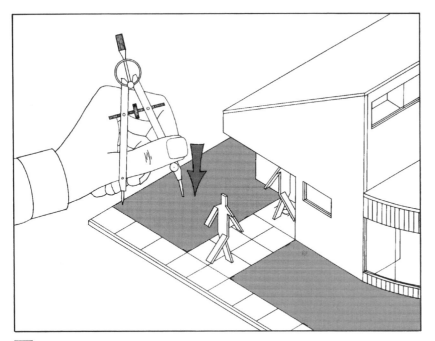

2 *Make a hole in the baseboard at the desired location with a sharp pointed object.*

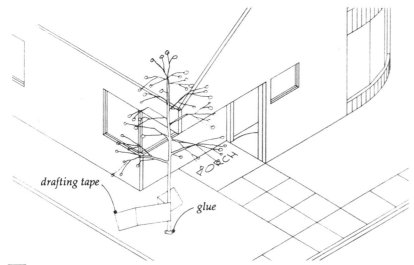

drafting tape

glue

3 *Set the tree in the hole and support it with drafting tape if necessary.*

Step 2   *Make a hole in the baseboard.*

Make a hole in your baseboard for the tree trunk to be inserted into. Since the baseboard is constructed of matboard it is difficult to penetrate. Set your model on top of your cutting board and push the sharp steel point of your compass into the matboard. Try not to make the hole any bigger than the tree trunk so that the tree will stand up by itself when inserted into the hole.

Step 3   *Attach tree to baseboard.*

Next, squeeze a small dab of white glue on top of the hole. Now, push the tree trunk through the glue and into the hole. Hopefully, the tree will stand up by itself. If it doesn't, apply a strip of drafting tape to the trunk and baseboard as illustrated to support it until the glue is dry.

Allow the glue to dry before moving the model. Once the glue has dried, carefully remove the tape and your tree is finished.

Once the tree is in place be careful not to accidentally hit it. The tree trunk is very brittle and will break easily.

Having completed our example model you now possess the basic skills of model making. Whether you are building architectural, interior, or engineering models the methods of cutting, glueing, and constructing the components are the same.

Let's move on now to the next chapter to learn how to make revisions to your model.

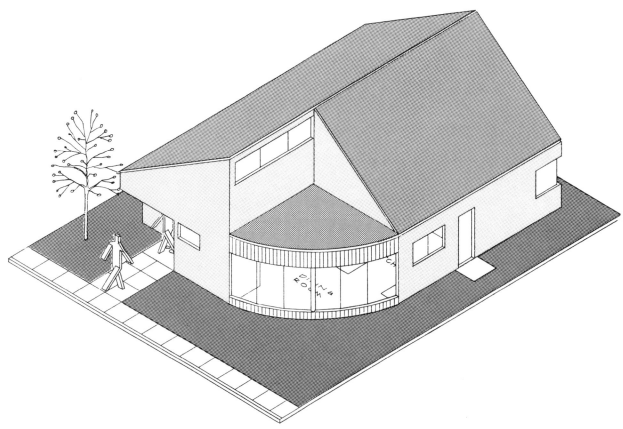

FINISHED SCHEMATIC STUDY MODEL

CHAPTER 3

Model Revisions

After spending many sleepless nights on your model, you carry it into class and are congratulated by your classmates and instructor on what a nice model it is.

But then your instructor starts to "hem" and "haw" over it and gives you suggestions on how to improve your design. You are shocked that after spending all that time and effort building the model, you now have to ruin it by moving a wall, reducing the size of a window, or, as I once encountered with a client on a presentation model, changing the color of the building.

Well don't be dismayed. Revisions are part of model making skills. You must be able to revise parts of the model, and do them cleanly. After all, a schematic study model is just what the name implies; a three-dimensional study of your design concept. Just as you redraw the elevations and floor plans over and over again you must also revise your three-dimensional representation.

Revisions can be easy. We will look at the techniques for revising a window, moving a wall, and removing a roof. The main objective behind every technique will be to show you how to make the revisions quickly and safely without causing anymore damage to the model than necessary. We will use our house model again for demonstration purposes.

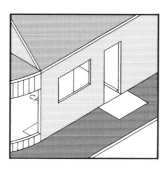

REVISING A WIDOW OPENING

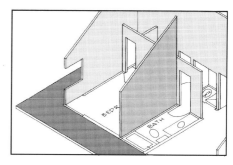

MOVING A WALL

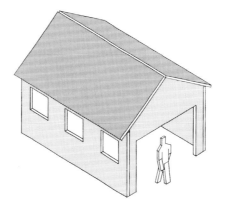

REMOVING A GABLE ROOF

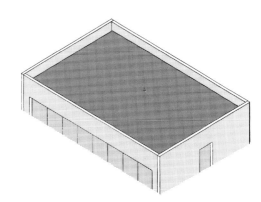

REMOVING A FLAT ROOF

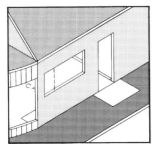

Increasing the Window Size by Removing a Portion of the Wall

Reducing the Window Size by In-filling

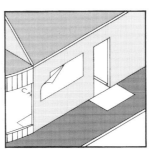

Increasing the Window Size by Applying a Larger Piece of Paper

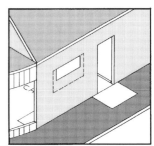

Reducing the Window Size by Applying a Smaller Piece of Paper

Changing the size of a window opening on a schematic model is a common revision performed during the design process. It can be either an easy process or an involved one, depending on the revision procedure. Increasing the window opening can be achieved by either cutting out portions of the wall adjacent to the opening, or applying a piece of plastic or paper over the opening. Reducing the opening size can be achieved by either adding a portion of wall into the opening, or replacing it with a smaller window. Let's look at each of these methods more closely.

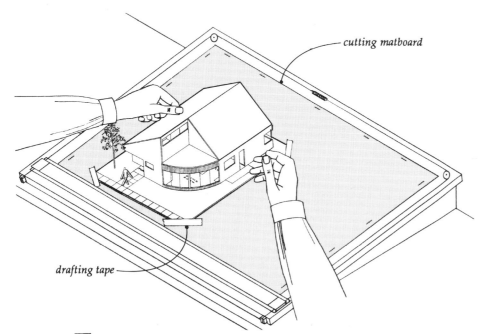

cutting matboard

drafting tape

1 Secure the model to your cutting board.

Increasing Window Size by Cutting Out Matboard

Removing portions of a wall adjacent to a window opening in chipboard involves a cutting technique that you will use over and over in making revisions. The objective is to cut a straight line through the chipboard wall that is glued to the baseboard without bending or ripping the wall from other components, such as your roof or floor. Let's look at this technique.

Step 1   Secure model to cutting board.

First, set the model on your cutting board in a position such that you can comfortably place both hands over or around it in a cutting position. You may want to tape the baseboard to your cutting board with drafting tape to keep it from moving around while you are working on it.

Step 2   Draw the cut lines.

With the use of your pencil and triangle draw the guidelines of the enlarged window opening onto the existing wall.

Step 3   Perform vertical cuts.

Place a small triangle against the wall with its edge lining up where you want to make your cut.

Now, making sure that the bottom of the triangle is sitting on the base so that you have a 90 degree angle, squeeze or push the triangle against the wall with your thumb and forefinger (stick your finger through an adjacent window or door opening if possible) to hold it in place while you make your first and second cut strokes. Use an Xacto knife with a sharp new blade and pull your stroke upward.

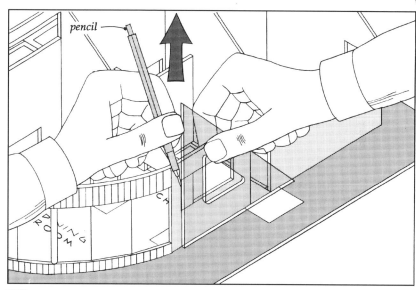

2 Draw the revision guidelines.

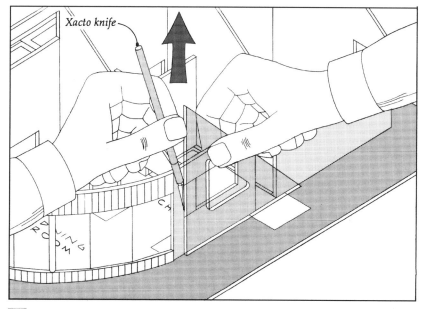

3 Perform the vertical cut.

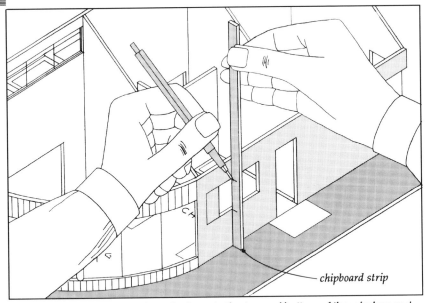

— chipboard strip

4a *Measure the distance from the base to the top and bottom of the window and cut out a piece of chipboard to use in performing the horizontal cuts.*

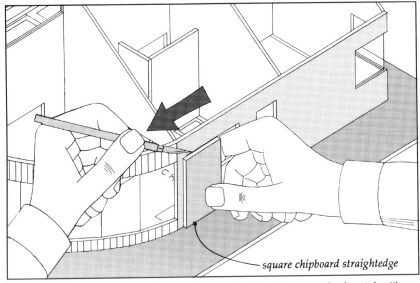

— square chipboard straightedge

4b *Hold the straightedge securely in place and perform the upper horizontal cutting strokes.*

Do not try to cut all the way through in one or two strokes. Just score along the cut line the first and second strokes and continue scoring until the blade goes through. Be patient and do not try to rush the technique. After three or four strokes the blade should penetrate, leaving the rest of your model still intact and undamaged. Now let's look at performing horizontal cuts.

Step 4 *Perform the upper horizontal cut.*

To perform straight horizontal cuts on an existing model wall, the procedure is the same as with vertical cuts: secure a straightedge against the surface of the wall to guide your Xacto knife blade during the first and second strokes.

For both horizontal and vertical cuts you can usually remove the straightedge from the wall after you have scored a groove deep enough to keep the blade from straying off course during your final cutting strokes.

Because a triangle is too big to set under the window and would not sit securely on the base, it will not be used for performing horizontal cuts. Instead, make a straightedge out of chipboard that will line up exactly at the cut line and rest on top of the baseboard.

To make sure that it is exactly the right height measure the distance from your base to the top of your window with a thin strip of matboard as illustrated, and cut out a piece of chipboard the required height. (ll. 4a)

Now set your straightedge against the wall and hold it in place the same way you held the triangle for vertical cuts. (ll. 4b) Perform the cut with a sharp Xacto knife and make a series of score cuts until you penetrate through. Once you have cut through you are ready to perform the lower horizontal cut.

Step 5   *Perform the lower horizontal cut.*

To perform the lower horizontal cut, follow the same procedures described for the upper horizontal cut. The same matboard straightedge can be cut down to the lower cut height and held firmly against the wall between your thumb and forefinger.

Once the piece is removed, smooth down the flaired edges with your fingernail and you have a finished window opening.

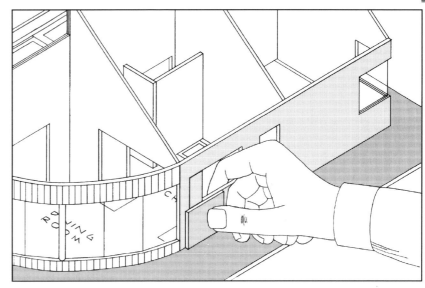

5 *Cut your straightedge down to line up at the bottom of your window and perform the lower horizontal cuts.*

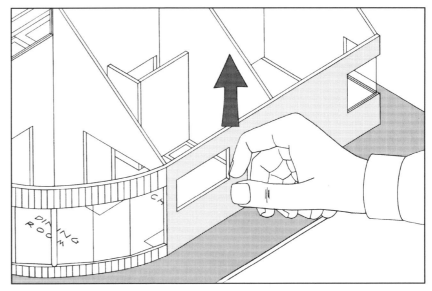

Smooth down the flaired edges by running your fingernail over them.

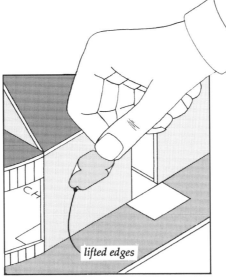

Increasing the size of a window can be achieved by applying a piece of paper or plastic over the existing opening.

colored paper or plastic window

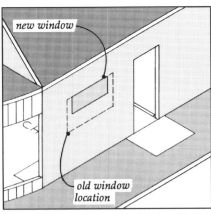

If your window is simulated with a piece of paper or plastic decal you can reduce the size by applying a smaller piece.

new window

old window location

Remove the paper window by lifting up each corner and pull toward the center.

lifted edges

Increasing Window Size by Applying Paper or Film to Matboard

Another method for revising window openings is to attach colored paper or plastic film over the opening to simulate the window glazing. This can save much time in the overall model construction and especially for revisions. You simply cut out the required window size and stick the paper or plastic film onto the chipboard wall. This way you do not have to cut any window openings in the walls, you simply spray the paper with Artists Adhesive spray glue and attach them to the wall. Or, in the case of plastic film, cut out your windows from sticky backed decals and apply them to the walls.

Design instructors encourage these types of time saving methods since they realize how valuable time is to students. Their main interest is to see your design intent, not to make more work for you. Remember, they were students once too.

Reducing Window Size by Revising Paper Window Size

If your existing windows are simulated with paper or plastic film attached to the matboard walls you can revise their size by simply removing the old window and replacing it with a smaller one. If, however, Super spray glue was used to attach them instead of Artists Adhesive you may not be able to remove them from the walls.

To remove the existing window, lift up one corner with your Xacto knife enough to grab it with your fingertips and then slowly pull it off. If it starts to lift off a portion of the matboard, stop and try another corner. If, after all the corners have been tried, you still cannot remove the window without tearing the matboard, try to control the ripping to an area that will be covered with your new window. Once the old window has been removed, apply the new window.

Reducing Window Size by Infilling

Window openings in a matboard wall cannot be reduced in size by applying paper over them and must therefore be filled-in with additional matboard. Let's look at this procedure:

Step 1 *Measure the infilling size.*

First, utilizing the 'thin strip of matboard' method measure the required size of infilling necessary to reduce the opening to its desired size. (ll. 1a & 1b)

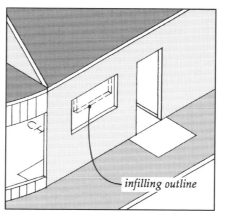

infilling outline

Actual window openings in a wall are reduced by filling in the opening with a piece of matboard.

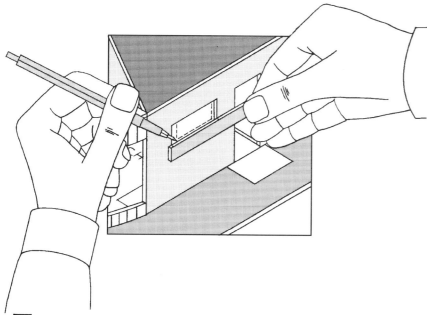

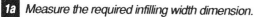
1a *Measure the required infilling width dimension.*

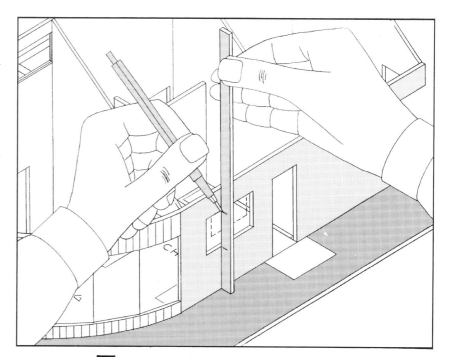

1b *Measure the required vertical dimension.*

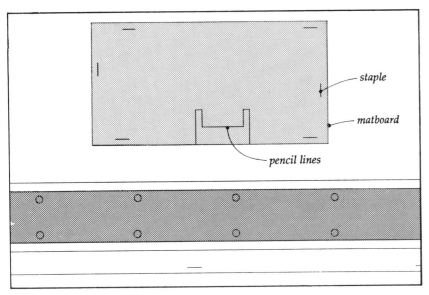

staple

matboard

pencil lines

2 Draw the infilling onto a piece of matboard and cut it out.

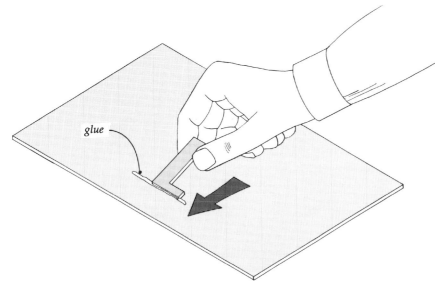

glue

3 Apply a thin layer of white glue to the edges by sliding them into a line of glue.

Step 2 Draw and cut out infilling.

Next, draw the infilling onto a piece of the same matboard that was used for the walls and cut it out. Smooth down the flaired edges with your fingernail. Set the piece in the opening and trim it if necessary.

Step 3 Apply glue to the piece.

Apply a line of white glue to the piece at the edges that will be in contact with the existing opening. The best method for applying the glue is to slide the edge through a line of glue as illustrated. Don't forget to remove some of the excess glue from the edges by tapping them down on a spare piece of matboard.

Step 4 Set the piece in place.

Next, set the piece in place in the existing opening. Position the piece so that it blends in with the existing wall as much as possible and remove any excess glue from the joint with one swipe of your finger. The main objective of the procedure is to hide the joint as much as possible. Let the piece set undisturbed for at least one hour.

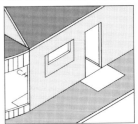

4 Set the piece in place and allow the glue to dry.

MOVING WALLS

The next procedure, relocating walls, involves separating a matboard wall from an adjacent wall and the model baseboard, without delaminating the outer layer of paper on the matboard. This procedure is the same for either matboard or Foamcore walls. The best method for doing this is as follows:

Step 1 *Score the joint.*

First, score the inside of the glued vertical joint with an Xacto knife so that when the boards are pulled apart the outer layer of matboard does not delaminate from the walls.

Step 2 *Separate the walls.*

Next, grasp both walls between your thumb and fingers with both hands and pull the wall to be moved in a downward motion with your left hand. Remember to pull downward so that the wall does not become separated from the base. Now that you have the two walls separated from each other you can remove the wall from the base.

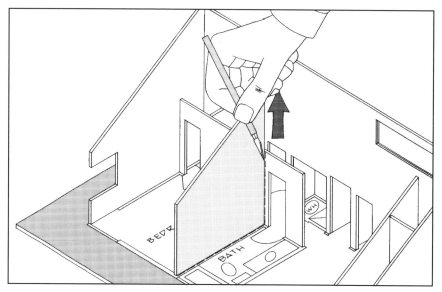

1 *Score the joint along the dotted line on both sides of the wall to be moved.*

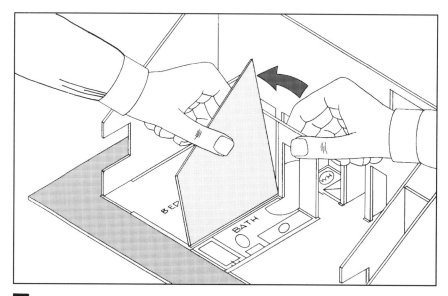

2 *Separate the two walls by pulling down on the wall to be moved.*

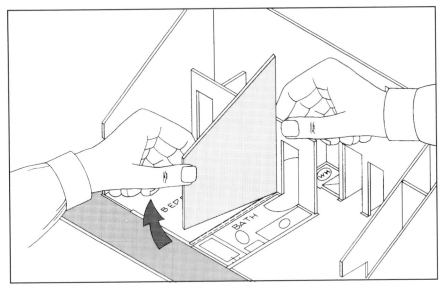

3 *Separate the wall from the baseboard by sliding it horizontally.*

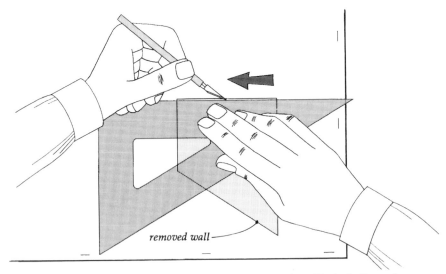

removed wall

4 *Trim off the rough edges of the wall with the use of an Xacto knife and straightedge.*

Step 3   Separate the wall from the base.

To remove the wall from the baseboard your main concern is to not allow the outer layer of the base matboard to delaminate. The procedure is the same as with separating the walls.

Score both sides of the joint with your Xacto knife only as deep as the outer layer of matboard paper. Again, pull the board downward, and then horizontally parallel to the baseboard surface. This will give you a clean break without ripping any paper. This is a typical technique for separating any two matboards joined together in a "T" connection.

You now have the wall separated from the baseboard and adjacent wall, and can prepare it to be relocated to its new position.

Step 4   Trim the rough edges.

Set the wall on top of your cutting matboard and trim the rough edges. With the use of a utility knife and triangle cut approximately 1/32" off the rough edges. You should now have sharp clean edges around the wall.

The wall is now ready to be relocated to its new position on the model.

REMOVING A ROOF

Removing a glued-down roof from a model is a difficult procedure which often leaves the roof in such condition that it can't be reused. By literally having to rip the roof from the top of the walls, it becomes bent and torn. Following are procedures for removing two types of roofs: a flat roof with parapet walls, and an overhanging gable roof.

Flat Roof with Parapet Walls

Step 1 Cut a hole in the roof.

First, using a utility knife cut a hole in the roof large enough to fit your index finger into.

Step 2 Rip the roof off.

Now, slowly and with as much care as possible rip the roof off the top of the walls. Push down on top of the parapet walls with your other hand to keep them from separating at the baseboard.

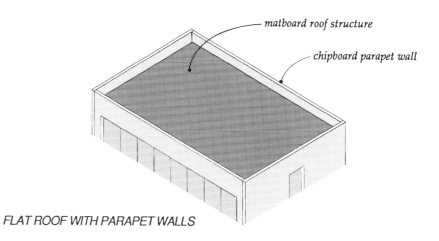

matboard roof structure

chipboard parapet wall

FLAT ROOF WITH PARAPET WALLS

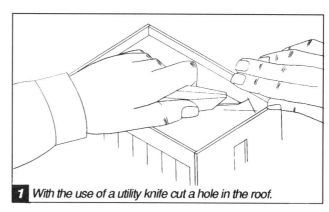

1 *With the use of a utility knife cut a hole in the roof.*

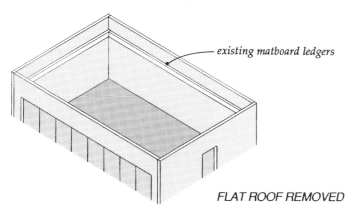

existing matboard ledgers

FLAT ROOF REMOVED

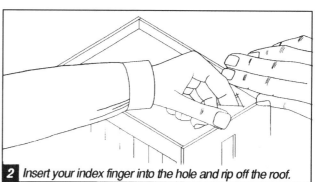

2 *Insert your index finger into the hole and rip off the roof.*

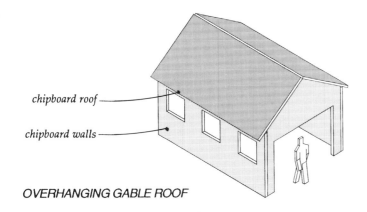

chipboard roof

chipboard walls

OVERHANGING GABLE ROOF

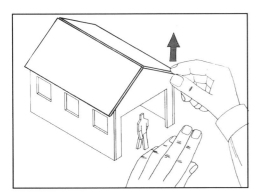

1 *Peel up one corner of the roof.*

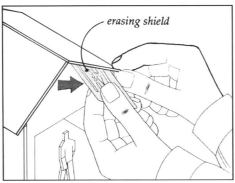

erasing shield

2 *Slide your erasing shield along the joint to separate the pieces.*

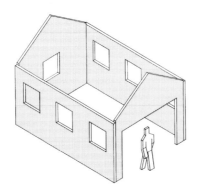

ROOF REMOVED

Overhanging Gable Roof

This type of roof is much easier to remove than the 'flat with parapet walls' since the roof is overhanging.

Step 1 Peel up one corner of the roof.

First, grasp one corner of the roof between your thumb and forefinger and peel the roof off at a corner of the supporting walls.

Step 2 Separate the roof from the walls.

With the corner lifted up, slide your erasing shield along the inside joint between the roof and walls to separate the two. Do this along the entire joint while gently lifting up the roof, being careful not to separate the walls from the baseboard.

Once the roof is separated, it may be reused if care was taken during its removal.

Now that we have covered how to construct and revise a schematic study model, let's take a look in the next chapter at some of the various materials available to the model maker for constructing models.

CHAPTER 4

Model Materials: Types and Their Uses

The number of model materials available to the model builder is limitless. Just as in full scale building construction where the number of building materials is only limited to your imagination, the same can be said for model materials.

For our purposes we will look at the basic materials used in model construction: cardboards, papers, plastics, knives, and glues. We will not only discuss their physical properties, but also their uses and availability.

The materials can be purchased at graphic art supply stores, hobby and craft shops, department and plastic supply stores and architectural model supply stores. Each supplier can be found by looking in the yellow pages of your phone directory. If you cannot locate a store in your area, such as an architectural model supply store, go to your city library and look in the yellow pages of a large metropolitan area close to you. The store will gladly send you a catalog.

Don't hesitate to ask questions of sales clerks, they are usually quite helpful in assisting you in finding materials and also have catalogs available from which to select needed supplies.

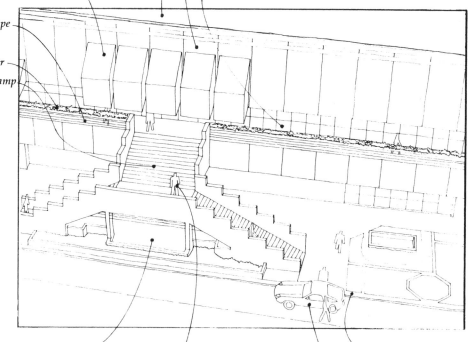

ROOF- grey Canson paper laminated to chipboard roof

STUCCO PANELS- rough finish cream colored matboard

CANVAS AWNINGS- hinged Canson paper

GLASS STOREFRONT- grey coated paper with inked lines laminated to chipboard backing

GUARDRAIL- clear styrene with green graphic tape

RAILING PLANTER- green flocking inside hinged Canson paper planter

STAIRS- pencil lines drawn on colored matboard ramp

FOUNTAIN POOL- blue plastic film laminated to white Strathmore board

PEOPLE- white Strathmore board

BRICK PAVING- brick pattern photocopied on Canson paper laminated to matboard

AUTO- store bought plastic

FINAL PRESENTATION MODEL

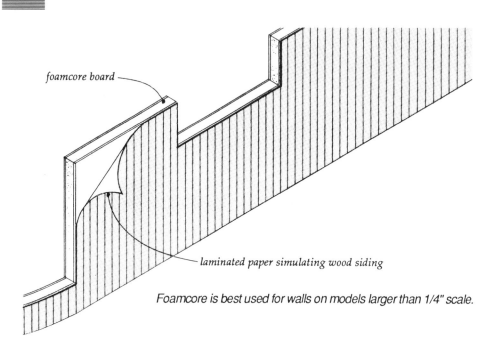

foamcore board

laminated paper simulating wood siding

Foamcore is best used for walls on models larger than 1/4" scale.

BOARDS

Boards and papers usually comprise at least 90% of the materials used on a model. Almost every component, from the baseboard to the roof, is constructed out of board or paper, with the exception of the windows and landscaping. (Refer to Chapter 6 for methods of simulating building materials with boards and papers).

They are available in many different textures, sizes, and thicknesses and can be attached to each other with white glue. Some of the boards we will look at are Foamcore, cardboard, chipboard, matboard and Strathmore board. The papers most commonly used are Canson paper and paint coated papers.

Foamcore

Foamcore board consists of two layers of white semi-porous paper or plastic film with a rigid plastic polystyrene foam sandwiched between them. It is available at graphic arts supply stores in thicknesses of 1/8", 3/16", 1/4" and 1/2", with two board sizes of 32"x40" and 40"x60". The board is best cut with an Xacto knife, and attached to the model with white glue. It is excellent for walls and roofs, and ideal for base construction.

On models larger than 1/4" scale, Foamcore is usually used for wall construction instead of matboard due to its available thicknesses which are equal to the scaled wall thickness. Colored paper or boards can be laminated to the Foamcore to simulate building material finishes. Curved walls cannot be created with Foamcore unless the outer layers of paper or film are removed.

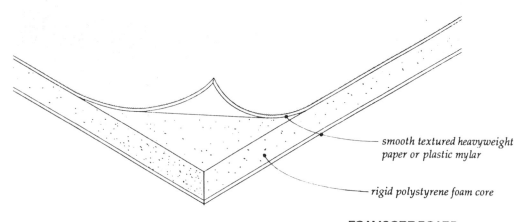

smooth textured heavyweight paper or plastic mylar

rigid polystyrene foam core

FOAMCORE BOARD

Cardboard

Corrugated cardboard consists of two outer layers of a heavy brown paper laminated to a corrugated paper core. It is most commonly found as the material used for constructing shipping boxes, and varies in thickness from 1/8" to 1/4". It is available at grocery and department stores usually at no cost, and is also available in 24"x72" sizes at graphic arts supply stores. It can be cut with a utility or Xacto knife and attached to other paper materials with white glue. Due to its crude nature it should not be used on final presentation models, but is an economical material for use on conceptual and schematic models.

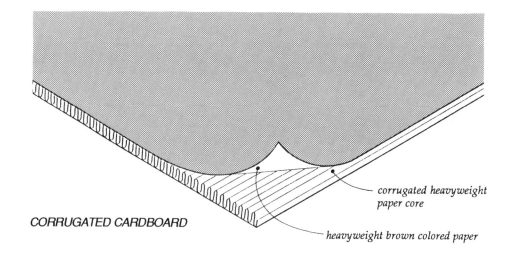

CORRUGATED CARDBOARD

corrugated heavyweight paper core

heavyweight brown colored paper

Chipboard

Chipboard is the most economical type of board and is excellent for design studio models. It is available in thicknesses varying from 1/32" to 1/8" with a board size of 32"x40" at graphic arts supply stores, and can also be found as the backboard of any tablet of paper. It has the same basic construction as matboard, two laminated layers of grey pulp paper, but does not have any outer layers of colored paper like matboard does.

The board is best cut with a utility knife and attached to the model with white glue. It can also be drawn on to simulate building materials such as wood siding or stone veneer, and colored paper can be laminated to it to create your own matboard finish. It can be utilized for walls, roofs, and floors, and can be scored to create curved surfaces.

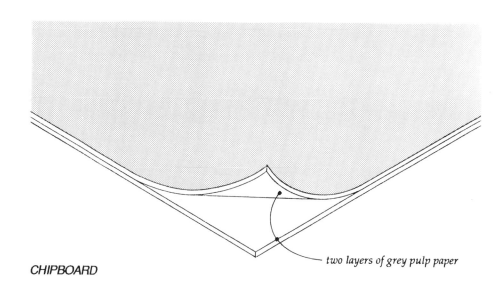

CHIPBOARD

two layers of grey pulp paper

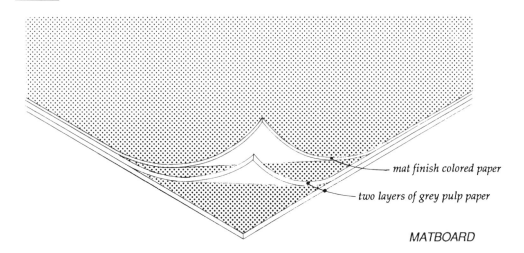

mat finish colored paper

two layers of grey pulp paper

MATBOARD

Matboard

Matboard, or museum board, as it is sometimes referred to, is generally available at graphic arts supply stores in a thickness of .055' (a little less than 1/16") with two board sizes of 30"x40" and 40"x60". The board is constructed of two layers of white pulp paper laminated to one exterior finish layer. The outside finish layer is available in a varied assortment of colors and textures, ranging from fabrics to mirror simulation. Ask a salesclerk in a graphic arts supply store for a sample catalog of matboards and you will see the wide range of design possibilities.

The board is best cut with a utility knife and attached to the model with white glue. It can be drawn on with ink or pencil to simulate various building materials and is used for walls, roofs, and floors.

Strathmore Boards

Strathmore is the company brand name of a series of boards available in thicknesses of 1/32" to 1/8", and are constructed of two to five plies of white paper laminated together. The board surface is available in two textures, plate (smooth) and regular (rough), and two colors, black and white. What makes the board ideal for models is the fact that the color is continuous throughout the core. Different color outer paper and core can be distracting on final presentation models.

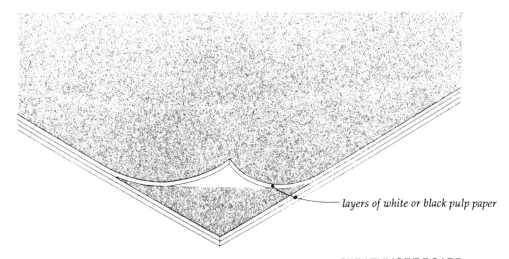

layers of white or black pulp paper

STRATHMORE BOARD

Strathmore is available at graphic art supply stores in sizes of 22"x30" and 30"x40". It is best cut with a utility knife and attached with white glue. It is excellent for wall construction due to its rough mat finish which can simulate plaster interior walls on a 1/4" scale model or stucco on a 1/8" model. For student design models, the thin 1/32" board is highly recommended since it can be cut more easily and faster than thicker boards. The board can be scored to create curved surfaces and is excellent for "hinged" wall construction.

Canson Paper

Canson paper is a company brand name and is available in a wide assortment of colors. Strathmore also has a paper of this type called 'charcoal paper'. It is of a heavier weight than regular colored paper and is available at graphic art supply stores in sheet sizes of approximately 20"x26" and 22"x30". It can be easily cut with an Xacto knife or scissors and is excellent for laminating to chipboard to create your own colored walls, roofs or floors. White glue is best used for attaching butted edges, but spray adhesive is best for laminating. It can be drawn on with ink or pencil to simulate building materials such as stone, wood, tile or concrete, and can be photocopied onto to create any pattern you desire.

Paint Coated Paper

Sheets of paper sprayed with a thin layer of paint are available in a wide assortment of colors at graphic art supply stores. It is available in sheet sizes of 10"x13" and 20"x26". It is excellent for laminating to chipboard to create any color board you desire. Due to its thinness it can be scored and bent around the corner of walls that are already constructed to create corners with no exposed board edges. This procedure enables the student model builder to achieve results equal in texture and shade definition to professionally spray painted plastic model construction.

Colored paper can also be obtained from paint supply stores. Paint supply companies provide architects with sheets of paint coated paper as samples of their product and are equal in quality to coated paper sold in graphic art supply stores. Thus, a model can be constructed in the exact color that the building will eventually be painted. The paper should be laminated to a matboard with spray adhesive, and can be drawn on with pencil or ink. Also, colored or patterned plastic decals can be applied to the paper to simulate windows and building materials.

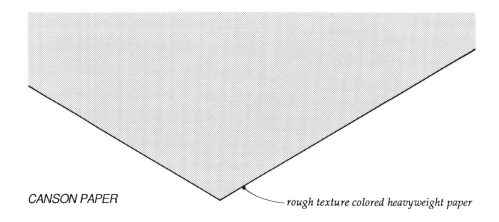

CANSON PAPER — *rough texture colored heavyweight paper*

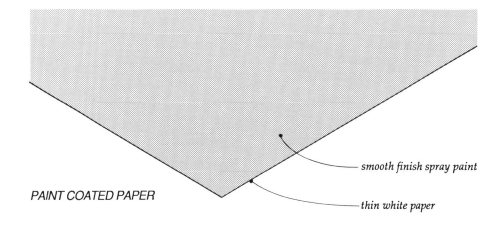

PAINT COATED PAPER — *smooth finish spray paint* — *thin white paper*

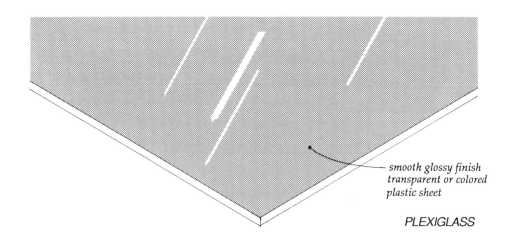

— plastic film decal pattern

— styrene or acetate windows

FINAL PRESENTATION MODEL

— smooth glossy finish
transparent or colored
plastic sheet

PLEXIGLASS

PLASTICS

Plastics bring a new dimension to a model. Their glossy appearance add to the authenticity of the scaled building components when used to simulate typical materials such as windows, skylights, and bodies of water. They can be used on all types of models from conceptual to final presentation and can be applied with various types of glue.

Plastics are available in many different forms. The types most commonly used in model construction are; Plexiglass, styrene, acetate, films, tapes, geometrical shapes, and structural steel shapes.

Plexiglass

Plexiglass is available in a large assortment of colors and finishes, with thicknesses of 1/8", 1/4", and 1/2". It can be purchased at plastic supply stores in any size up to 4'x8' and can be cut at the store. Due to the difficulty in cutting Plexiglass, I recommend having the store cut it for you. Plexiglass is excellent for simulating bodies of water such as oceans, lakes and swimming pools, but it is much too thick to serve as small windows on student models.

Super glues are used to attach it to other components and plastic tapes can be applied to it to simulate mullions on a large window wall. It can be cut with a Plexiglass cutting knife, but only if it is the 1/8" thickness. The 1/4" and 1/2" thicknesses must be cut with electric power saws.

Styrene

Styrene is a thin transparent sheet of plastic that is excellent for schematic and final presentation models. Its 1/32" thickness and soft density provides model builders with excellent window and skylight material that can be cut easily with an Xacto knife. The 8"x10" sheet size can be taped to your cutting board with drafting tape. It can be bought at hobby stores specializing in model airplane parts, and attached to other components with white glue. Window mullions can be etched into the plastic with an Xacto knife, or drawn on with an ink pen. (Technical pen and india ink is recommended).

Acetate

Acetate is a thin plastic sheet that comes in a roll form and is therefore not thick enough to serve as windows or skylights unless it is laminated to a chipboard backing. Once laminated it takes on the appearance of a thick sheet of Plexiglass and can be easily cut with a utility knife. It is available in one thickness and approximately four colors, and can be purchased at graphic art supply stores.

Plastic Films

Plastic films (or 'decals' as they are commonly referred to) can be purchased in sheet sizes of 10"x15" or 20"x26" and are available in a wide selection of colors and patterns. They are provided with an adhesive on the back for laminating to a backing board, and can be cut with an Xacto knife. They can be drawn onto with pencil or technical pen to simulate material patterns and mullions.

Patterns available range from brickwork to roofing shingles so that actual building materials can be depicted at a selected scale. The sheets are available at graphic art supply stores and can be selected from a catalog.

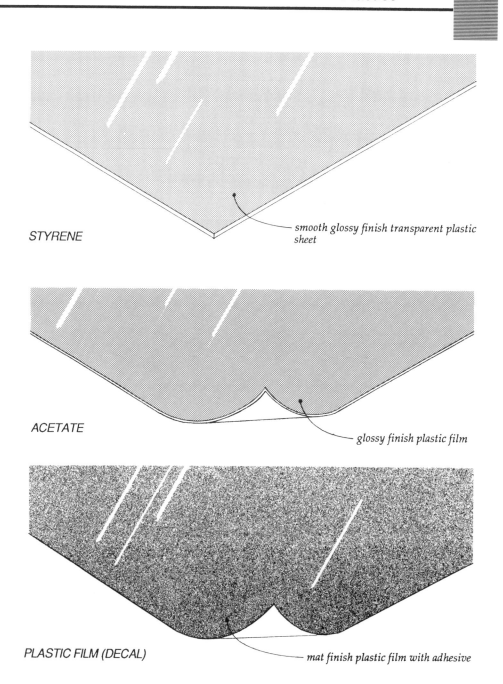

STYRENE
smooth glossy finish transparent plastic sheet

ACETATE
glossy finish plastic film

PLASTIC FILM (DECAL)
mat finish plastic film with adhesive

PLASTIC GRAPHIC TAPES

Plastic tapes are available in a wide variety of widths, patterns, and colors and can be cut with an Xacto knife. They have adhesive on the back enabling them to be attached to other components. Ask your graphic art supply store clerk for a catalog.

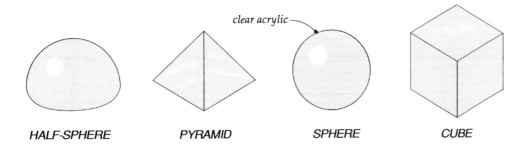

HALF-SPHERE   PYRAMID   SPHERE   CUBE

clear acrylic

Geometrical Plastic Shapes

Clear acrylic plastic shapes such as cubes, pyramids, spheres, half spheres, cylinders, tubes, and rods are available in a variety of shapes and sizes at plastic supply stores. They are usually made of the same plastic as Plexiglass and are therefore difficult to cut without an electric power saw. But, the rods can be bent into any shape you desire by heating them. They are best attached to other plastic components with Super glue.

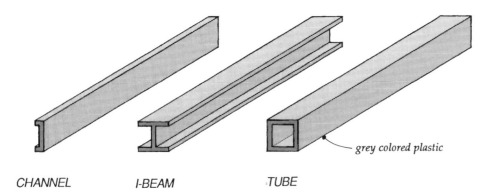

CHANNEL   I-BEAM   TUBE

grey colored plastic

Plastic Structural Shapes

Plastic structural steel column and beam shapes can be purchased at hobby stores to simulate a buildings' structure at scales of 1/8"=1'-0" and larger. The plastic is graphite in color and can be cut with a hack saw blade. They can be attached to each other with Super glue and can be spray painted when assembled.

KNIVES

Basically there are two types of knives used in model construction: the utility knife and the Xacto knife. Each should be used for its specific uses.

Extreme care must be taken when using a knife of any type and safety glasses must be worn. You must think about a cutting procedure before performing it to avoid any possible danger. No model component is more important than your physical safety.

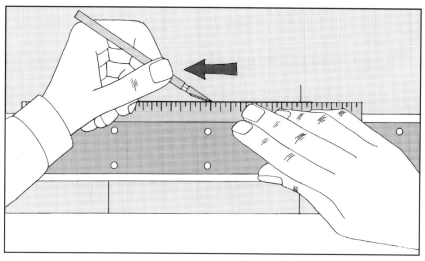

Extreme care must be taken when using a knife of any type and safety glasses must be worn.

Utility Knife

The utility knife is used for cutting cardboard, matboard, or any other type of heavy, thick board. It can also cut paper and light boards, but is cumbersome for such purposes. Xacto knives are best used for these purposes. There are basically two type of utility knives available; the fixed blade and the retractable blade.

The fixed blade type can be purchased in hardware stores, graphic art supply stores and some supermarkets. It is limiting in its speed of use since it has to be taken apart to change the blade. This can be a time consuming task considering how often you have to change blades when constructing a model. The blade should be changed as soon as the tip gets dull or broken.

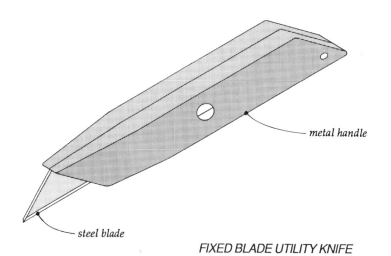

metal handle

steel blade

FIXED BLADE UTILITY KNIFE

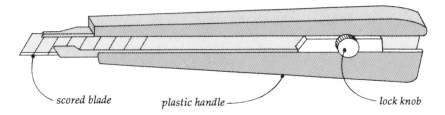

scored blade *plastic handle* *lock knob*

RETRACTABLE BLADE UTILITY KNIFE

The retractable utility knife (often referred to as a 'matknife') can be purchased at graphic art supply stores and hobby shops. It is used for the same purposes as the fixed blade, but is more versatile due to the ease of obtaining a fresh point. The blade is broken off at the prescored break line, thus saving you a lot of time during construction. When buying the retractable type make sure it has a pressure knob to lock the blade into position.

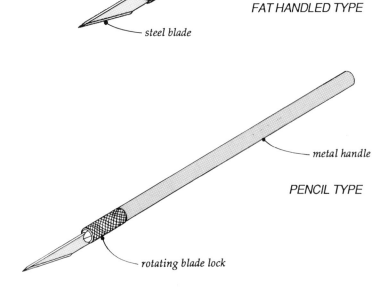

plastic handle

FAT HANDLED TYPE

steel blade

metal handle

PENCIL TYPE

rotating blade lock

Xacto Knife

The Xacto knife is a company brand name knife and is available in two forms, the pencil type and the fat handled type. The different styled handles have different uses. The pencil type is best used for cutting paper and very thin boards. This is the type used most often in model building. The fat handled type is intended for use in cutting matboards, and should only be used for that purpose with the appropriate blade type. It is available in many different blade tips, but the one illustrated with an * adjacent to it is the most versatile for model building.

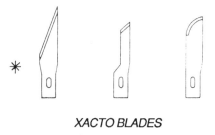

*

XACTO BLADES

GLUES

There are many different types of glue available on the market for model construction. Some are used for laminating sheets of matboard or plastic, and others are used for edge application. Each has its own chemical makeup and thus its own uses. You as the model builder must choose the appropriate glue according to the desired results and the type of model material being utilized. For example, on a schematic study model built of matboard, a thick white glue or glue gun is best used. While on a final presentation model constructed of plastics, a super glue should be used. It is important to decide which type of glue will be used during the planning stages of a models' construction when you are selecting the model materials. Let's now look at some of the glues available for constructing your model.

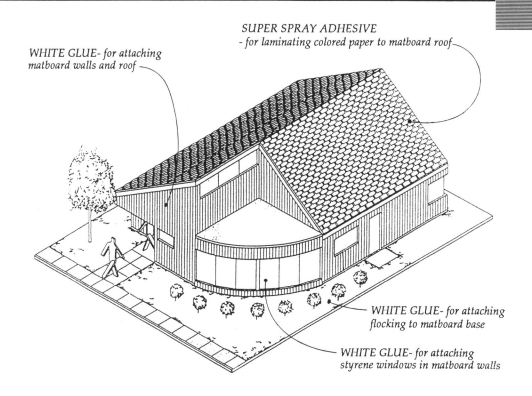

SUPER SPRAY ADHESIVE
- for laminating colored paper to matboard roof

WHITE GLUE- for attaching matboard walls and roof

WHITE GLUE- for attaching flocking to matboard base

WHITE GLUE- for attaching styrene windows in matboard walls

White Glue

White glue such as Elmers and Tacky vary in their thicknesses and thus their strengths. Usually, the thinner the glue is the longer it will take to dry, but the longer it will last. Elmers is ideal for matboard, chipboard and Strathmore construction because it dries relatively quickly and can be applied in thin lines. It also does not 'string', which is when a thin string of glue trails from the model to the bottle. These strings leave a messy appearance and are common with thick white glues.

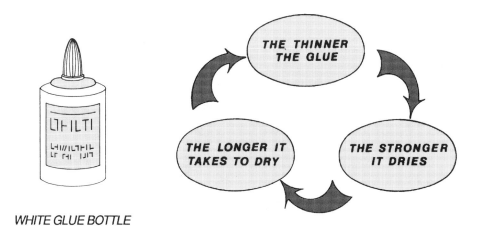

WHITE GLUE BOTTLE

THE THINNER THE GLUE

THE STRONGER IT DRIES

THE LONGER IT TAKES TO DRY

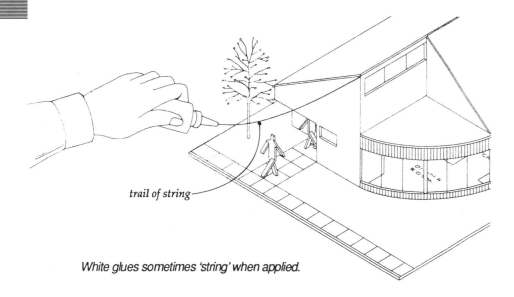

trail of string

White glues sometimes 'string' when applied.

Due to the water base chemical makeup of white glue it is not recommended for laminating sheets of paper or matboard together. The paper pulp absorbs the water from the glue and expands, creating waves and ripples across the matboard surface if it is not applied in an even layer. Spray adhesives are recommended for laminating. White glues are best used for edge applications, such as bonding a wall to a baseboard.

Thick white glues can actually dry too fast. Usually when **attaching** two boards together, it is necessary to adjust their position slightly, but with thick glues you do not get the time to make adjustments. It will dry very quickly and become brittle.

White glues can be purchased at grocery stores, department stores, and hardware stores.

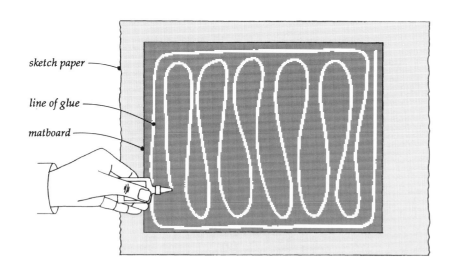

sketch paper

line of glue

matboard

Waves in the surface of the matboard will appear in the pattern of the glue if it is applied in a wavy pattern and not smoothed out.

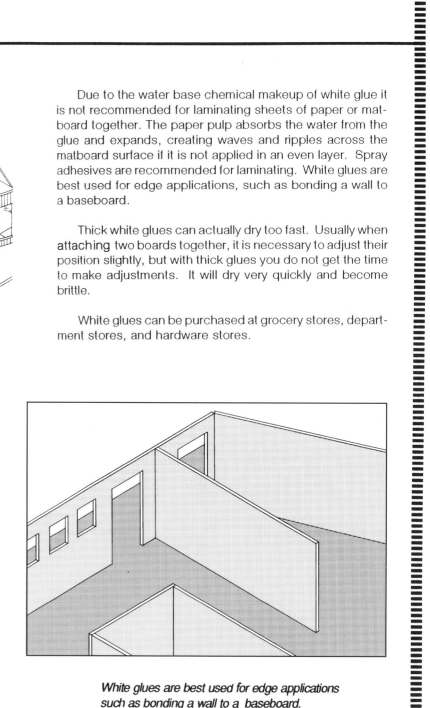

White glues are best used for edge applications such as bonding a wall to a baseboard.

Glue Gun

A glue gun is best used when the speed of construction is most important. The hot glue dries very quickly (2 to 3 seconds) and is thus appropriate for bonding edge applications on conceptual and schematic models. Due to the speed at which it dries it cannot be used for laminations.

The glue gun and glue refills can be purchased at most hardware and department stores. The gun itself is an electric hand held heating element that melts the hard glue capsule when activated by the user. The glue is dispensed at a very high temperature and burns when it comes into contact with the skin. During model construction it is very difficult to keep the glue from coming into contact with your skin no matter what type of glue you are using.

One disadvantage is that the glue dries very quickly, sometimes before you have a chance to bond the two model components together. It is a rubber base glue that does not absorb into porous materials such as matboard and therefore does not stay bonded for long periods of time. It becomes stiff and brittle after a couple of weeks and is therefore not appropriate for final presentation models.

Another disadvantage is that the glue 'strings' during application. Whenever a dab of hot glue is applied to a model component a hair thin string of glue trails from the gun tip when you pull it away from the model. The string dries immediately and does not stick to the model, but you end up with messy strings on yourself and the model.

Despite all the disadvantages of the hot glue gun, it is still the fastest method for bonding two components together, and is appropriate for use on conceptual or schematic models which need not last a long time.

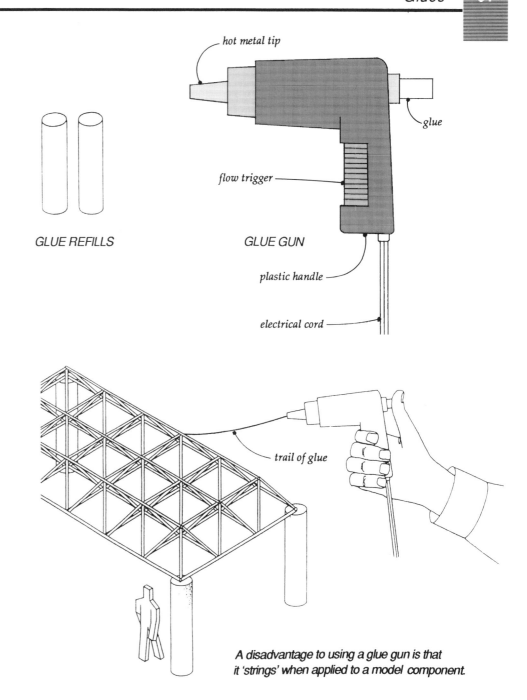

GLUE REFILLS   GLUE GUN

hot metal tip

glue

flow trigger

plastic handle

electrical cord

trail of glue

A disadvantage to using a glue gun is that it 'strings' when applied to a model component.

Spray Glues

Spray glues are best used for laminating two sheets of paper or matboard together. Lamination is necessary when applying paper to model components, such as blueprint paper to the model base. The glue dries relatively fast (10 to 15 seconds) and should be applied very lightly. It is available at graphic art supply stores and some department stores. There are two types of spray glue used in model construction: Artist's Adhesive and Super Spray Glue.

— matboard walls

— hinged paper window

— matboard base

SPRAY GLUE CAN

Artists adhesive spray glue is excellent for applying paper windows to the walls of a study model allowing for removal to alter their size or location.

Artist's Adhesive spray glue is used in graphic design paste-up preparation where a temporary application is desirable. Sheets of paper can be applied to a surface and lifted up again for repositioning. This concept can be applied in model construction wherever a temporary application is required, such as applying colored paper windows to walls on a study model. The windows can be lifted off and revised in size and location. The glue should be applied as described in the directions on the can, and it should be noted that only a light application is necessary. Do not saturate the surface with glue. It will ooze out at the edges after the paper has been smoothed out, leaving a messy appearance.

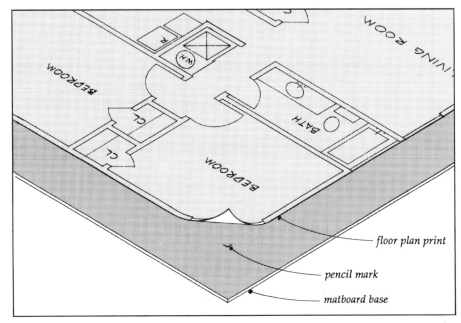

Super Spray Glue is used for permanent applications such as applying a floor plan to a baseboard. It cannot be used for temporary applications since it will pull up the paper if an attempt is made to relocate it. As with any spray glue it should be used only for laminating purposes since it cannot be sprayed onto a board edge. It should be applied according to the manufacturers' directions on the can.

— floor plan print

— pencil mark

— matboard base

Super spray glue is excellent for permanent applications such as attaching a floor plan to a baseboard.

Super Liquid Glue

Super liquid glues are best used on plastic components such as Plexiglass and styrene, but are not suggested since they 'cloud' the transparency of the plastic. Capillary action causes the glue to spread across the plastic surface and it then dries opaque. It dries very quickly and can be used for laminating or edge applications where transparency is not required. The chemical makeup may irritate the eyes and should not come into contact with your skin. There are many different types of liquid super glues available to bond paper, plastic, and wood, and can be purchased at most department stores.

SUPER
LIQUID GLUE

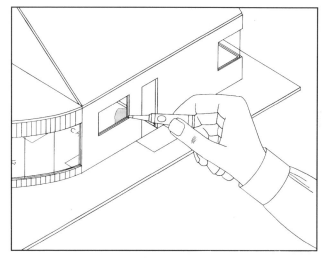

Due to capillary action, liquid super glue spreads across the surface of a plastic window and dries opaque.

ADHESIVE TAPES

There are many different types of adhesive tape available to the model builder that can be used for various purposes. Some can be applied to hold model components together while glue dries, while others can be used to hold components together in place of glue. Let's look at the various types of tape available for model construction and their uses.

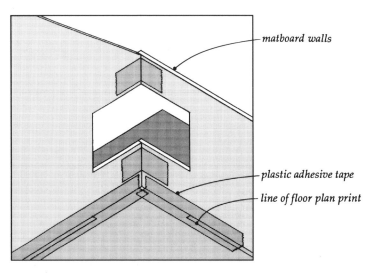

matboard walls

plastic adhesive tape

line of floor plan print

Adhesive tapes can be used to hold model components together in place of glue.

Drafting Tape

Drafting tape is the type most commonly used in model building and is available at graphic art supply stores. It is a paper-backed tape with a light coat of rubber based adhesive sprayed on it. Since it is not as tacky as most adhesive tapes it is excellent for temporary applications and will not damage the matboard finish when carefully removed. Most other tapes will pull some of the paper finish off matboard components when removed.

cardboard dispenser

metal cutting edge

tape roll

DRAFTING TAPE

Masking Tape

Masking tape looks exactly like drafting tape but has a much tackier glue applied to it. It also is paper backed and is available at grocery and department stores. Since it is so tacky it will damage a matboard finish if removed and should only be used for permanent applications. It can be applied anywhere on a model that will not be visible to the viewer.

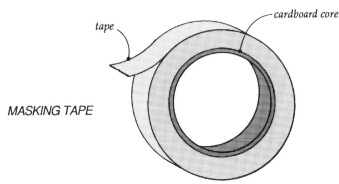

tape

cardboard core

MASKING TAPE

Transparent Tape

Transparent tape is also used for permanent applications and adheres best to plastic components. It is a plastic backed tape with a tacky rubber-based adhesive and is available at most department and grocery stores. Even though it is supposedly transparent it is not recommended for applications visible to the viewer. It will also damage a matboard finish if removed.

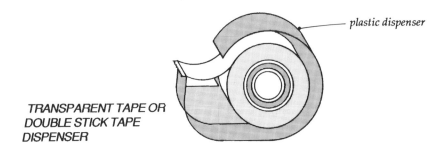

plastic dispenser

TRANSPARENT TAPE OR
DOUBLE STICK TAPE
DISPENSER

Double Stick Tape

Double stick tape looks like transparent tape but is used to laminate two surfaces together. It is a plastic backed tape with a very tacky rubber based glue. Once the tape is applied to a surface the plastic is lifted up and you are left with a strip of glue to laminate your other surface to. It is excellent for laminating two layers of plastic or paper together and is available at most department stores.

Packing Tape

Packing tape is available in a 2" width at grocery or department stores. Since its main purpose is for securing cardboard boxes for shipping it is a very strong tape that adheres well to plastic sheets. It is an opaque plastic backed tape with a tacky rubber based adhesive. It is excellent for securing two sheets of Plexiglass together temporarily, or securing Foamcore to your cutting board.

Duct Tape

Duct tape is a fabric backed plastic tape with a very tacky adhesive applied to it, and is available in a 2" width at hardware stores. It is probably the strongest tape available to the model builder and excellent for hinged Plexiglass wall joints not visible to the viewer.

So, as you can see there are many different types of materials available to assist you in constructing your model. Each has its own characteristics and therefore its own particular uses, which must be considered in the planning stages of constructing your model.

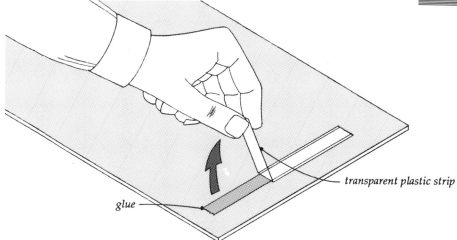

transparent plastic strip

glue

Double stick tape can be applied to a surface for laminating purposes in place of spray glue.

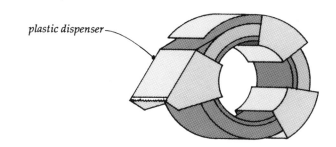

plastic dispenser

PACKING TAPE

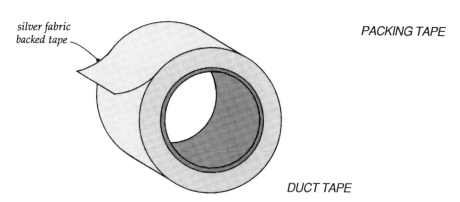

silver fabric backed tape

DUCT TAPE

CHAPTER 5

Thinking To Scale

In order to construct models with a professional appearance the model maker must 'think-to-scale'. They must visualize in their minds how the building materials will appear at the model scale and what model materials will best simulate them. Factors that must be considered in selecting an appropriate model material are such things as: the matboard thickness in relation to the model walls; the matboard finish in relation to the simulated wall finish; the need for scaled objects such as trees or people; and the need for color variations and patterns. Let's now take a closer look at these factors.

Matboard Thickness

The thickness of the model walls should be equal in scale to the actual building walls. Therefore, the thickness of the matboard that will be simulating the model walls must be considered in the planning stages of the model making process. For example, a 6" thick wall at 1/8" scale is best represented with a 1/16" thick matboard. A 6" thick wall at 1/4" scale is best represented with a 1/8" thick Foamcore board, since 1/8" thick matboard is much too difficult to cut.

Most building walls are on an average 6" thick and for most models both the exterior and interior walls can be constructed this thick. For a schematic study model the wall thickness is not as important as speed of construction, so a thinner matboard can be utilized. But on a final presentation model the walls should be built at the same scale as the actual building walls.

A 1/32" thick wall on a 1/8" scale model represents a 3" thick wall. This may be a little too thin on a final presentation model but is acceptable for a schematic study model where speed of construction is most important.

A 6" thick wall on a 1/8" scale model is best represented with a 1/16" thick matboard.

A 6" thick wall at 1/4" scale is best represented with a 1/8" thick Foamcore board, since 1/8" thick matboard is much too difficult to cut.

EXTERIOR STUCCO WALL

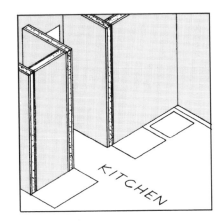

INTERIOR PLASTER WALL

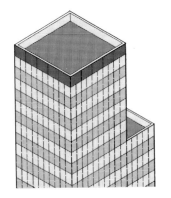

STOREFRONT WINDOW WALL

CONCRETE BLOCK WALL

As with the matboard wall thickness, the matboard finish should also be equal to the texture of the actual building wall. This must be considered in the planning stages of model construction. Let's look at some examples:

- Interior plaster walls painted with a flat white paint are best simulated with Foamcore board on a 1/4" scale model.

- An exterior stucco wall at 1/4" scale is best represented bya rough textured Strathmore board, while a medium texture should be used on a 1/8" scale model.

- A large glass and aluminum storefront window wall at 1/4" scale is best simulated with one sheet of Plexiglass, while a sheet of acetate laminated to chipboard should be used on a 1/8" scale model.

- A concrete block wall at 1/4" scale can be simulated by removing the paper from Foamcore and scoring the exposed core at the mortar joints.

Scaled Objects

The best way to give a model scale is to attach scaled objects to it. People, cars, trees, and other landscaped items give the model a human-size scale that the viewer can relate to. Without scaled objects the model does not have a human scale; it may be misinterpreted by the viewer as being at another scale than what it is built at. All of the items can be built by the model maker or purchased at hobby and architectural model supply stores.

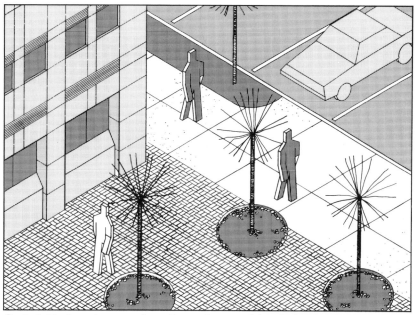

Scaled objects such as people and trees give a model scale that the viewer can relate to.

Color & Patterns

Color and pattern variations on the walls and floor give the model scale and make it 'read' better. It also 'reads' better if the walls and floor are of a differing color or pattern to give the intersecting planes more definition. Models constructed of all one color matboard lack the visual contrasts necessary for a model to 'read' clearly. Let's look at some examples:

- A ceramic tile floor at 1/8" or 1/4" scale will contrast well with white interior model walls. The tile can also be colored by photocopying the pattern onto a sheet of colored paper.

- A red tile roof on a 1/8" or 1/4" scale model will accentuate the roof against the white exterior walls. The tile roof pattern can also be photocopied onto colored paper.

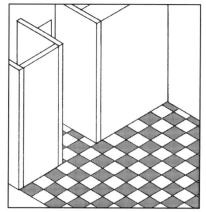

A patterned floor material contrasts well with solid color walls.

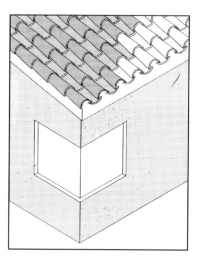

A colored roof material contrasts well with white exterior walls.

Hopefully you now have an understanding of what must be considered when selecting your model materials. The main objective is to select the materials that will best simulate your building's materials at the model scale, and thus provide the most realistic simulation.

Now, with this concept of 'thinking to scale' in mind, let's take a look in the next chapter at methods of constructing scaled building components.

BEAMS- laminated sheets of white Strathmore board

DRYWALL- white Strathmore matboard

WINDOWS- scored transparent styrene

HANDRAIL- balsa wood strip

GUARDRAIL- styrene

GRANITE FLOOR- colored paper with inked score lines

PEOPLE- store bought white plastic figures

FINAL PRESENTATION INTERIOR MODEL

CHAPTER 6

Constructing Scaled Building Components

Constructing scaled building components is a combination of art and science; artistically you develop a concept in your mind to simulate a building material and then construct it with model building materials. The main objective is to simulate the full scale component as closely as possible at the smaller model scale. In this chapter we will look at methods for constructing the most common building components: columns and beams, walls, windows, floors, roofs, skylights, space frames, trellises and stairs.

COLUMNS AND BEAMS

Columns and beams are usually round, square, or rectangular in cross-sectional shape and can be simulated on a model with common household items. Cotton swabs, drinking straws, and wooden dowels can be utilized for round columns, while balsa wood, chipboard, Foamcore, and plastic extrusions can be used for square columns and beams. Choose the object that will best simulate a column or beam at the selected scale of the model.

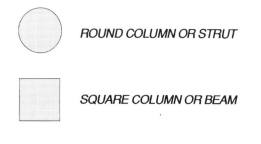

ROUND COLUMN OR STRUT

SQUARE COLUMN OR BEAM

RECTANGULAR COLUMN OR BEAM

1/4"

ELECTRIC ERASERS are made
of a soft rubber.

1/8" TO 1/2"

DRINKING STRAWS are available
in plastic or paper.

PENCIL LEADS are available in
plastic and graphite.

COTTON SWABS are available in
paper or plastic sticks.

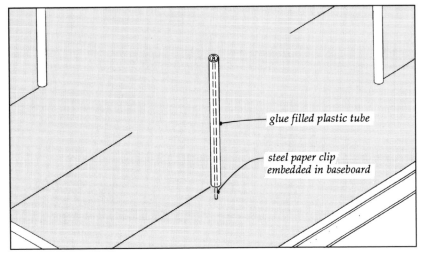

— glue filled plastic tube

— steel paper clip
embedded in baseboard

STEEL & GLUE REINFORCED PLASTIC TUBE COLUMN

Round Columns and Struts

Round shaped columns and struts are best simulated on
a model with cotton swab sticks, drinking straws, electric
erasers, pencil leads, or wooden dowels. Following is a brief
discussion of the use of each item on the model.

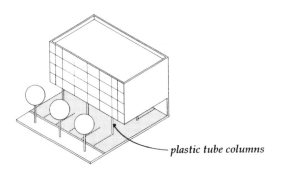

plastic tube columns

Cotton Swabs

Cotton swabs are available in paper or plastic and can
be bought at any grocery store. They are 1/16" in diameter
and are therefore excellent for simulating a 6" diameter
column at 1/4" scale, or a 12" diameter column at 1/8" scale.
The paper sticks are solid core and generally white in color,
while the plastic are hollow and blue or white. Both can be
cut with scissors or an Xacto knife and the paper can be
attached to the model with white glue. Procedures for construction of paper sticks are discussed in Chapter 2.

Since white glue does not adhere to the plastic sticks a
combination of white glue and paper clips must be utilized to
attach the plastic columns to the model. The paper clip is
straightened out and run inside the hollow stick to hold it in
place on the model base until the glue dries. This enables
you to build the rest of the model on top of your columns
without having to wait hours for the glue to dry as required for
paper columns. Let's look at this construction procedure
more closely:

Step 1 *Mark required column length on chipboard.*

First, make two marks on your cutting board spaced apart the desired length of the columns.

Step 2 *Cut the plastic sticks.*

Cut the plastic swab sticks at the required length by holding each stick adjacent to the two marks and pushing your utility knife through at each end. Try to get all of the columns as close to the same length as possible.

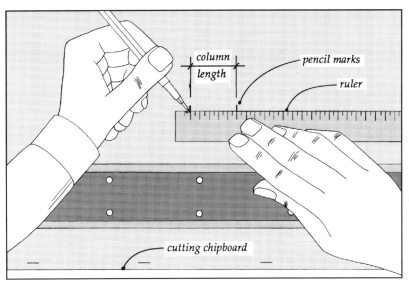

1 With the use of a pencil and ruler make two marks on the cutting matboard the length of the columns.

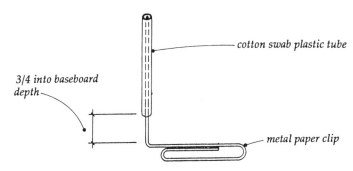

3 Cut the paper clip long enough for it to protrude from the bottom of the column three-fourths into the baseboard.

Step 3 *Cut the paper clips.*

Next, straighten out the paper clips the best that you can with your fingertips.

Cut them with wire cutters so they are long enough to penetrate at least 3/4 of the way into the baseboard and up inside the column to the top.

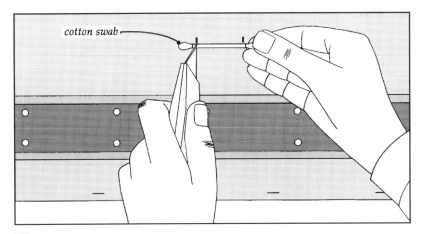

2 Cut the columns to the desired length with a utility knife.

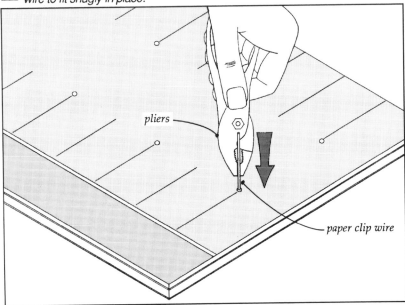

4 Punch a hole in the baseboard with a sharp pointed object deep enough for the wire to fit snugly in place.

— column locations

— matboard laminated to foamcore base

— pliers

— paper clip wire

5 Push the wire into the baseboard until it stands snugly in place.

Step 4 Punch holes in baseboard.

With the use of a sharp pointed object such as your compass point, punch a hole into the baseboard at the column locations. If your baseboard is only the thickness of one matboard you will have to penetrate all the way through to get enough depth for the matboard to support the wire in a vertical position. The ideal baseboard construction is one layer of matboard laminated to the top of a sheet of Foamcore. This gives you a much more desirable penetration depth. Do not make the diameter of the hole larger than the diameter of the wire since the wire will be relying on a snug fit to hold it upright.

Step 5 Attach wires to base.

Using a pair of pliers, push the wire into the hole until it stands snugly in place on its own. With a small triangle check its verticality so that it stands at a 90 degree angle to the baseboard.

Step 6 Set the columns in place.

Place the hollow plastic stick over the wire, allowing it to penetrate up through the center.

Now, squirt white glue down into the plastic tube until it starts to come out at the bottom. Try not to get glue on the sides of the column and wipe any excess glue from the base.

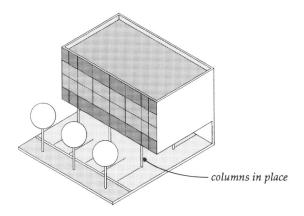

columns in place

The column is now complete and can be built on top of.

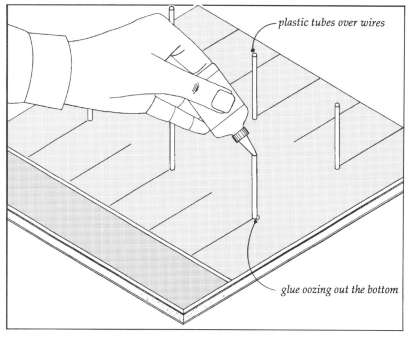

plastic tubes over wires

glue oozing out the bottom

6 Set the plastic tubes over the wires and squirt white glue into each tube.

Drinking Straws

Drinking straws are available in paper or plastic and come in many different colors. They range in size from 1/4" to 1/2" in diameter thus making them ideal for columns on 1/8", 1/4", and 3/8" scale models. Since the straws are hollow, their strength in compression decreases as their height increases so use shorter ones. They can be bought at grocery stores and cut to their desired length with scissors.

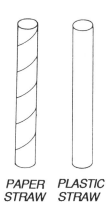

PAPER   PLASTIC
STRAW   STRAW

COLUMN
plastic straw

Drinking straws are generally 1/4" in diameter and thus ideal as a 12" diameter column on a 1/4" scale model.

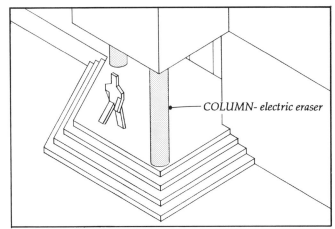

Electric erasers are usually 1/4" in diameter and can therefore simulate a 12" diameter column on a 1/4" scale model, or a 24" diameter on a 1/8" scale model.

COLUMN- *electric eraser*

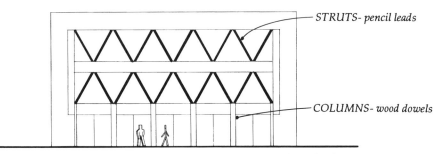

STRUTS- *pencil leads*

COLUMNS- *wood dowels*

Pencil leads are generally 1/16" in diameter and can therefore simulate 12" diameter columns or struts on 1/8" scale models.

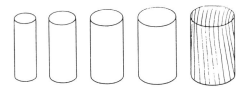

WOODEN DOWELS range in diameters from 1/8" to 1" and are therefore excellent for simulating columns and struts on models 1/16" scale and larger.

Electric Erasers

Electric erasers are made of soft rubber and are available in five different colors; pink, white, grey, green and yellow. Their diameter is usually 1/4" and easily cut with an Xacto knife. They can be bought at architectural drafting supply stores and attached to the model with white glue.

Pencil Leads

Pencil leads are available in graphite or plastic and can be bought at architectural drafting supply stores. Their diameter is 1/16" thus making them ideal for 1/8" and 1/4" scale models. They are available in many different colors (black, red, yellow, blue, green, etc.), and can be attached to the model with white glue. They are best cut by scoring them with an Xacto knife at the desired cut line and then breaking.

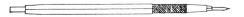

DRAFTING PENCIL

Wooden Dowels

Wooden dowels can be bought at hobby stores and are available in diameters of 1/8" to 1". They are best cut with a hacksaw and attached to the model with white glue. They can be spray painted any color you desire.

Square Columns and Beams

Square or rectangular shaped columns and beams can be simulated on a model with balsa wood, matboard, Foamcore, or plastic extrusions. Following is a brief discussion of each and their uses on a model.

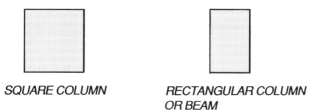

SQUARE COLUMN   RECTANGULAR COLUMN OR BEAM

Balsa Wood

Balsa wood is available at hobby stores in both square and rectangular shapes with dimensions of 1/8" square and larger. It can be cut with an Xacto knife but is best cut with a balsa wood saw available at the hobby store. Since it is unfinished wood it can be spray painted to any color you desire. Balsa wood can be attached to itself or to paper components with white glue or Super glue made for wood.

Chipboard

Chipboard may be utilized for square or rectangular shapes but must be laminated together for shapes larger than 1/16" since the chipboard is only 1/16" thick. It can be cut with a utility knife and attached to the model components with white glue.

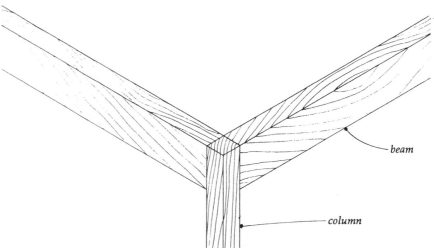

Columns and beams can be constructed with balsa wood available at hobby stores.

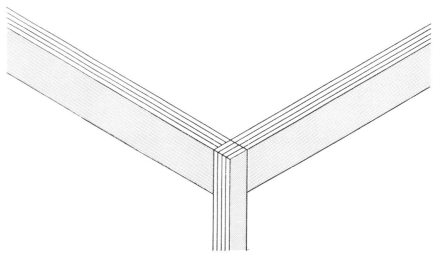

Columns and beams can also be constructed with chipboard. For shapes wider than 1/16" strips of chipboard will have to be laminated together.

Foamcore board can also be used to construct columns and beams, but is limited to a maximum thickness of 3/8".

Plastic structural shapes can be bought at hobby stores to simulate columns and beams. Since the shapes are large in size they are appropriate for model scales 1/4" and larger.

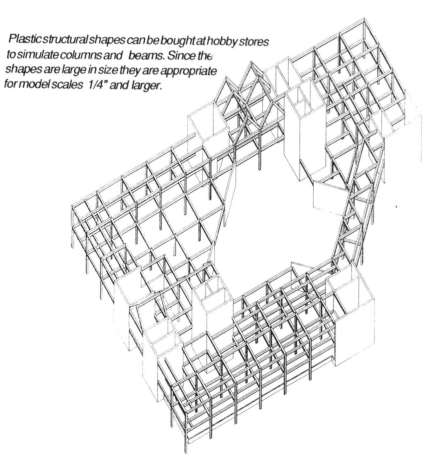

Foamcore

Foamcore board can be utilized for square and rectangular shapes but must be laminated together for shapes larger than the board thickness of 3/8". It can be cut with an Xacto knife and attached with white glue.

Plastic Extrusions

Plastic extrusions shaped in tubes and structural sections are excellent for simulating steel columns and beams on models 1/4" scale and larger. (See page 86 for an illustration of the shapes). They are best cut with a hacksaw and attached to each other with Super glue. They are grey in color but can be spray painted to any desired color.

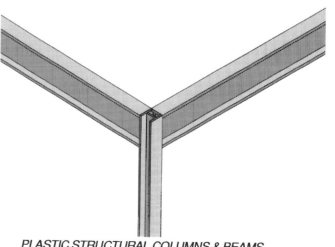

PLASTIC STRUCTURAL COLUMNS & BEAMS

Domes and Spherical Shapes

Domes, awnings, and other building components that are spherical in shape are the most difficult forms to simulate on a model. It is nearly impossible to construct a spherical shape out of a sheet of paper or plastic and much too time consuming for a student to consider. Therefore, preformed objects such as ping-pong balls, racquetballs, tennis balls, Plexiglass balls, Styrofoam balls, plastic aerosol caps, and light bulbs can be used to simulate spherical shapes on models. The ease of cutting the object must be taken into consideration when selecting a shape.

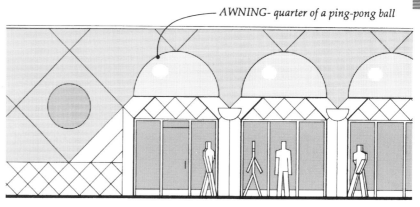

AWNING- quarter of a ping-pong ball

SHOPPING CENTER MODEL ELEVATION AT 1/4" SCALE

Ping Pong Balls

Ping-pong balls are probably the most commonly used spherical shape for models. At 1/8" scale its diameter is 13', and therefore 6'-6" for 1/4" scale. They are available in white or yellow and can be cut with a utility knife as illustrated below. A ping-pong ball cut into fourths can be utilized as awnings, or, cut in half, can serve as a dome. Use white glue to attach to the model. Please use the utmost care when cutting ping-pong balls.

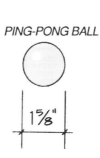

PING-PONG BALL

$1\frac{5}{8}"$

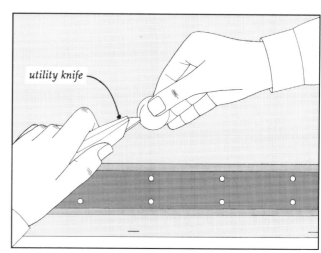

utility knife

Extreme care must be taken when cutting a ping-pong ball.

Raquetballs

A racquetball can also be cut in halves or fourths and serve as an awning or dome. It is constructed of a soft rubber outer layer 1/8" thick with a hollow center. Raquetballs are found at sporting good stores and are available in blue or black. It is difficult to obtain a consistent cut around the perimeter of the ball due to the thickness of the rubber, but is still best cut with a utility knife. They can be attached to the model with rubber cement or white glue.

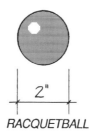

$2"$

RACQUETBALL

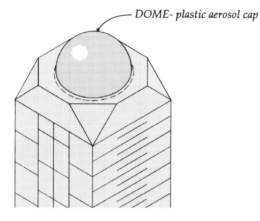

DOME- *plastic aerosol cap*

AEROSOL CAN CAP

Plastic Aerosol Caps

Plastic aerosol caps found on spray cans can be used as a dome but are most likely too difficult to cut without power tools. They are usually appropriate only on conceptual or schematic models since they are difficult to disguise as something other than an aerosol can cap.

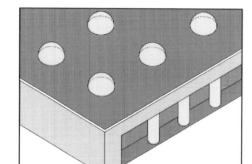

PLEXIGLASS DOME

PLEXIGLASS SPHERE

Clear Plexiglass half-spheres can be used to simulate skylights on a 1/8" scale model and larger.

Plexiglass Balls

Plexiglass balls and half spheres can be bought in diameters ranging from 1/4" to 2" and are excellent for simulating domes, skylights, and light fixtures. They are made of a very hard plastic and cannot be cut to a smaller size. They can be bought at plastic supply stores and are only available in a clear transparent color. Due to their smooth glossy finish they are appropriate for final presentation models and add a professional look to any model.

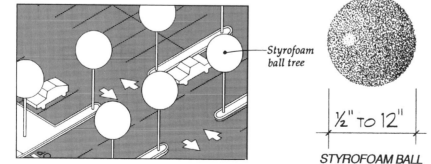

Styrofoam ball tree

½" TO 12"

STYROFOAM BALL

Styrofoam Balls

Styrofoam balls are available in many diameters ranging from 1/2" to 12", and can be bought at craft stores. They are generally white or green in color and should be cut with a hot wire by the craft store. They have a very rough texture and are therefore appropriate only for conceptual or schematic models. They can be attached to other model components with white glue.

WALLS

Interior and exterior building walls are usually the largest category of components on a model. Scaled material indications can be achieved with the use of any one of a variety of papers, cardboards, plastic films, and Foamcore board. The main objective is to select one that most simulates the building material you are trying to represent on the model. Following is a brief description of typical building wall materials and the papers, cardboards, and plastic films available to represent them on a model.

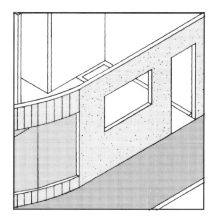

A rough texture Strathmore board is excellent for simulating an exterior stucco wall.

Stucco

An exterior stucco wall is best represented with white Strathmore matboard. Available in various surface finishes from smooth to rough, the finish selected should be appropriate for the scale of the model. On a 1/4" scale model the roughest finish should be used, while a smoother finish is best for 1/8" scale and smaller.

Drywall

Interior plaster walls are best simulated by white Foamcore board. Its color and texture are perfect for simulating the finish of painted gypsum board and the available thicknesses correspond to actual model wall thicknesses. Interior plaster walls can also be simulated with white Strathmore board.

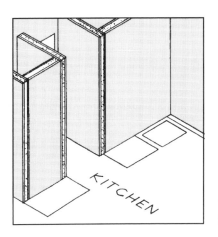

The 'flat' white color of Foamcore board is excellent for simulating painted drywall.

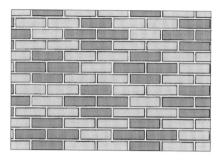

BRICK WALL IN ELEVATION

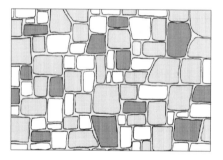

STONE WALL IN ELEVATION

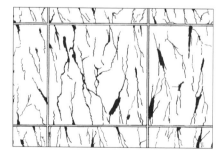

MARBLE PANELS IN ELEVATION

Brick

Brick walls can be simulated by drawing grey or black lines in ink or pencil for the mortar joints onto colored matboard. The smoother the surface, the easier and more quickly the lines go on. Unfortunately this is a very time consuming method.

A much faster method is to buy a plastic decal with the brick pattern already printed on it and laminate it to a matboard backing.

Note: Feel free to photocopy any of the material patterns on this page onto a colored paper. This will enable you to reduce the pattern to your selected scale.

Stone

Stone walls are best represented by drawing the joints in pencil or ink onto a piece of colored matboard. Drawing all of the joints of a stone wall at a small scale can be very time consuming and must be considered in the planning stages of the model construction.

Marble

Marble walls are best simulated by drawing veins onto a colored matboard or plastic film in pencil or ink at the model scale. It can also be drawn at a large scale and reduced on a photocopy machine to obtain sharper lines.

Concrete Block

Exterior concrete block walls at 1/8" or 1/4" scale are best simulated with scored Foamcore. This is achieved by stripping the white paper or plastic film off the Foamcore board and scoring the block joints into the plastic foam with an Xacto knife. Obviously this can be a time consuming procedure and should be experimented with before committing yourself to a large wall. The paper is usually difficult to pull off the plastic Foamcore, but generally the older the Foamcore is the easier it is to remove. The plastic film lifts off easily. White glue is used to attach Foamcore but takes a long time to dry, usually overnight.

Concrete block can also be simulated by drawing or photocopying the concrete block pattern onto matboard. The block pattern illustrated at the right is drawn at 1/2" scale and can be enlarged or reduced on a photocopier to whatever scale you desire. The paper can then be laminated to your model walls.

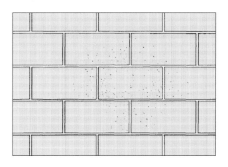

CONCRETE BLOCK 8"x16" PATTERN

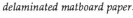
delaminated matboard paper

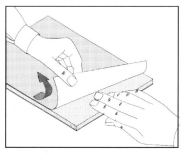

The outer layers of paper on Foamcore board can be removed by pulling it off the plastic core.

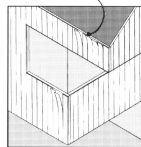

Matboard scored to simulate wood siding may delaminate if the scores are too close together.

Wood Siding

Interior and exterior wood siding can be simulated by scoring colored matboard with an Xacto knife at the board joints. But, be careful. If the scorelines are any closer together than 1/8" the outer layer of paper on the matboard may delaminate when scored. The textured wall is then set into place with white glue.

The wood siding can also be drawn onto the matboard with pencil or ink, or photocopied onto a colored paper which is then laminated to the matboard walls.

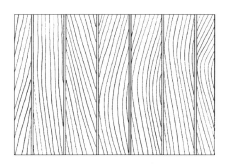

WOOD SIDING IN ELEVATION

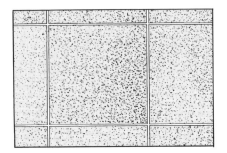

GRANITE PANELS IN ELEVATION

Granite

Granite walls can be simulated with colored paper or plastic film that is lightly sprayed with paint. Because the paint specks are relatively large in scale the simulated wall should be at a large scale, such as 1/4" or more. Simple colored Canson paper is best used for smaller scales.

Metal Panels

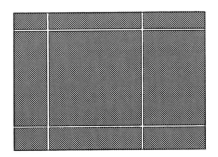

METAL PANELS IN ELEVATION

A metal clad exterior wall of stainless steel, copper, or painted metal can be simulated by drawing the joints in pencil or ink onto a colored plastic film or coated paper. The texture and finish of the film is appropriate for simulating a smooth, glossy building material finish. The film will have to be laminated to a smooth backup board, such as Strathmore matboard, in order to make the wall rigid enough for constructing the model. The smooth surface of the backup board will keep the finished surface smooth. Films and papers are available with glue on the back, or they can be sprayed with adhesive and attached to the backup board. Also available is a Bainbridge matboard that has a silver or bronze finished outer layer, enabling you to draw the joint lines directly on it.

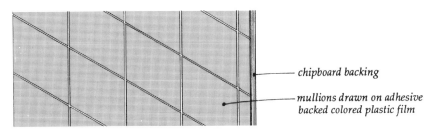

chipboard backing

mullions drawn on adhesive backed colored plastic film

Metal panels can be simulated with a colored plastic film laminated to a chipboard backing.

Mirrors

A mirror can be simulated on a model with either a sheet of Plexiglass or a reflective mylar sheet. Due to the difficulty of cutting Plexiglass it is not recommended for use on a model unless the mirror is 4" square or larger. It is excellent though for simulating a large exterior reflective window wall such as on an office building model.

For smaller sized windows and mirrors, a thin sheet of reflective mylar laminated to a smooth backup board is recommended. This allows the model builder to cut the mirror down to any size they desire with the use of a utility knife and metal ruler. The mylar can be bought at graphic arts supply stores and laminated to a smooth finish matboard such as Strathmore with Super spray adhesive. A smooth matboard should be used since the mylar is paper-thin and will take the shape of whatever it is attached to. A rough finish will give you a distorted image.

Joints between the mirrors can be scored into the Plexiglass or mylar with an Xacto knife, but care must be taken when scoring the mylar to not cut all the way through it.

HANDRAIL- *thin black plastic graphic tape*

GLASS- *scored transparent styrene*

MIRROR- *scored reflective mylar sheet laminated to smooth board*

PEOPLE- *matboard*

ESCALATOR MODEL ELEVATION AT 1/4" SCALE

A mirror can be simulated with either a sheet of Plexiglass with a reflective finish, or a reflective sheet of mylar laminated to a backing board.

Colored Walls

Paint coated papers are available to make a wall any color you desire. The paper is coated with paint and has a texture and finish ideal for small scale models. The exact paint color selected by a designer of a building can be used on a model to get an exact replica.

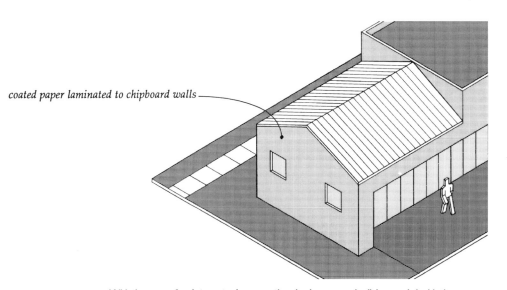

coated paper laminated to chipboard walls

With the use of paint coated papers the designer can build a model with the exact paint color that will be used on the building.

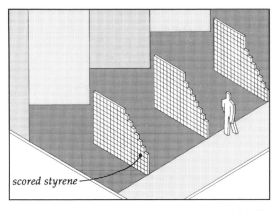

Glass block walls can be simulated on a model 1/8"
scale and larger by scoring the pattern onto a sheet
of styrene.

scored styrene

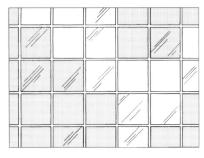

GLASS BLOCK IN ELEVATION

Glass Block Walls

A wall constructed of glass block is best simulated on
a 1/8" or 1/4" scale model with a scored sheet of clear
plastic styrene. The glossy finish of the plastic simulates the
smooth clear finish of the glass block and the joints can be
scored into the plastic with an Xacto knife. Generally, actual
glass block is 4", 6", or 8" square and 4" thick. A clear sheet
of styrene is recommended since it can be easily cut with
a utility knife.

Hinged Wall Construction

In Chapter 2 we described how to attach two perpendicular walls to each other by applying glue to their edges
and butting them up against each other. This is the most
common method for attaching two perpendicular walls and
is used extensively in the construction of a model. It is also
very time consuming.

A much faster method is to create a hinged wall joint at
corners, thus eliminating the glueing procedure for each
joint. On a large model this can save hours of time applying
and waiting for glue to dry before proceeding with the
construction. Since the vertical edges of the wall board are
left exposed, the method is only recommended on schematic models, or on final presentation models when a thin
colored paper is hinged and applied over matboard walls.
Let's look at the procedures for constructing hinged joints
on the exterior walls of our schematic study model:

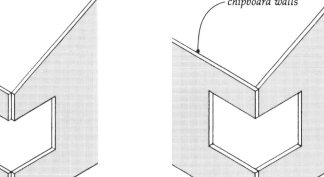

HINGED WALL JOINT

chipboard walls

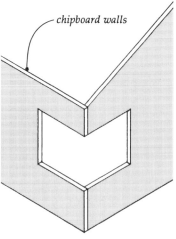

BUTTED WALL JOINT

Step 1 *Draw wall locations on floor plan.*

The first step is to obtain a photocopy or blueprint of your floor plan and draw on the plan where each wall will be placed. Take note of their intersection with each other. Since the chipboard is only 1/16" thick and the walls drawn on the plan are 1/8" thick, we will place the chipboard walls at the outside perimeter line.

Once this is done we will now draw the walls adjacent to each other onto a sheet of chipboard and cut them out as one large piece.

Step 2 *Draw wall elevation 1 onto chipboard.*

Staple a sheet of chipboard to your cutting board and draw wall 1 in elevation taking note of how it will intersect with wall 2. As you can see due to the hinged joint the end of the wall will have to be drawn 1/16" shorter than it was on your floor plan. Do not draw the curved portion of wall 1. It will be included as part of wall 4. Draw wall 1 at the far right side of the chipboard sheet since the remaining three walls will be drawn to its left.

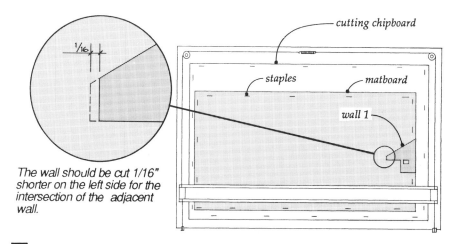

Walls are hinged, not butted and therefore must be cut shorter.

1 *Draw wall locations and their intersections on the floor plan.*

The wall should be cut 1/16" shorter on the left side for the intersection of the adjacent wall.

2 *Draw wall elevation 1 onto a sheet of chipboard at the far right hand edge of board.*

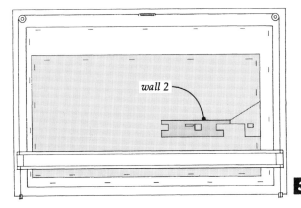

3 Draw wall 2 onto the chipboard adjacent to wall 1.

Step 3 Draw wall 2 onto chipboard.

Moving in a clockwise direction, draw wall 2 in elevation adjacent to wall 1. Again, take note of how wall 2 will intersect with wall 1 and 3. Due to the hinged joints, both ends of wall 2 will have to be drawn 1/16" shorter than what is indicated on your plan.

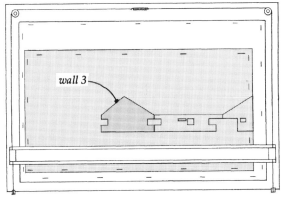

4 Draw wall 3 adjacent to wall 2.

Step 4 Draw wall 3 onto chipboard.

Again, moving in a clockwise direction, draw wall 3 in elevation adjacent to wall 2, 1/16" shorter on both ends.

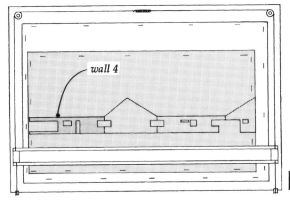

5a Draw wall 4 adjacent to wall 3.

Step 5 Draw wall 4 onto chipboard.

Draw wall 4 in elevation adjacent to wall 3 taking note of how it will intersect with walls 3 and 1. Due to the hinged joint it will have to be drawn 1/16" shorter at wall 3 only. The curved portion will be glued to wall 1 with a butted joint. (Il. 5a)

To obtain the true radiused length of the curved portion of wall 4 use the 'thin strip of matboard' method of measuring and bend it around the curve. (A flexible plastic architectural scale can also be used to measure a curved line). (Il. 5b)

Now, with all four walls drawn in elevation adjacent to each other, you are ready to cut them out in one large piece and attach them to the model baseboard.

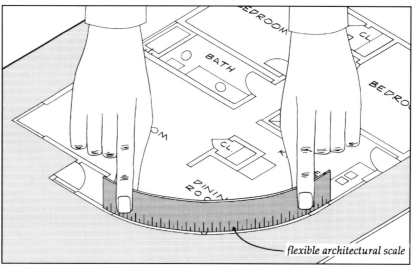

flexible architectural scale

5b Measure the 'true' radiused length of the curved portion of wall 4 with a flexible architectural scale.

Step 6 Cut out and bend the walls.

First, with the use of a utility knife and triangle cut out and remove all window and door openings. Then, perform vertical scorelines at 1/8" apart along the curved portion of wall 4.

Also, perform a vertical scoreline at each hinged joint location between the walls. Try not to penetrate all the way through the board, but if you do the mistake can be mended with transparent tape placed on the back.

Finally, cut out the entire piece along the perimeter and remove it from your cutting board. Smooth down the flaired edges and bend the walls at the scored hinged joints. Now you are ready to attach it to the model baseboard.

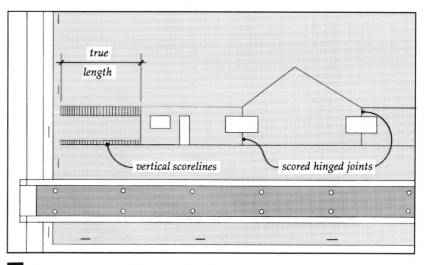

true length

vertical scorelines   *scored hinged joints*

6 Cut out and remove all door and window openings first.

Step 7 Attach walls to baseboard.

In this step we will apply glue to the baseboard and set the walls in place. Since the entire piece is too large and clumsy to apply glue to the entire bottom edge at one time, we will apply a thin line of white glue to the baseboard along each wall and set them in place in order.

Apply a thin line of white glue along the base of wall 1 on the floor plan, and set wall 1 in place, adjusting any portion of it that is out of line. (Il. 7a) Apply a piece of drafting tape to secure wall 1 while placing the others.

Next, apply a thin line of white glue along the base of wall 2 and rotate wall 2 into position. As the wall moves into place it will push a lot of the glue to the inside of the joint which should be quickly removed using a square piece of matboard as illustrated. (Il. 7b)

Apply a line of glue along the base of wall 3 and rotate it into position. Remove the excess glue with a fresh piece of matboard.

floor plan print

matboard base

drafting tape

7a *Apply a line of glue to the baseboard where wall 1 is to be located and set wall 1 in place.*

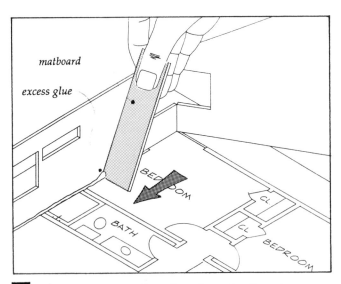

matboard

excess glue

7b *Remove the excess glue with a piece of matboard.*

Finally, apply a line of glue along the base of wall 4 including the curved portion and rotate the wall into place. Bend the curved wall into place and attach it to wall 1 with a small amount of glue on the vertical edge. Apply a piece of drafting tape across the joint if necessary. (Il. 7c)

Now you have all the exterior walls in place with sharp, clean vertical joints strong enough to support construction of the roof on top.

Another time-saving method that could be used in the hinged joint procedure would be to apply photocopies of the exterior elevations to the chipboard instead of redrawing them. But, you must remember to cut 1/16" off each end of the walls as described in step 2 to compensate for the adjacent wall thickness. Remember to verify the wall lengths with your floor plan, especially at the curved portion of wall 4. Attach the photocopies to the chipboard with Super spray glue if you want to leave the paper on, or Artists Adhesive if you want to remove them after the walls are cut out.

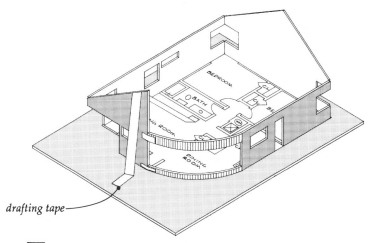

drafting tape

7c *Apply glue to the vertical edges of the radiused wall and attach them to wall 1.*

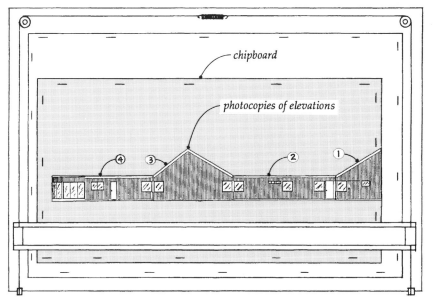

chipboard

photocopies of elevations

A time saver to the hinged joint procedure is to apply photocopies of your already drawn elevations to the chipboard.

1/4" FOAMCORE

1/8" FOAMCORE

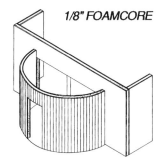

CORRUGATED CARDBOARD

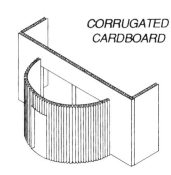

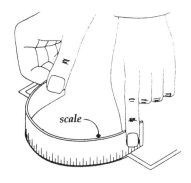

1 *Measure the 'true' radiused dimension with a thin strip of matboard or flexible architectural scale.*

CURVED WALL CONSTRUCTION

Radiused curved walls are more difficult and time consuming to construct than straight walls, but they add a dramatic, playful appearance to the model. What makes them time consuming is the fact that they have to be scored along the entire wall surface that is to be curved in order to make the board stay in a radiused shape once it is applied to the baseboard.

Radiused walls can be constructed with any type of board: chipboard, matboard, Strathmore, Foamcore, and corrugated cardboard. Let's look first at constructing a chipboard curved wall:

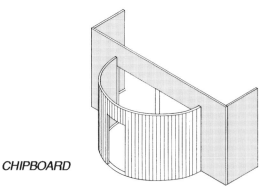

CHIPBOARD

Curved Wall: Chipboard Construction

Step 1 *Measure the curved wall dimensions.*

With the sheet of chipboard already lined up with your parallel bar and stapled to your cutting board, use the 'thin strip of matboard' method to measure the dimensions of the curved wall and draw them onto the chipboard. (A flexible architectural scale can be used). To measure the required length of the curved wall, you will have to bend the strip of matboard to follow the curve so that you have the exact required length. You may want to add an extra 1/4" to the dimension at both ends to make sure the wall will be long enough. If it is too long you can simply trim it to the required length, but if it is too short you will have to cut out an entirely new wall.

1 Draw the curved wall elevation onto a sheet of chipboard.

Step 2 *Cut the vertical scorelines.*

Next, with the use of an Xacto knife and triangle cut vertical scorelines approximately 1/8" apart along the curved portion of the wall. Try to score only half-way through the board, not all the way through.

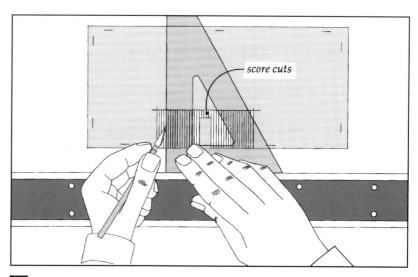

2 Perform vertical score lines 1/8" apart.

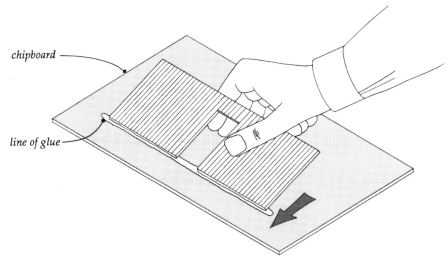

3 Cut out the wall and set it in place without glue to make sure it is the correct size.

existing column

existing chipboard walls

chipboard

line of glue

4 Apply a small amount of glue to the bottom of the wall by sliding it through a line of glue.

Step 3 Cut out the wall.

Once you have performed all the scorelines cut out the wall from the stapled down chipboard and smooth down the flaired edges.

Before attaching it to the model set it in place and verify that it is cut to the correct dimensions. Check to make sure the curved portion is not too long, and trim it if it is.

Step 4 Apply glue to bottom of wall.

Now you are ready to attach the wall to the model. Apply a thin line of white glue to the bottom edge by sliding it through a line of glue as illustrated. Remove the excess glue by tapping the edge down on a spare piece of chipboard.

Step 5 Attach wall to model base.

Set the wall down on the baseboard along the radiused wall line by holding the wall in a curved shape above the baseboard and then setting it down as close to the curved line as possible. You won't be able to set it down exactly along the curved line so adjust its location wherever necessary, so that it follows the curve.

Hold the wall in place for a few minutes by pushing down on it to achieve a strong bond. Once in place it should stay by itself without the need of drafting tape to hold it. Now attach the vertical edges.

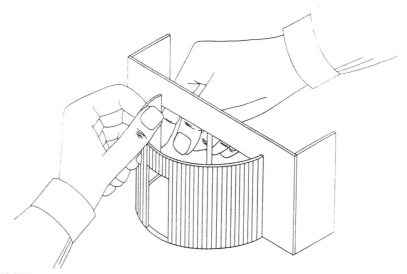

5 **6a** *Set the wall in place and apply glue to the vertical edges with your fingertips.*

Step 6 *Attach vertical edges to model.*

The vertical edges will be attached to existing matboard walls and will hold the wall in a vertical position. Begin by applying a thin line of white glue to the vertical edges with your fingertip. Don't forget to remove the excess glue from your fingers. (ll. 6a)

Now, push the curved wall up against the existing wall and hold it for one minute to get a strong bond. Remove any excess glue from the joint by running your fingertip across it in one swipe. Apply strips of drafting tape across the joint if necessary to hold it in place while the glue dries. (ll. 6b)

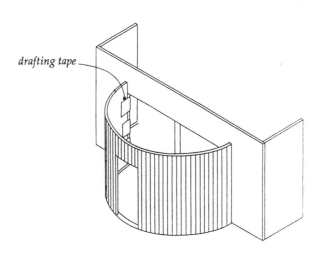

drafting tape

6b *Attach the vertical edges and apply drafting tape to hold it in position.*

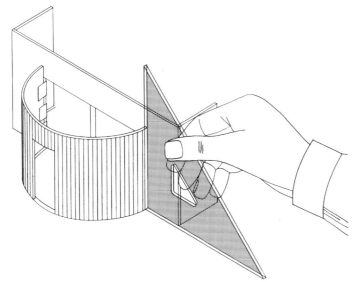

7 *Check the verticality of the wall with a small triangle and adjust it if necessary.*

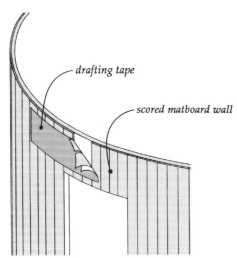

— *drafting tape*

— *scored matboard wall*

Care must be taken when removing drafting tape from a scored wall to not damage the scored outer layer.

Step 7 *Check the vertical angle.*

Check the verticality of the wall with a small triangle and adjust the wall if necessary. Your curved wall is now complete.

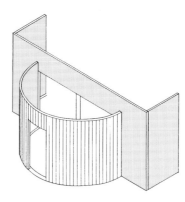

FINISHED CHIPBOARD CURVED WALL

Curved Wall: Matboard Construction

Curved wall construction with matboard or Strathmore is the same as with chipboard, but with matboard you must remember not to space your scorelines any closer together than 1/8". If they are any closer the outer layer of paper on the matboard will delaminate. The outer layer is usually a thin colored paper that is laminated to a sheet of chipboard and delaminates when cut into small pieces. This should also be remembered when applying drafting tape to the scored wall. The tape must be carefully removed so as not to damage the scored outer layer of paper.

Curved Wall: Foamcore Construction

The construction technique selected for constructing a curved Foamcore wall depends on the wall thickness and thus the scale of the model. For example, on a 1/4" scale model with radiuses of no less than 10'-0" a 1/8" thick Foamcore with the paper removed from both sides can be curved to follow the radiuses without scoring it; but a 1/4" thick Foamcore with the paper removed on one side only, must be scored to curve properly. For 1/4" models using 1/4" Foamcore, the paper must be left on the inside wall surface to hold the scored wall together.

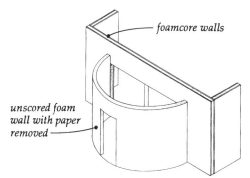

foamcore walls

unscored foam wall with paper removed

On a 1/4" scale model a 1/8" thick Foamcore with both layers of paper removed can be curved without having to score it.

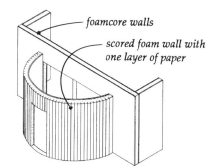

foamcore walls

scored foam wall with one layer of paper

On a 1/4" scale model a 1/4" thick Foamcore with one layer of paper removed must be scored to curve properly.

Curved Wall: Cardboard Construction

Creating a curved wall with corrugated cardboard is a simple process of removing one of the outer layers of paper and bending the wall to its desired form. Unfortunately though, the paper does not come off easily and you are left with a rough corrugated finish that distracts from the design intent. Also, the corrugated vertical pattern is not to scale if used on a 1/8" or 1/4" scale model. For these reasons it is not recommended for use on final presentation models, but is fine for schematic models. It can be attached to the model with white glue and cut with a utility knife.

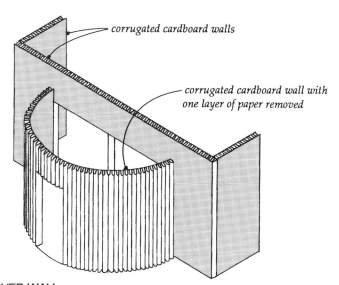

corrugated cardboard walls

corrugated cardboard wall with one layer of paper removed

CARDBOARD CURVED WALL

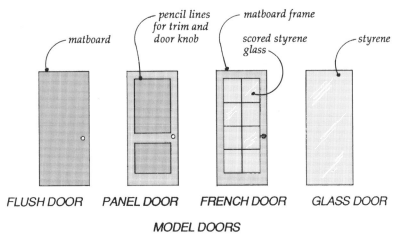

matboard — pencil lines for trim and door knob — matboard frame — scored styrene glass — styrene

FLUSH DOOR   PANEL DOOR   FRENCH DOOR   GLASS DOOR

MODEL DOORS

DOORS

Interior and exterior doors can be simulated with a number of materials such as matboard, chipboard, Canson paper, or clear plastic styrene, depending on the type of door being represented. Illustrated, are a number of door types and the materials used to construct them. They can be simulated at 1/8" or 1/4" scale.

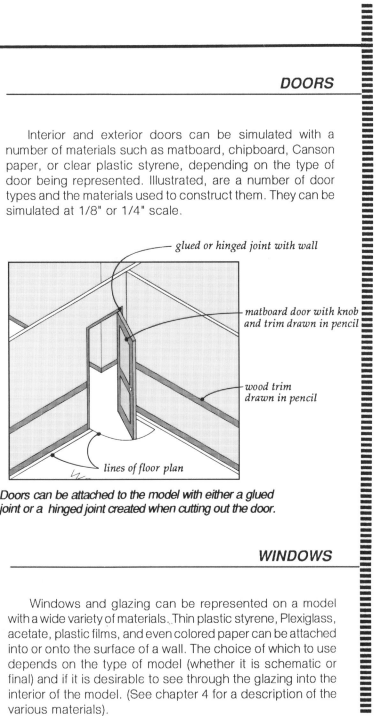

glued or hinged joint with wall

matboard door with knob and trim drawn in pencil

wood trim drawn in pencil

lines of floor plan

Doors can be attached to the model with either a glued joint or a hinged joint created when cutting out the door.

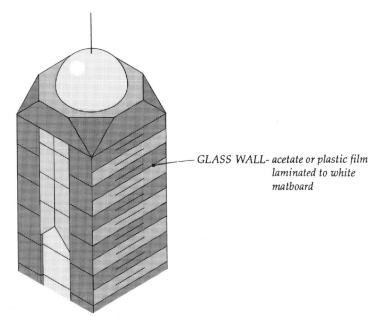

GLASS WALL- *acetate or plastic film laminated to white matboard*

A glass wall can be simulated with a sheet of laminated acetate.

WINDOWS

Windows and glazing can be represented on a model with a wide variety of materials. Thin plastic styrene, Plexiglass, acetate, plastic films, and even colored paper can be attached into or onto the surface of a wall. The choice of which to use depends on the type of model (whether it is schematic or final) and if it is desirable to see through the glazing into the interior of the model. (See chapter 4 for a description of the various materials).

Plastic Film

Plastic film sheets with the adhesive already on the back, (commonly referred to as 'decals'), and coated papers can also be used for window glazing on models of any size in the same manner as acetates. Aside from being able to be laminated to backing board and attached into the window opening, it is also possible to attach the film or paper directly to the wall without cutting any openings. This provides flexibility in changing the size of the windows on a schematic model where the main purpose is to study the 'mass-to-void' proportioning.

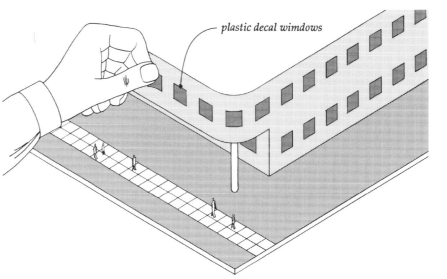

plastic decal wimdows

Plastic films and coated papers with adhesive on the back can be applied to the model walls to simulate windows.

Plexiglass

Plexiglass is excellent for simulating window walls on large scale schematic or final presentation models, but it is not recommended for small windows where the piece is smaller than 4" square. This is due to the fact that the Plexiglass sheets are too thick to cut without power tools. I recommend using styrene or laminated acetate for small pieces, and having the plastics store cut the Plexiglass for you to the desired size.

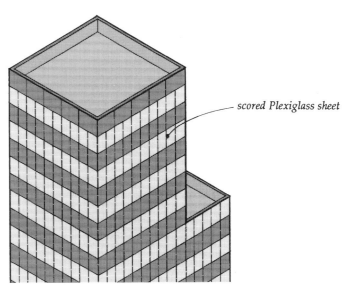

scored Plexiglass sheet

Sheets of Plexiglass can be used to simulate large window walls.

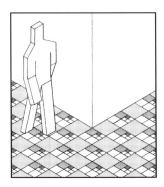

CERAMIC TILE FLOORING

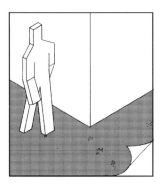

CARPET FLOORING

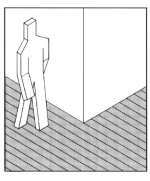

WOOD STRIP FLOORING

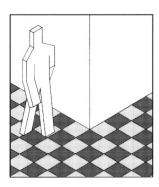

VINYL TILE FLOORING

Flooring adds color and scale to a model and is appropriate for both schematic and final presentation models. There is a vast array of different types of flooring materials available to the model designer. Some of the materials we will look at are ceramic tile, vinyl tile, wood strips, and carpet.

Ceramic Tile

Ceramic tile flooring is available in many different colors and sizes. It is best simulated on a model by drawing or photocopying the various patterns onto colored film or paper.

The semi-glossy finish of the film simulates the smooth surface of the ceramic tile at 1/8" or 1/4" scale. Canson paper has a rough finish to it but can be drawn on with pencil or ink. Both are available in a wide assortment of colors at graphic arts supply stores.

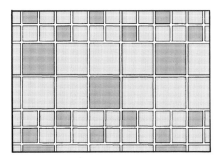

CERAMIC TILE

Vinyl Tile

Vinyl floor tile is simulated in the same manner as ceramic tile, with plastic film being the best material to use because of its semi-glossy finish.

Another method for simulating vinyl tile in a checkerboard pattern is to use gift wrapping paper. Your local gift store may have a variety of patterned papers to use as floor and wall coverings on your model. Take your scale with you and measure patterns to make sure they fit your selected model scale.

VINYL TILE FLOORING

Wood Floor

Wood flooring is available in a variety of styles and is best simulated on your model by drawing or photocopying the pattern onto colored paper. The paper you select should be the color of the finished wood.

WOOD STRIP FLOORING

Carpet

Carpeting is available in a wide assortment of colors and patterns and is best simulated on a model with colored paper. Canson paper is excellent to use since it has a rough texture that is ideal for simulating at 1/8" or 1/4" scale.

Another method is to use some type of fabric, such as velvet or felt. Due to their texture they would be more appropriate on a large scale model such as 1/2". These are available at your local fabric store.

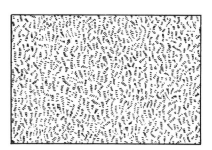

CARPET FLOORING

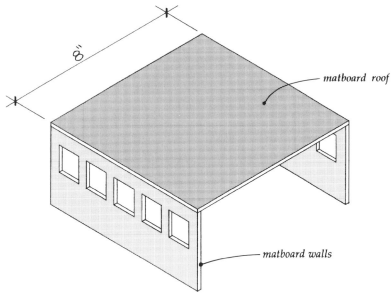

8"

matboard roof

matboard walls

Roofs with long spans (8" or more) should be constructed with Foamcore. Those less than 8" can be built with matboard.

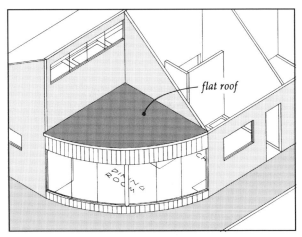

flat roof

FLAT ROOF TO THE EDGE

ROOFS

The roof of a building is usually the last component attached, but must be considered in the early planning stages of your models' construction. You must decide what board thickness should be used and whether or not the roofing material will be simulated.

Generally, whatever type of board (matboard or Foamcore) was used for the walls is also used for the roof. But roofs with long spans (8" or more) should be constructed with Foamcore to avoid deflection.

Usually, roofing materials such as clay tile, shingles, or metal panels are only applied to final presentation models, but they can be applied to a schematic model to hide a revision to the roof such as moving a skylight.

Let's look at the construction procedures for a flat roof, flat roof with parapet walls, gable roof, hip roof, and curved roof. (Refer to Chapter 2 for construction of a gable roof).

Flat Roof

There are two types of flat roofs used on a building: flat to the edge, and flat with a parapet wall. The 'flat to the edge' type of roof is easiest of the two to construct; its construction procedures are described in Chapter 2. Let's look at the construction procedures for a 'flat with a parapet wall' roof.

Flat Roof with Parapet Walls

A flat roof with parapet walls is difficult to construct because you must cut the roof to fit exactly within already constructed walls that do not always line up. Discrepancies during wall construction cause the tops of the walls to not be parallel and square with each other. The best method for constructing a roof to fit precisely within the parapet walls is as follows:

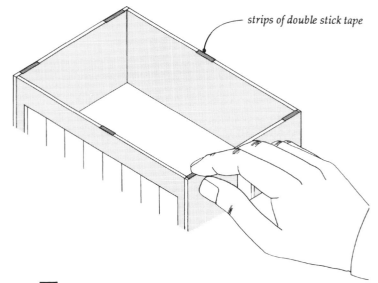

strips of double stick tape

1a *Apply pieces of double stick tape to the top of the parapet walls.*

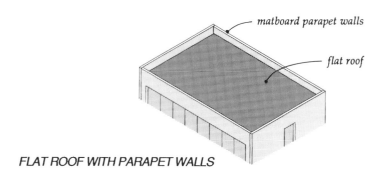

matboard parapet walls

flat roof

FLAT ROOF WITH PARAPET WALLS

Step 1 *Draw the roof outline onto matboard.*

Apply pieces of double-stick tape to the top of the walls as illustrated. (Il. 1a)

Next, set a sheet of matboard on top of the walls so that it is overhanging them by at least 1/2" all around. Press down at the tape locations to set the board in a fixed position.

With a pencil draw the outline of the perimeter of the roof on the underside of the matboard. Do not press so hard that the walls move inward, a light guideline is sufficient. (Il. 1b)

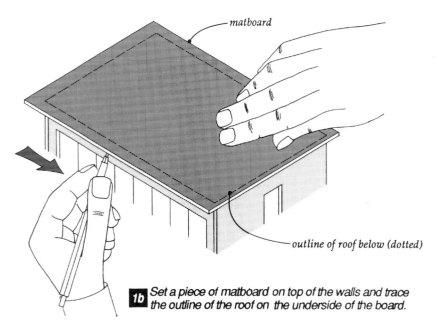

matboard

outline of roof below (dotted)

1b *Set a piece of matboard on top of the walls and trace the outline of the roof on the underside of the board.*

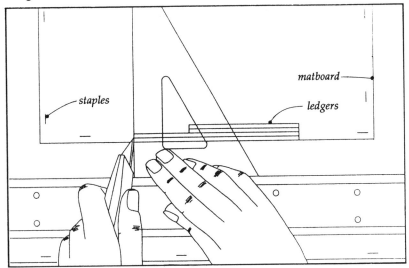

drawn pencil outline

cut along dotted line

1/16"

matboard

staples

2 Secure the matboard to your cutting board and cut the roof out 1/16" in from the guidelines.

staples

matboard

ledgers

3 Cut out matboard ledgers.

Step 2 *Cut out the roof.*

Carefully remove the board from the walls and line up the roof lines with your parallel bar before stapling it to your cutting board. Using a utility knife and triangle cut out the roof 1/16" in from the guidelines. The 1/16" is the wall thickness if you are using 1/16" matboard, if not adjust to whatever your model wall thickness is. You may notice that some of the right angles are not exactly 90 degrees or that some of the walls are not straight. This is typical for paper models and must be compensated for when cutting out the roof. Follow the guidelines even though they are not straight . Once the roof is cut out smooth down the flaired edges with your fingernail.

Step 3 *Cut out and attach ledgers.*

Next, cut out 1/8" wide strips of matboard and attach them to the walls at the roof line corner to corner to serve as ledgers. Make pencil lines at the roof line to get the ledgers level with the top of the wall. Attach the ledgers with a thin line of white glue.

Step 4 *Set the roof in place.*

Set the roof in place on top of the ledgers. Do not apply any glue yet. Trim any edges that need to be cut for the roof to fit snugly in place, but do not cut off anymore than you have to. You will be surprised to find that when you trim one side of the roof it will affect the fit on the other side as well.

4 Set the roof in place on top of the ledgers and trim any edges to make it fit.

Step 5 *Glue roof to ledgers.*

This step is optional. If you want to be able to remove the roof and see the interior of the model, do not glue the roof down.

However, if you would like the roof to be permanently fixed, lift the roof out of the model by pushing it up from underneath if possible or attaching strips of drafting tape to the top of it and lifting it up.

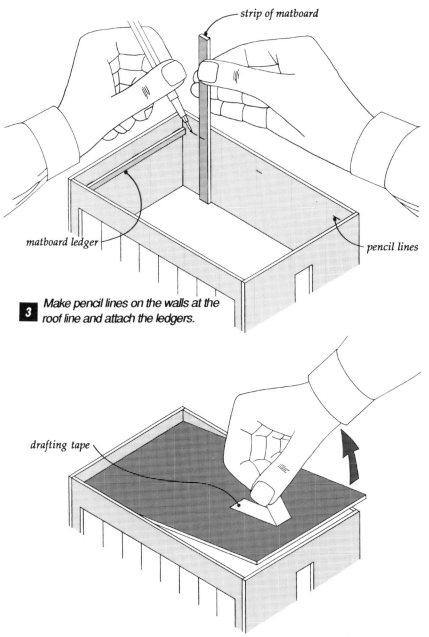

strip of matboard

matboard ledger

pencil lines

3 Make pencil lines on the walls at the roof line and attach the ledgers.

drafting tape

5 Lift the roof out of the model by attaching a strip of drafting tape to the top of it and pulling it up.

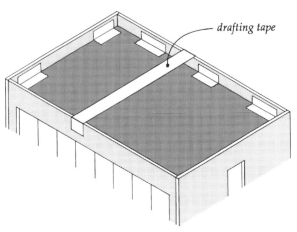

drafting tape

6 *Apply strips of drafting tape along the edge to hold it in place until the glue is dry.*

Apply a thin layer of white glue to the top of the ledgers all the way around the walls, and set the roof down pushing on it for a strong bond.

Apply drafting tape wherever necessary to hold the roof in place while the glue dries. Long strips of tape spanning from parapet wall to parapet wall will pull the walls together giving you a tight joint between the roof and wall. Tape applied to the joint as illustrated will hold the roof down.

Allow the glue to dry for a couple of hours before removing the tape. Your flat roof with parapet walls is now complete.

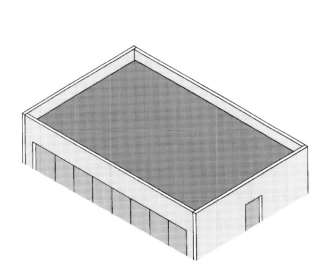

**COMPLETED FLAT ROOF
WITH PARAPET WALLS**

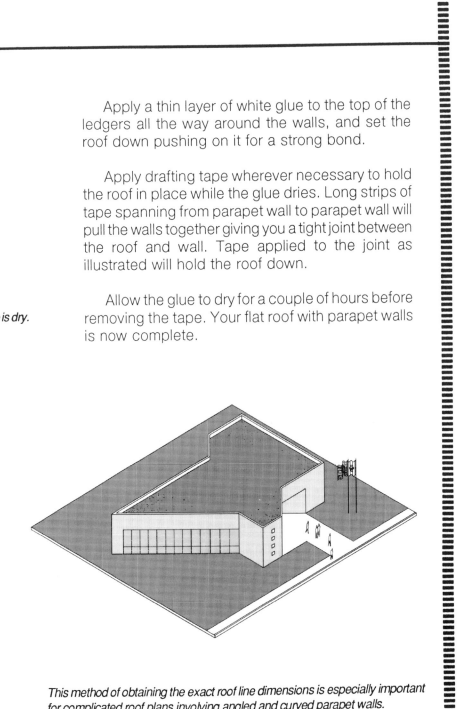

This method of obtaining the exact roof line dimensions is especially important for complicated roof plans involving angled and curved parapet walls.

Hip Roof

A hip style roof is similar in construction to a gable roof, but for a hip roof you must add a sloping roof at each end. Since you are using the actual sloping dimensions of the sloped roof planes, you cannot simply cut out a roof plan and bend it at the ridge lines. Instead, you must measure the 'true' dimensions of the roof from its elevations and plan views. Let's look at this procedure:

HIP STYLE ROOF

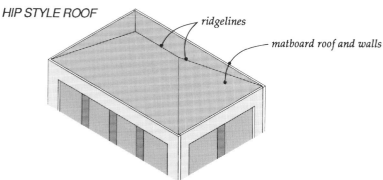

ridgelines

matboard roof and walls

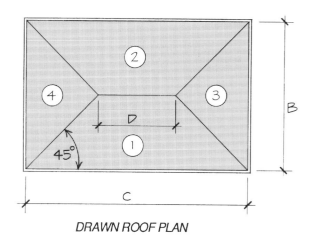

DRAWN ROOF PLAN

Step 1 Attach matboard to cutting board.

First, staple a sheet of matboard to your cutting board. Select a matboard color that corresponds to the actual roof material. (Dark red for clay tile; grey for shingles; light blue for slate; etc.)

Step 2 Draw roof panel #1.

To start, we will draw roof panel #1 onto the matboard. Begin by measuring distances C, D and A from your roof plan and elevations with a 'thin strip of matboard'. (Il. 2a) In order to determine at what angle

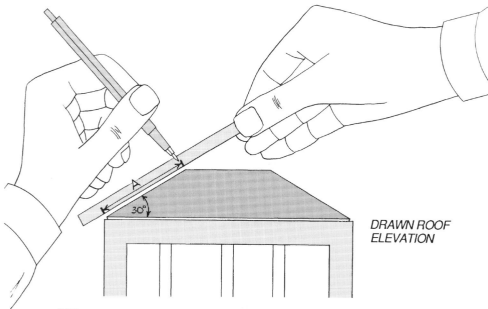

DRAWN ROOF ELEVATION

2a *Measure distances C, D and A from your roof plan and elevations.*

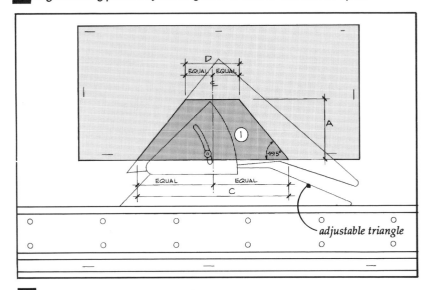

2b *Begin drawing panel 1 by drawing lines 'C' and 'D' distance 'A' apart.*

2c *Draw the sloping sides of panel 1.*

the sloping sides of panel #1 should be drawn at you must first draw lines D and C parallel and centered with each other distance A apart. (Il. 2b) Then, with your adjustable triangle draw a line from one end of D and C on both sides. (Il. 2c) Both angles should be the same. On our example roof the angle is 49.5 degrees, and this could be used again on any hip roof with a 30 degree slope. (Below is listed other roof slopes and their corresponding ridge angles).

25 degree roof slope = 47.5 degrees
35 degree roof slope = 50.5 degrees
40 degree roof slope = 52   degrees
45 degree roof slope = 54   degrees

Step 3 *Draw roof panel #2 onto matboard.*

Since panel #2 is a mirror image of panel #1, draw panel #2 with the same dimensions and angles as panel #1 directly above it. The line between them is going to be a hinged joint.

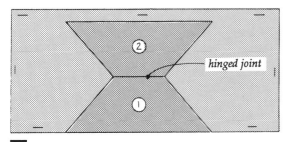

3 *Draw roof panel 2 above panel 1.*

Step 4   *Draw panel #3 onto matboard.*

Next, draw panel #3 adjacent to panel #1. To do this you must first rotate panels #1 and #2 around on your cutting board so that the sloping side of panel #1 is parallel with your parallel bar. Now draw a line the length of dimension B at 49.5 degrees from panel #1 with your adjustable triangle. (Il. 4a)

Once that is done you can draw the other sloping wall to complete panel #3. (Il. 4b)

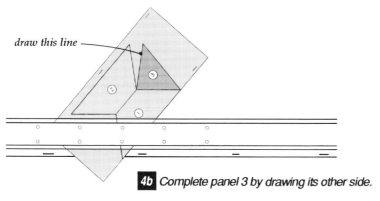

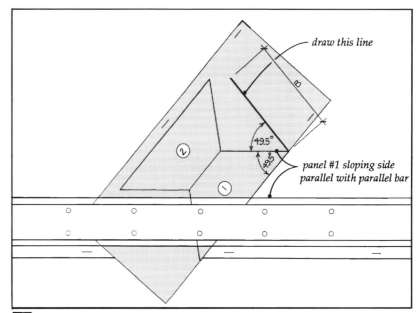

4a *Draw line 'B' at 49.5 degrees from panel 1.*

4b *Complete panel 3 by drawing its other side.*

Step 5   *Draw panel #4 onto the matboard.*

Rotate the plan back into its original position and draw panel #4. It should be drawn on the opposite side of panel #1, as a mirror image of panel #3.

Now, with your entire roof pattern drawn with actual dimensions, score the three ridge lines and create hinges for their connection. Now you only have two ridge joints to glue and tape.

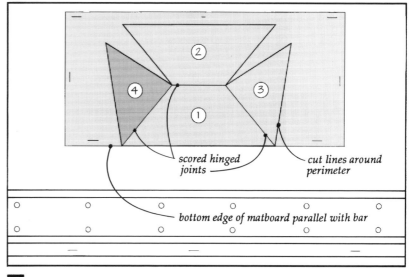

5 *Draw roof panel 4 as a mirror image of panel 3, and perform the score and cut lines.*

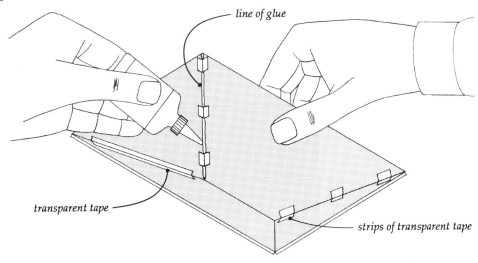

Bend the roof at the ridge lines and apply strips of transparent tape at the joints.
6 Apply a thin line of glue to the joints.

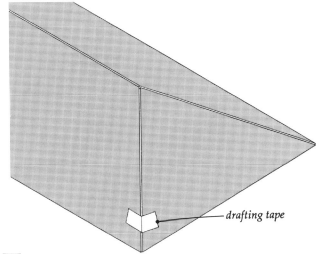

7 The drafting tape can be removed after the glue has dried.

Step 6 *Cut out the roof and bend at the ridge lines.*

Using a utility knife cut out the roof, and flatten down the flaired edges with your fingernail. Next, bend the board at the ridge lines into the desired shape. If any of the scored joints break while bending simply apply a strip of transparent tape along the underside of the joint.

Attach a piece of transparent tape at the bottom of the open joint to hold it in place while you apply three short strips of tape along the inside of the joint. Short strips of drafting tape can also be applied to the outside of the joint to hold it together while the glue dries.

Step 7 *Apply glue to the joint.*

Apply a thin line of white glue along the inside of the joint between the short strips of tape. Adjust the nozzle if the flow of glue from the bottle is to much.

After the glue has dried the drafting tape can be removed but the transparent tape on the inside of the joints must remain. Since the tape is holding the joint together you can now set the roof in place on the model.

Step 8 *Apply glue to the top of the walls.*

If you want to be able to remove the roof to see the model's interior do not glue the roof to the walls. If you want it attached apply a thin line of white glue to the top of the walls with the 'fingertip' application.

Step 9 *Set the roof on top of the walls.*

Set the roof in place making sure that it is parallel with the walls. You may have to apply drafting tape at the edges to hold the roof down firmly until the glue dries.

Let the roof set undisturbed for at least two hours until the glue is dry. Remove the tape and your hip roof is complete.

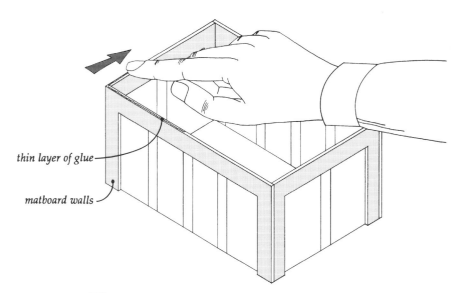

thin layer of glue

matboard walls

8 *Apply a thin layer of glue to the top of the walls with your fingertip.*

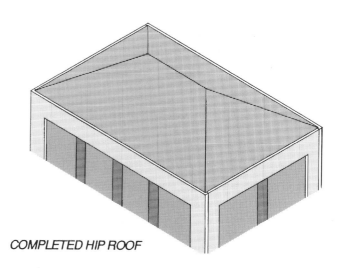

COMPLETED HIP ROOF

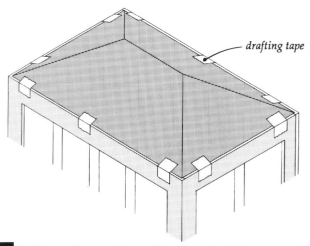

drafting tape

9 *Set the roof on top of the walls and apply drafting tape to the edges.*

A
B

CURVED ROOF

C

scored matboard roof

matboard walls

Curved Roof

A curved roof is different in construction than any other roof type. In order to keep the roof in a curved shape, matboard ribs or end walls must be attached to the roof diaphragm. Lets look at the construction procedures for the curved roof as illustrated:

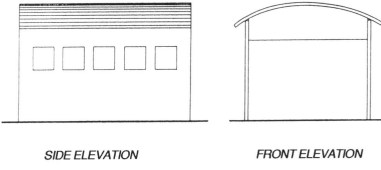

SIDE ELEVATION

FRONT ELEVATION

staple

A

matboard

B

cutting matboard

1 *Draw the roof in plan with actual dimensions onto matboard.*

Step 1 Draw the roof plan onto chipboard.

First, measure and draw the roof onto a sheet of chipboard stapled to your cutting board. Measure the true width 'A' by bending a thin strip of matboard along the roof line on the roof elevation. Measure distance 'B' from the roof plan or side elevation.

Step 2 *Score and cut out the roof.*

With the use of a utility knife and triangle, perform scorelines along the roof at 1/8" apart so that it will curve to the desired shape. Then, cut out the roof from the chipboard and flatten down the edges with your fingernail.

Step 3 *Draw the end walls on the chipboard and cut out.*

Next, measure and draw both end walls onto the sheet of chipboard. Use the dimensions from the front elevation. Cut the end walls with a utility knife and flatten their edges with your fingernail.

Step 4 *Attach the end walls to your side walls.*

Next, attach the end walls to the existing side walls butted together, with a thin layer of white glue. Apply drafting tape across the joint to hold it in place while the glue dries.

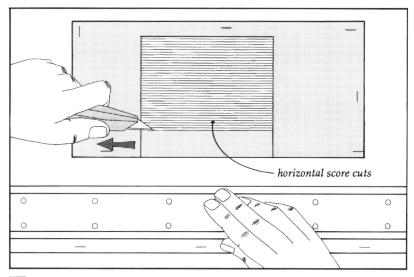

horizontal score cuts

2 *Perform horizontal score lines 1/8" apart and cut out roof.*

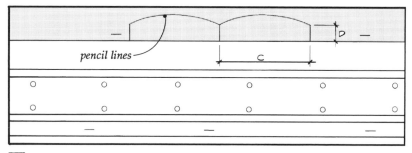

pencil lines

3 *Draw end walls onto matboard.*

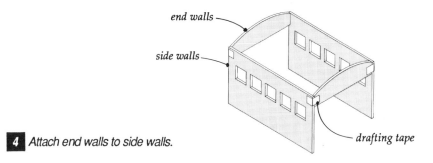

end walls

side walls

drafting tape

4 *Attach end walls to side walls.*

Step 5   *Attach roof to walls.*

Finally, set the roof diaphragm in place to make sure it is the right size. If any of the score lines penetrated through the board apply transparent tape to the back. If the roof fits properly, apply a thin layer of white glue to the top of the walls with your fingertip and set the roof in place. If it does'nt, trim the edges as much as necessary and attach it to the walls.

Apply drafting tape at the edges to hold it down while the glue dries.

Once the glue has dried, carefully remove the tape and your curved roof is complete.

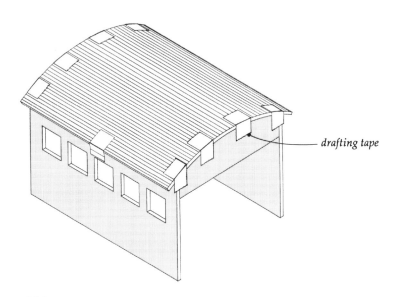

drafting tape

5 *Apply glue to the top of the walls and set the roof in place.*

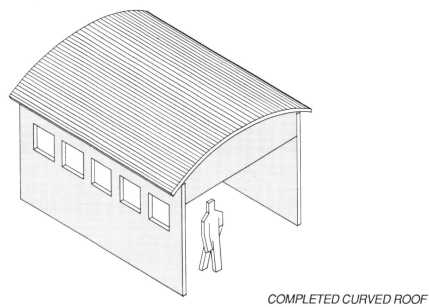

COMPLETED CURVED ROOF

ROOFING MATERIALS

A roof can be covered with a variety of different materials, each tailored for either a flat or sloping roof. Clay tiles, shingles, wood shakes, slate and metal panels are usually applied to sloping roofs, while built-up and single-ply membranes are applied to flat roofs. Let's look at these materials and how they are best simulated on a model.

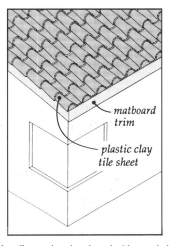

Clay tile can be simulated with a red plastic sheet available at architectural model supply stores.

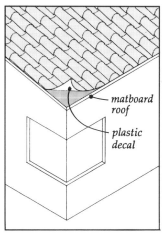

Clay tile can also be simulated with a plastic decal available at graphic arts supply stores.

Clay Tile

Clay tile roofing for a model is available in many different styles and colors, and can be bought at any architectural model supply store, or simulated by applying a plastic decal onto colored matboard.

The type of clay tile most commonly available at stores is the red barrel type. It is made of a thin plastic sheet, available in 1/8" or 1/4" scale and can be cut with a utility knife. It is quickly attached to the model roof with white glue, and is excellent for final presentation models, but may be too expensive for a schematic study model.

Plastic decals with the clay tile pattern printed on them are available in many different styles and scales at graphic supply stores. The plastic sheets are self-adhesive and can be attached to colored matboard to simulate any color tile you desire. Attach the decal to your matboard before cutting out the roof panels, making sure to smooth out all of the bubbles with a straightedge. This method is excellent for both schematic and final presentation models.

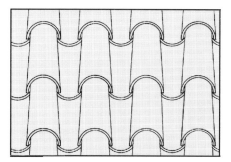

CLAY TILE IN ELEVATION

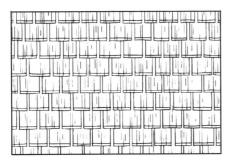

SHINGLE PATTERNS IN ELEVATION

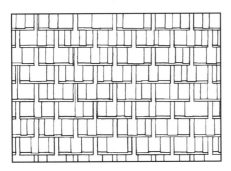

WOOD SHAKES IN ELEVATION

SLATE TILES IN ELEVATION

Shingles

Shingle patterns are also available on decals at graphic arts supply stores and can be applied to a model in the same manner as clay tile decals.

A much more realistic method is to photocopy a shingle pattern onto colored paper and laminate it to a sheet of chipboard. Canson paper is excellent for this method and is more realistic looking than a decal since it is not shiny. Its texture is rough and porous, making it ideal for simulating composition shingles on a 1/8" or 1/4" schematic or final presentation model.

Wood shakes

Wood shake patterns are very similar to shingles, so they can be easily substituted for the other. The only difference is that the color should simulate weathered wood, so, select a matboard of that color.

Slate Tiles

Slate roofing tiles are usually blue or grey in color and are similar in pattern to shingles. Slate tile is best represented on a model with a shingle pattern photocopied onto colored paper and laminated to chipboard. (Feel free to photocopy the various material patterns on these pages for use on your models).

Metal Panels

Metal roofing panels are available in many different styles and colors, and are best simulated on a model with colored plastic film. You can draw the pattern directly on the film with ink, or photocopy onto it. Use a technical pen with india ink to draw the seams, battens, or ribs onto the smooth decal. The semi-glossy finish is excellent for simulating painted metal at 1/8" or 1/4" scale.

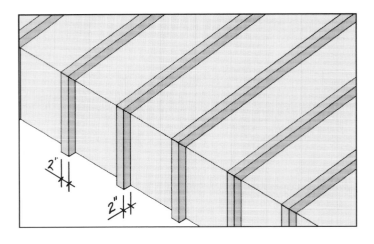

FULL SCALE BATTEN SEAMS

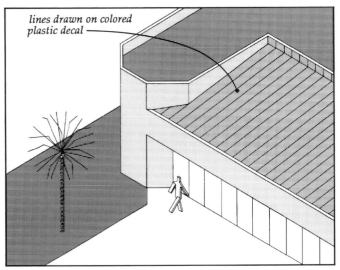

Metal roofing can be simulated by drawing or photocopying lines onto a colored plastic decal.

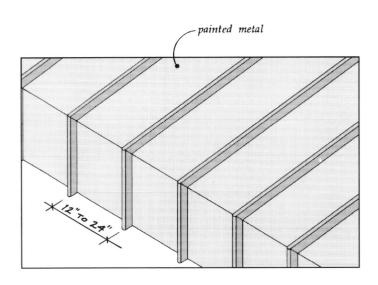

FULL SCALE STANDING SEAMS

Built-up Roofing

A built-up roof on a building is constructed of gravel on top of coal tar, on top of roofing felt, respectively. It is best simulated on a 1/8" or 1/4" model with a grey colored Canson paper laminated to a chipboard roof.

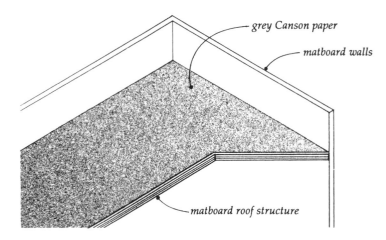

MODEL ROOF SECTION

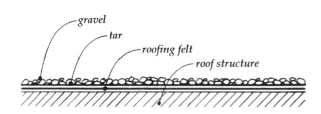

BUILT-UP ROOFING SECTION

Single Ply Roof

A single-ply roof on a building is constructed of large sheets of thick plastic vinyl attached to the roof and is generally white or grey in color. It is best simulated on a model with a plastic film laminated to a chipboard roof.

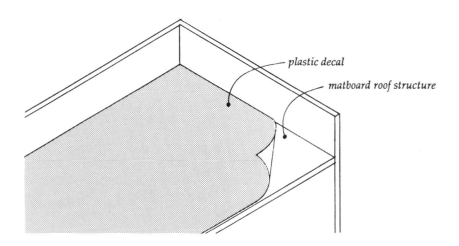

MODEL ROOF SECTION

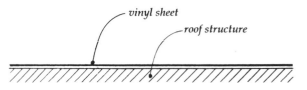

SINGLE PLY ROOFING SECTION

SKYLIGHTS

There are five types of skylights commonly used on buildings: the gable, the hip, the octagon, the shed, and the dome. All can be constructed of matboard and styrene, or bought at an architectural model making supply store. All five types consist of two components: the parapet base, and the glazing. The base is usually made of matboard and is either set on top of, or penetrating through the roof. The glazing is constructed of scored styrene sheets and is attached to the parapet base with white glue. Let's look at the method of construction for each component:

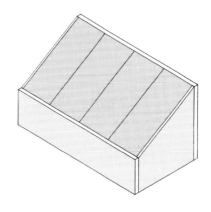

SHED TYPE

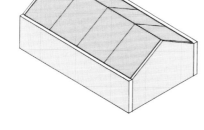

GABLE TYPE

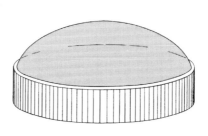

DOME TYPE

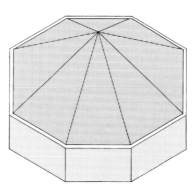

OCTAGON TYPE

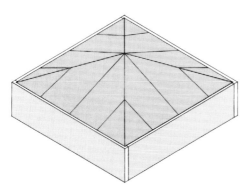

HIP TYPE

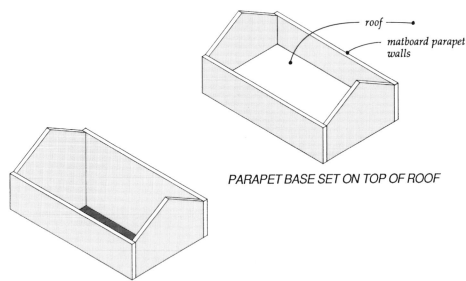

roof

matboard parapet walls

PARAPET BASE SET ON TOP OF ROOF

PARAPET BASE PENETRATING ROOF

Parapet Base Construction

The parapet base can be either set on top of the roof or penetrate through it. Each method is appropriate for different types of models. For example, if the model type is a quick schematic study then the base can be set on top, the glazing being simulated with an opaque plastic film. Or, if the model type is for a final presentation then the base should penetrate through the roof with transparent glazing on top enabling the viewer to see the interior of the model. Either way it is not feasible to apply an opaque glazing on top of a base that penetrates the roof since you will not be able to see the interior through the glazing.

Let's look first at the construction procedures for the base set on top of the roof, then the base penetrating through the roof.

Roof-Top Mounted Parapet Walls

Step 1 *Draw the walls onto matboard.*

First, staple a sheet of matboard to your cutting board making sure to line up the bottom with your parallel bar.

Next draw the parapet walls in elevation onto the matboard. Draw the walls adjacent to each other. Then draw the bottom of the base.

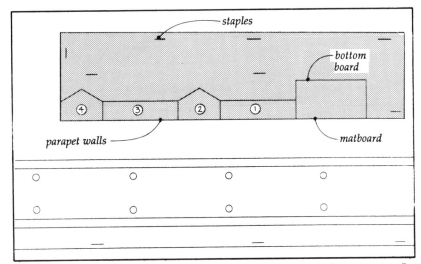

staples

bottom board

parapet walls

matboard

1 Secure a sheet of matboard to your cutting board and draw the parapet walls adjacent to each other.

Step 2 Cut out walls and bottom.

Cut out the walls and bottom board with a utility knife and smooth down the flaired edges with your fingernail.

Step 3 Attach walls together.

Apply a thin layer of white glue to the vertical edges of the walls and attach them to each other around the bottom board as illustrated. Once all the walls are together apply a thin layer of glue to the inside wall and bottom baseboard joint.

Once the glue has dried you are ready to apply glazing to the top of the walls and attach the skylight to the roof with white glue.

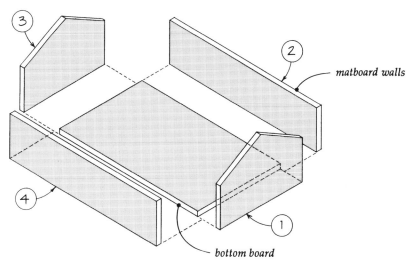

matboard walls

bottom board

2 **3** *Cut out the walls and bottom board and attach them together.*

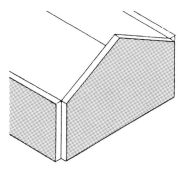

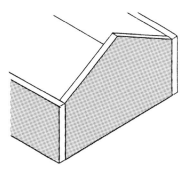

FINISHED GABLE TYPE PARAPET BASE WITH HINGED JOINTS

FINISHED PARAPET BASE WITH BUTTED JOINTS

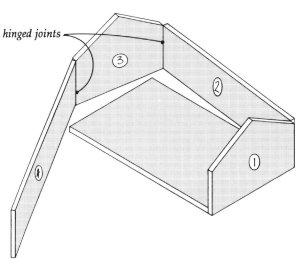

hinged joints

You may want to construct the walls with hinged joints to save time. If so don't forget to reduce the wall lengths by 1/16" at each end.

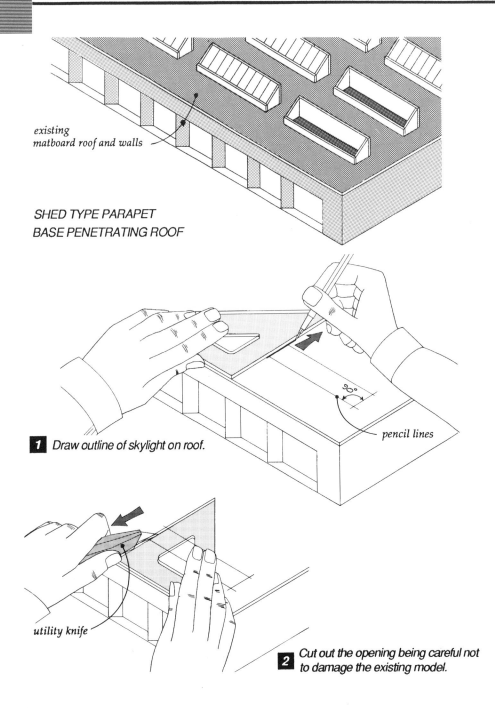

existing
matboard roof and walls

SHED TYPE PARAPET
BASE PENETRATING ROOF

90°

pencil lines

1 Draw outline of skylight on roof.

utility knife

2 Cut out the opening being careful not
to damage the existing model.

Parapet Walls Penetrating the Roof

In order to construct parapet walls penetrating the roof a hole must be cut in the roof the size of your skylight. This is much easier to perform if the roof is removable from the model walls. You simply attach it to your cutting board with drafting tape and perform the cuts. But, if it is not removable you must place your drafting and cutting tools on top of the fragile model roof being careful not to damage the already built model. Let's look at the construction procedures for this type of parapet wall:

Step 1 *Draw skylight opening on roof.*

First, with a pencil and triangle draw the skylight opening on top of the roof making sure that all inside angles are 90 degrees.

Step 2 *Cut out opening.*

Cut out the opening with a utility knife and triangle being careful not to damage the existing model roof. Be patient and perform a number of slow cutting strokes with light pressure on the knife until you have cut through the board. Remove the piece and flatten down the flaired roof edges with your fingernail.

Step 3 *Draw the parapet walls in elevation.*

Next, draw the parapet walls in elevation onto a sheet of matboard stapled to your cutting board. Since the walls will be penetrating through the roof structure its depth must be added to the height of the parapet walls. Measure the required wall lengths from the opening in the roof with a thin strip of matboard.

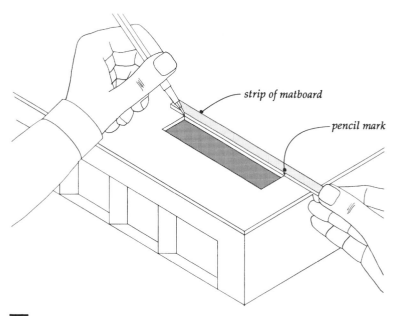

strip of matboard

pencil mark

3a *Measure the required wall lengths from the opening.*

Step 4 *Cut out walls and set in place.*

Cut out the walls with a utility knife and flatten down the flaired edges. Set the walls in place within the opening without any glue on them to make sure they fit snugly.

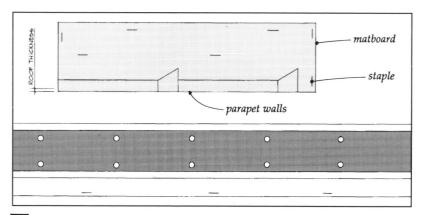

ROOF THICKNESS

matboard

staple

parapet walls

3b *Draw parapet walls onto matboard, and cut them out.*

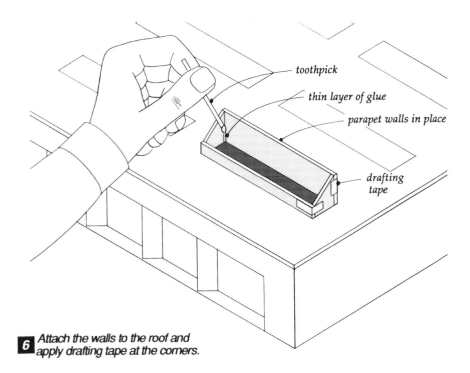

layer of glue

glue on spare chipboard

5 *Apply a thin layer of glue to the inside of the roof structure.*

toothpick

thin layer of glue

parapet walls in place

drafting tape

6 *Attach the walls to the roof and apply drafting tape at the corners.*

Step 5 Apply glue to the roof structure.

Next, apply a thin layer of white glue to the sides of the roof structure that will be in contact with the walls by dabbing it on with your fingertip.

Step 6 Attach walls into the opening.

Now, attach all of the walls to the sides of the opening being careful not to get any glue on a portion of wall that will be exposed. Apply drafting tape across the top of the walls to hold them in place with 90 degree corners, and apply a thin line of glue to the inside wall corners.

Once the glue has dried you can remove the drafting tape and attach glazing to the top of the walls.

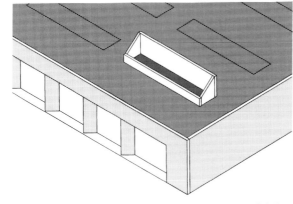

FINISHED PARAPET BASE PENETRATING ROOF

Glazing Construction: Gable Type

Step 1 *Measure the glazing dimensions.*

Begin by measuring the required length and width of the glazing with a thin strip of matboard as illustrated.

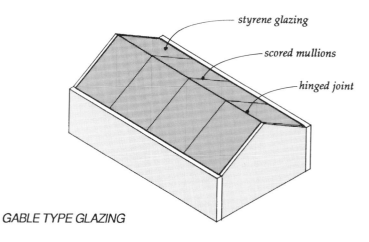

GABLE TYPE GLAZING

styrene glazing

scored mullions

hinged joint

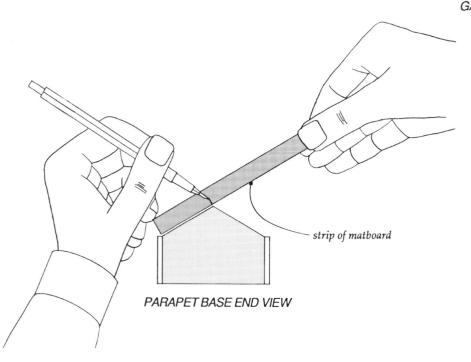

strip of matboard

PARAPET BASE END VIEW

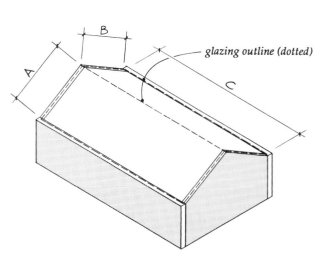

glazing outline (dotted)

1a *Take the measurements off the already constructed walls.*

1b *Measure the required glazing dimensions with a thin strip of matboard.*

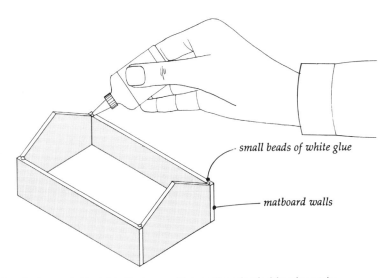

2 Etch the overall size and mullion locations into the styrene, and score the ridge line.

mullions

drafting tape

ridge line

styrene sheet

small beads of white glue

matboard walls

3 Cut out the glazing and attach it to the base with small beads of white glue at the corners.

Step 2 Etch mullions into styrene and score ridge line.

Next, attach a clear sheet of plastic styrene to your cutting board with drafting or masking tape, and with the use of an Xacto knife and triangle etch the overall size and mullion locations into the plastic. Score the ridge line deep enough into the plastic so that it will bend but not break, creating a hinged joint. Keep the sheet taped to your cutting board and square to the parallel bar during all cuts.

Step 3 Cut out the glazing.

Next, cut all the way through at the outside lines and remove the glazing from the plastic sheet. Place small beads of white glue at the corners to secure the glazing to the base. Bend the plastic at the ridge line to the desired angle and set it on top of the parapet base. After the glue has dried, the finished skylight can be set on top of the roof and glued down.

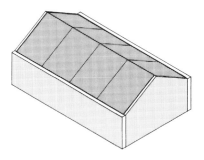

COMPLETED GABLE TYPE SKYLIGHT

Glazing Construction: Hip Type

The fastest, easiest, and most professional method for constructing the glazing of a hip style skylight is to cut and score a pattern onto one piece of plastic styrene and then bend it at the desired ridge lines into a pyramid shape. Let's look at this procedure:

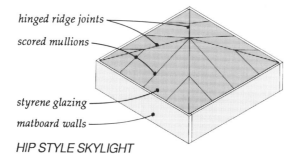

hinged ridge joints
scored mullions
styrene glazing
matboard walls

HIP STYLE SKYLIGHT

Step 1 Measure the glazing dimensions.

Begin by measuring the slope and base dimensions of the glazing from an elevation view of the skylight as illustrated.

Step 2 Etch the first triangle into the styrene.

With the use of an adjustable triangle and Xacto knife etch the first skylight triangle into a sheet of styrene taped to your cutting board. To draw the triangle you must first locate the top of the triangle at the centerline of dimension 'A' distance 'B' from the bottom edge. You will not be able to determine the angle until you have the top located.

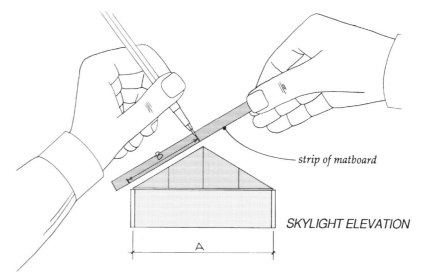

strip of matboard

SKYLIGHT ELEVATION

A

1 Measure the lengths of the sloped glazing and base from a drawn elevation. Verify that dimension 'A' is the same as the already built parapet base.

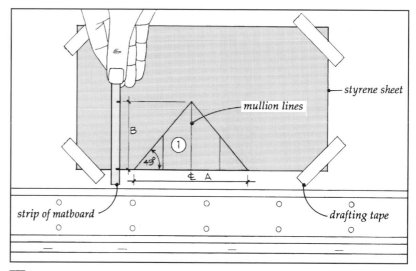

mullion lines
styrene sheet
B
49°
1
℄ A
strip of matboard
drafting tape

2 Etch the first glazing triangle into the styrene.

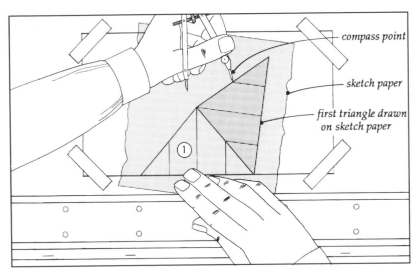

3a *The second triangle can be located by drawing the first triangle on a piece of sketch paper and locate the pencil lines by piercing the paper with a compass point.*

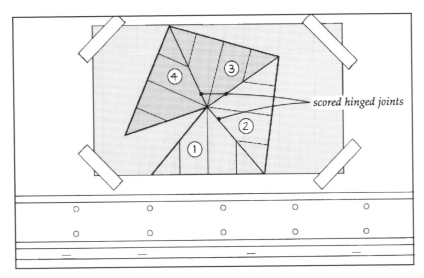

3b *Etch the three remaining triangles adjacent to the first one into the styrene.*

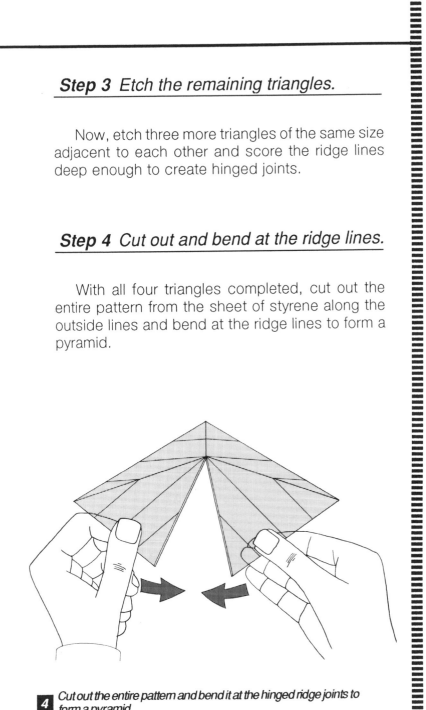

Step 3 *Etch the remaining triangles.*

Now, etch three more triangles of the same size adjacent to each other and score the ridge lines deep enough to create hinged joints.

Step 4 *Cut out and bend at the ridge lines.*

With all four triangles completed, cut out the entire pattern from the sheet of styrene along the outside lines and bend at the ridge lines to form a pyramid.

4 *Cut out the entire pattern and bend it at the hinged ridge joints to form a pyramid.*

Step 5 Apply glue to the joint.

Now, apply small beads of white glue to the edges and join them together. If the ridge lines are scored deep enough the pyramid should be able to stand alone while the glue dries. Otherwise, the edges should be held together with drafting tape until it dries. Now the glazing is ready to be attached to the parapet base.

Step 6 Attach glazing to base.

Place a small bead of white glue at each corner of the parapet base and set the glazing on top of the base. Allow the glue to dry before touching the skylight.

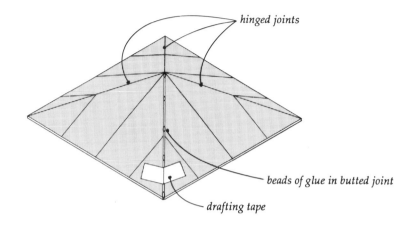

5 *Apply small beads of glue along the butted edges and apply a strip of drafting tape to hold it together until the glue dries.*

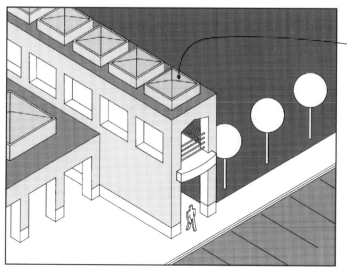

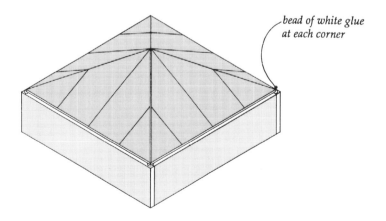

6 *Place a bead of glue at each corner of the base and set the glazing on top.*

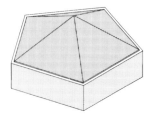
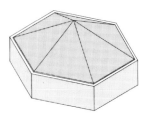
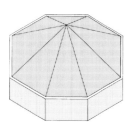

PENTAGON STYLE   *SEXAGON STYLE*   *OCTAGON STYLE*

Glazing Construction: Octagon Type

The same procedures for constructing a hip style skylight (four sided) can also be used for constructing an octagon style skylight (eight sided), or a pentagon style (five sided), or even a sexagon style (six sided). It does not matter how many sides there are to the skylight as long as you carefully follow the measuring technique of the glazing and etch the triangles adjacent to each other on the sheet of styrene.

clear acrylic dome

scored matboard base

DOME TYPE SKYLIGHT

Glazing Construction: Dome Type

The glazing for a spherical shaped dome skylight should be bought at an architectural model supply store and set on top of your matboard parapet base. It is virtually impossible to form your own plastic dome with styrene.

Another method is to buy a Plexiglass half-sphere at a plastic supply store and attach it to your roof. Although the plastic will be distorted visually it is excellent on models 1/4" scale and smaller.

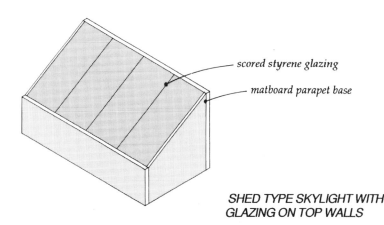

scored styrene glazing

matboard parapet base

SHED TYPE SKYLIGHT WITH GLAZING ON TOP WALLS

Glazing Construction: Shed Type

The glazing for a shed type skylight is different from the other types since it does not have a scored ridge line. The single sheet of plastic is set on top of the sloped parapet walls and attached with very small dots of white glue at the corners. After the glue has dried the joints are very fragile and care should be taken to not disturb the glazing.

SPACE FRAME

A space frame is one of the most difficult building components to simulate on a scaled model. If the model scale is smaller than 1/4", it is virtually impossible to construct a space frame using individual strut members. In these cases it is recommended to draw the struts in ink on plastic film or etch them onto a clear styrene sheet, both being transparent enough for the viewer to see through.

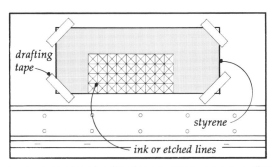

The structure can be simulated most simply on a two dimensional plane by etching square boxes with 45 degree diagonals in them.

When drawing the structural pattern onto plastic I recommend using a technical pen with india ink. It dries quickly and produces sharp straight lines. The structure can be represented most simply on a two dimensional plane by drawing square boxes with 45 degree diagonals in them as illustrated.

For a model 1/4" or larger the strut members are best represented with cotton swab sticks, and the bottom chords with 1/16" diameter wooden dowels. The swab sticks and dowels are the same diameter and when spray painted will appear to be the same material. Paper and wood are the easiest to work with since they can be cut with an Xacto or utility knife and attached with white glue. The construction procedure is as follows:

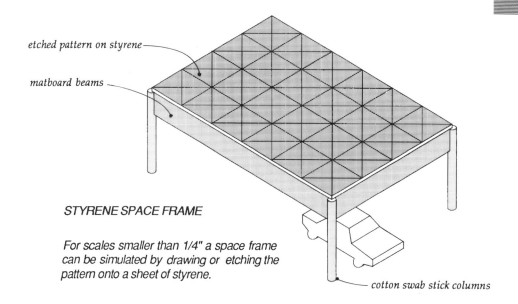

STYRENE SPACE FRAME

For scales smaller than 1/4" a space frame can be simulated by drawing or etching the pattern onto a sheet of styrene.

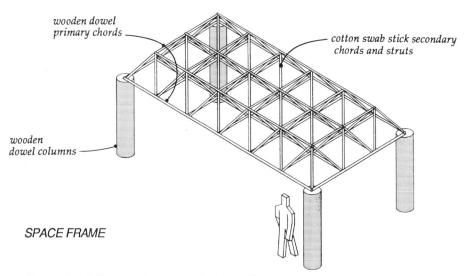

SPACE FRAME

For models 1/4" scale or larger an actual space frame can be built with wooden dowels and cotton swab sticks.

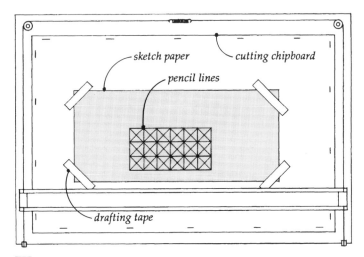

1 Draw the space frame in plan onto a sheet of sketch paper.

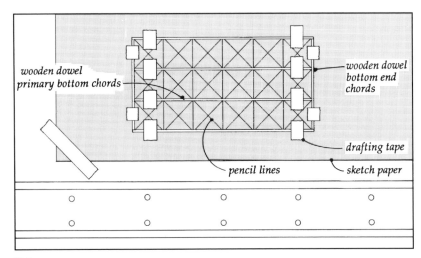

2 Secure the four primary bottom chords and end chords to the sketch paper.

Step 1 *Draw space frame in plan.*

First, with the use of your triangles, draw the space frame in plan at the desired scale onto a piece of sketch paper.

Step 2 *Attach primary chords to plan.*

Next, tape the four primary bottom wooden dowels and both ends to the paper at their proper length with drafting tape, and apply a dab of white glue at each intersection.

Step 3 *Cut and glue the secondary members together.*

Cut the secondary bottom chords out of paper cotton swab sticks all the same length and set them in place between the primary chords. Place a small dab of white glue on top of each joint so that the glue penetrates into the joint. Don't be afraid to let the glue run down onto the paper below, but don't allow pools to form. After the space frame is built the paper will be cut away from around the joints. Allow the glue to dry for at least one hour or longer until it is strong enough to begin constructing the vertical struts on top of the joints.

Step 4 *Measure and cut the vertical struts.*

Next, determine the required length of the struts by drawing a portion of the space frame in elevation. The elevation should be drawn parallel to the struts in plan. Once the strut length is determined, cut all of the struts out of paper swab sticks the same length.

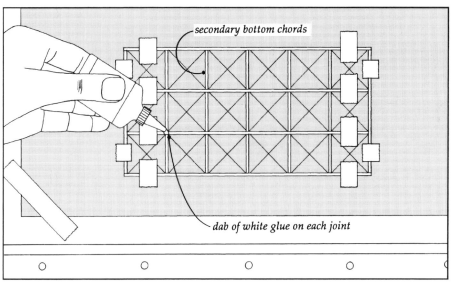

secondary bottom chords

dab of white glue on each joint

3 *Cut out and set the secondary bottom chords between the primary chords, and apply a small dab of glue on each joint.*

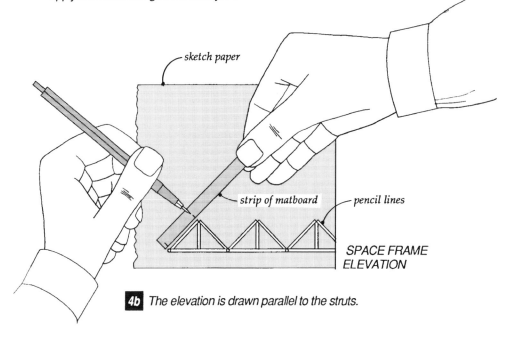

sketch paper

strip of matboard — *pencil lines*

SPACE FRAME
ELEVATION

4b *The elevation is drawn parallel to the struts.*

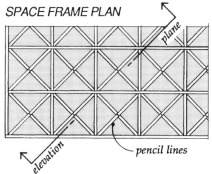

SPACE FRAME PLAN

plane

elevation — *pencil lines*

4a *Measure the required length of the struts from an elevation of the space frame.*

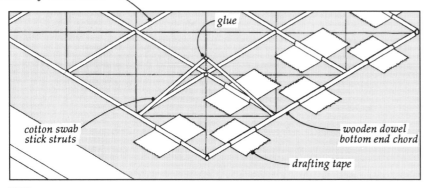

cotton swab stick
secondary bottom chord

glue

cotton swab
stick struts

wooden dowel
bottom end chord

drafting tape

5 Attach the first two struts to the bottom chords.

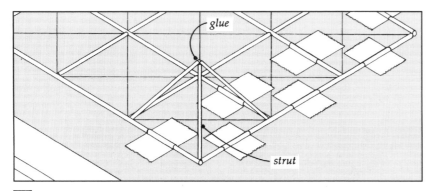

glue

strut

6 Attach the next two struts to the bottom chords and first two struts.

Step 5 *Attach the first two vertical struts.*

Apply a small dab of white glue at two opposite corners and lean two struts against each other at the corners. Apply a small dab of white glue at the top to help the struts stand up.

Step 6 *Attach the next two struts.*

Now, with the first two struts supporting each other, apply the next two struts, leaning them against the first two. Apply a dab of glue at the top of the four leaning struts.

Step 7 *Attach all struts.*

Attach all of the space frame struts to the bottom chords in groups of four as described in the last two steps. After all of the struts are in place, allow the glued joints to dry for at least one hour.

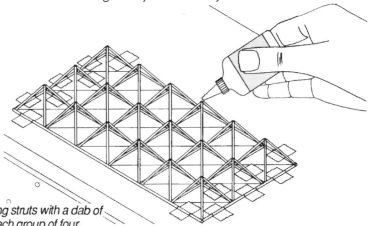

7 Attach the remaining struts with a dab of glue at the top of each group of four.

Step 8 Measure and cut top chords.

After allowing all vertical struts and bottom chords to completely dry, it is time to attach the top chords. The primary top chords run parallel with the primary bottom chords and are also continuous pieces.

Measure the required length from one ridge end to the other and cut a dowel to that length. Measure the required length of the chord from the model, not the drawing.

Step 9 Attach top chords to struts.

Apply a small dab of white glue to the top of the strut ridges and set the primary chords on top. Stick a small piece of drafting tape around the chord and strut wherever the two do not touch.

Next, cut and apply the secondary top chords between the primary chords in the same manner as the bottom chords were constructed.

Allow the glue to dry for at least one hour before carefully removing the drafting tape.

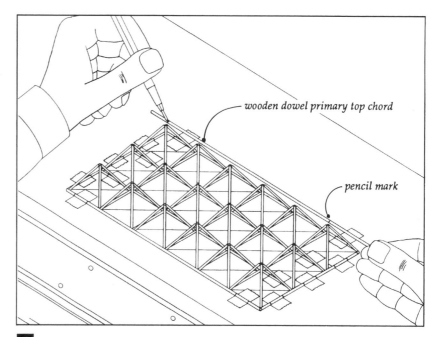

wooden dowel primary top chord

pencil mark

8 Measure and cut the three top primary chords.

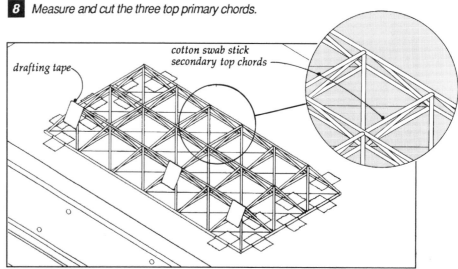

cotton swab stick secondary top chords

drafting tape

9 Attach the primary top chords and secondary top chords to the struts.

— sketch paper

10 Remove the sketch paper from the bottom of the space frame by cutting it away with an Xacto knife.

Step 10 *Remove paper from space frame.*

Finally, with all of the members attached the paper can be removed. Remove the drafting tape at the corners of the paper and turn the space frame over so the paper can be cut away from the chords with an Xacto knife. Once the paper is removed, the joints can be sanded smooth if desired.

Your space frame is now complete and can be spray painted if desired.

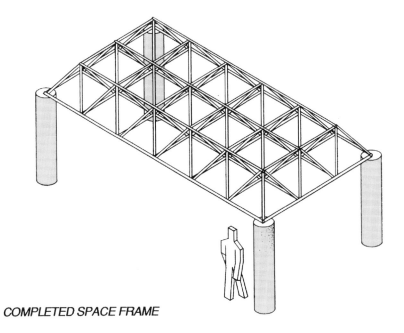

COMPLETED SPACE FRAME

TRELLISES

A scaled wood trellis in model form is usually done only on large scale models (1/4" and larger), since the construction of the individual members is tedious work and is difficult to achieve professional-looking results. Small scale trellises can be bought at architectural model supply stores but are expensive.

A typical trellis constructed on a building is usually built out of 2"x2" wood slats spaced 4" apart on top of 4"x6" wood rafters spaced 4'-0" apart. Whatever size and spacing your trellis is to be, the construction method described below would be the same. The trellis can be constructed of Strathmore board, balsa wood, or plastic strips. We will look at the procedures of constructing a Strathmore trellis at 1/4" scale:

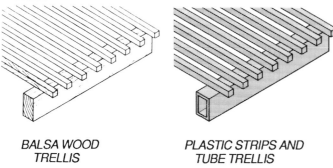

BALSA WOOD TRELLIS   **PLASTIC STRIPS AND TUBE TRELLIS**

Trellises: Strathmore Construction

Step 1 Attach Strathmore board to cutting board.

First, select a Strathmore board thick enough to simulate the scaled size of 2"x2" slats. At 1/4" scale a Strathmore board 1/32" thick would be appropriate. Staple the four corners of the Strathmore board to your cutting board.

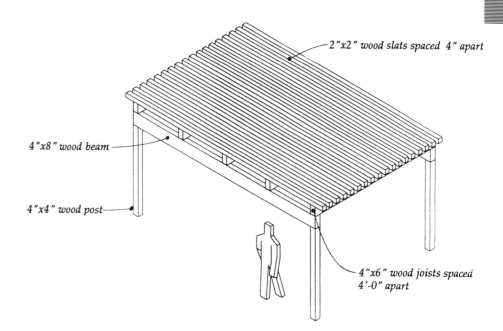

2"x2" wood slats spaced 4" apart

4"x8" wood beam

4"x4" wood post

4"x6" wood joists spaced 4'-0" apart

TYPICAL FULL SCALE TRELLIS CONSTRUCTION

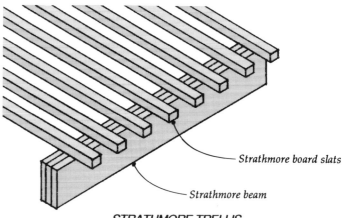

Strathmore board slats

Strathmore beam

STRATHMORE TRELLIS

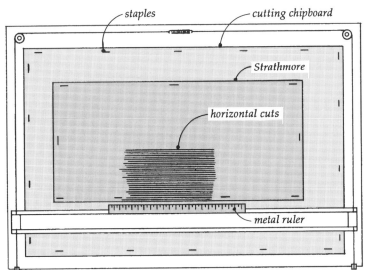

staples — cutting chipboard

Strathmore

horizontal cuts

metal ruler

1 **2a** *Secure the Strathmore board to your cutting board and perform the horizontal cuts.*

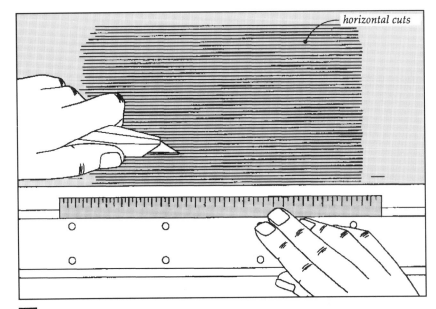

horizontal cuts

2b *Perform the horizontal cuts spaced approximately 2" on center at 1/4" scale.*

Step 2 Perform horizontal cuts.

With the use of your metal ruler and matknife cut horizontal lines at approximately 2" on center at 1/4" scale into the Strathmore board. Because the strips are so narrow you must cut all the way through on the first stroke. Therefore it is not feasible to use a Strathmore board thicker than 1/32".

While cutting the horizontal lines do not cut all the way to the edge of the board. Leave the strips attached to the Strathmore board as illustrated. After you have made the cuts make sure you have cut all the way through on all the cuts.

Step 3 Attach sketch paper to slats.

Now, spray a light coat of Artists adhesive onto a sheet of sketch paper and apply the paper to the top of the Strathmore board. Press down very hard on the paper to achieve a strong bond. It is important to apply only a small amount of spray glue so that the sketch paper can be removed easily.

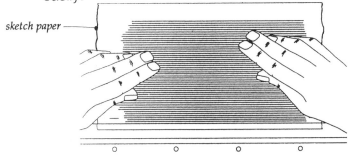

sketch paper

3 *Laminate a sheet of sketch paper to the slats.*

Step 4 *Cut out trellis.*

Cut the desired trellis size from the paper covered Strathmore board within the ends of the cuts. Remove the paper covered strips in one piece and discard the remainder of the Strathmore board.

Step 5 *Remove every other strip.*

Turn the trellis over and pull every other strip off the paper so that you have strips attached to the paper with a space between them.

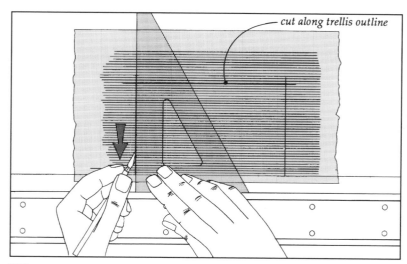

cut along trellis outline

4 *With an Xacto knife and triangle cut out the trellis.*

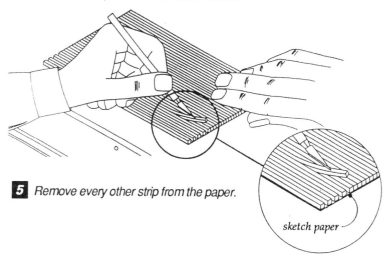

sketch paper

5 *Remove every other strip from the paper.*

Step 6 *Cut out and attach rafters.*

Now, cut the 4"x6" rafters out of a 1/16" thick Strathmore board. Apply a thin layer of white glue to the entire length of one side of the rafter and set

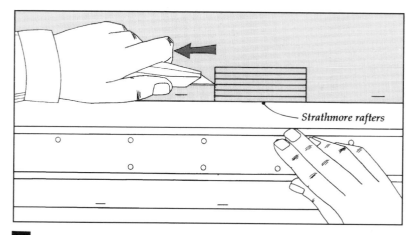

Strathmore rafters

6a *Cut out Strathmore board rafters.*

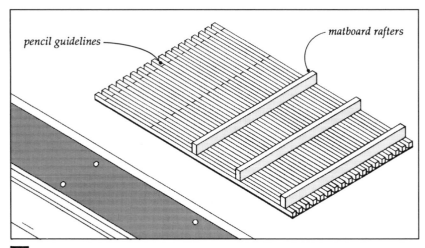

6b *Attach rafters to top of strips at desired spacing.*

it on top of the spaced strips. Repeat this procedure with the other rafters at their desired spacing. Allow the glue to dry completely before trying to remove the paper from the strips.

Step 7 *Remove paper from trellis.*

Finally, remove the sketch paper from the trellis. Peel the paper off the trellis slats in one piece if possible. If too much Artists Adhesive was applied the paper will be difficult to remove in one piece.

Your trellis is now complete and can be spray painted if desired.

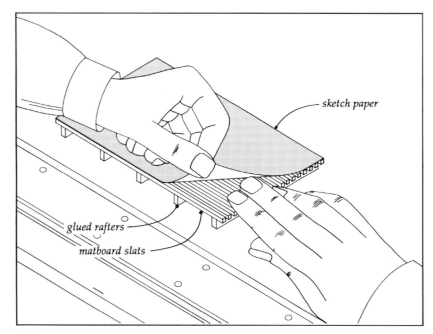

7 *Remove the sketch paper from the strips.*

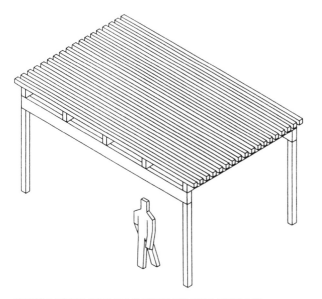

COMPLETED STRATHMORE BOARD TRELLIS

Trellises: Balsa Wood and Plastic Construction

Strips of balsa wood or plastic strips the scaled size of the trellis members can be used to construct the trellis in much the same manner as matboard construction. Let's look at their construction procedures:

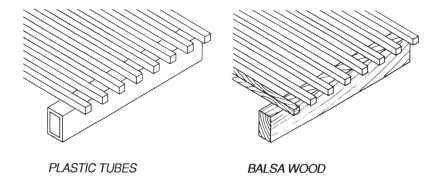

PLASTIC TUBES   BALSA WOOD

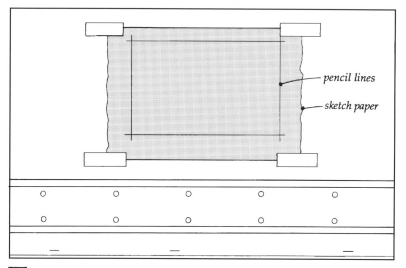

1 *Draw the outline of the trellis onto a piece of sketch paper.*

Step 1 Draw trellis onto sketch paper.

First, draw the trellis outline onto a sheet of sketch paper taped down to your cutting board.

Step 2 Apply adhesive to paper and attach to cutting board.

Next, remove the paper from your cutting board and apply a light coat of Artists Adhesive spray glue to the back of it. Reattach the sketch paper to your cutting board, with the sticky side up.

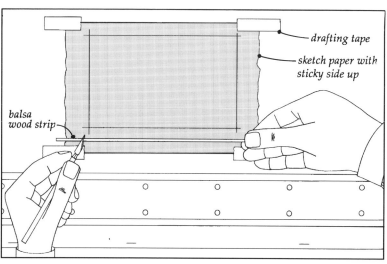

2 **3a** *Attach the sketch paper to your cutting board with the sticky side up, and cut three balsa wood strips longer than the trellis.*

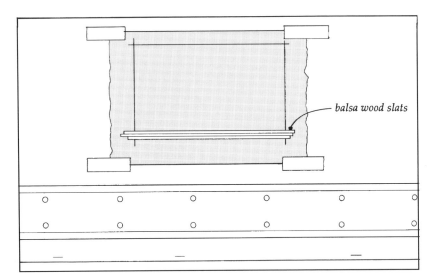

balsa wood slats

3b *Attach the three slats to the sketch paper.*

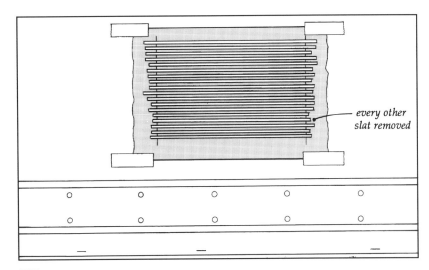

every other
slat removed

4 *Remove the middle strip at every other slat to get them evenly spaced.*

Step 3 *Attach wood strips to paper.*

Cut three wood strips longer than the trellis width and attach them to the sketch paper adjacent to each other as illustrated.

Step 4 *Remove middle strip.*

Next, lift up and remove the middle strip leaving the other two strips attached to the paper evenly spaced apart. Place three more strips directly adjacent to each other and repeat this procedure until you have all the slats in place on the paper.

Step 5 *Cut the slats along the sides.*

With the use of an Xacto knife and triangle cut through the slats along the side guidelines. Remove the cut out trellis and discard the remaining sketch paper.

5 *Cut through the slats along each side.*

Step 6 *Attach wood rafters to slats.*

Attach wood rafters to the slats with white glue as described for matboard trellises and allow the glue to dry for at least one hour.

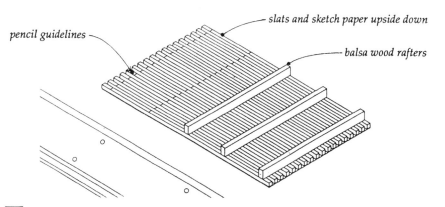

pencil guidelines

slats and sketch paper upside down

balsa wood rafters

6 *Cut and attach rafters to the top of the slats.*

Step 7 *Remove the sketch paper.*

Finally, carefully remove the sketch paper from the back of the trellis. Again, as with matboard trellises, if too much glue was applied to the paper it will be difficult to remove.

Once the paper is removed your trellis is complete and can be spray painted if desired.

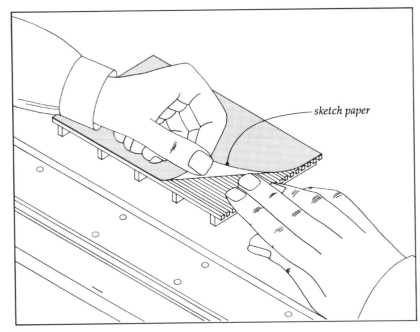

sketch paper

7 *Remove the sketch paper from the back of the slats.*

COMPLETED BALSA WOOD TRELLIS

STAIRS

Stairs, whether they be long staircases or only a few steps, add a human scale to a model, giving the viewer a physical object they can visually relate to. Everyone subconsciously knows the height and depth of a step, and can therefore relate to the scale of the model when they see a staircase within it.

There are basically three types of stairs built for a model: straight, curved, and spiral. All are available in plastic at an architectural model supply store or can be constructed with matboard, Foamcore, or paper. Let's look at their construction procedures:

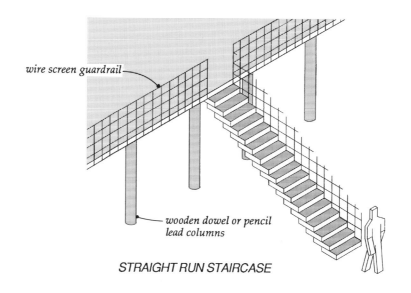

wire screen guardrail

wooden dowel or pencil lead columns

STRAIGHT RUN STAIRCASE

Straight Stairs

The 'straight run' staircase is the most common and easiest type to build. It can be constructed of chipboard, Foamcore, or paper. Since cutting out and attaching every tread and riser is a very time consuming task I recommend using this construction technique only on a final presentation model or a schematic study model that will later be transformed into a final presentation model.

For schematic study models, most instructors will allow a staircase to be simulated with a matboard ramp from floor to floor with the treads drawn in pencil. Ask your instructor which they prefer.

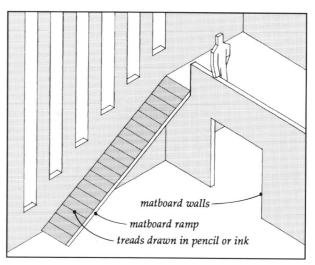

matboard walls
matboard ramp
treads drawn in pencil or ink

For schematic models a staircase can be simulated with a matboard ramp with steps drawn in pencil.

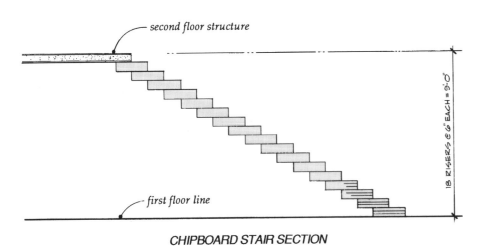

STAIR PLAN

17 TREADS @ 11" EACH = 15'-5"

3'-0"

UP

second floor structure

first floor line

18 RISERS @ 6" EACH = 9'-0"

CHIPBOARD STAIR SECTION

1 Determine the number of steps by drawing the stair in section and plan.

Straight Stair : Chipboard Construction

A 1/16" thick chipboard is excellent for simulating a 6" step on a 1/8" scale model, and a 1/8" thick Foamcore board on a 1/4" scale model. Each step is cut out and attached to each other to form a staircase. Let's look at the procedures for constructing a chipboard staircase:

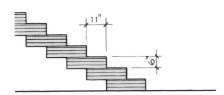

1/16" chipboard simulates a 6" step on a 1/8" scale model.

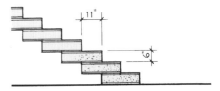

1/8" Foamcore board simulates a 6" step on a 1/4" scale model.

Step 1 *Determine the number of steps.*

First, calculate the number of steps you have from floor to floor. For a 9'-0" distance there would be 18 risers at 6" each and 17 treads at 11" each. (There is always one less tread than the total number of risers).

Step 2 *Draw the stairs onto chipboard.*

On a sheet of chipboard or Strathmore board secured to your cutting board, draw the stairs in plan, twice, with 11" treads at 1/8" scale. The reason you draw them twice will become evident in later steps.

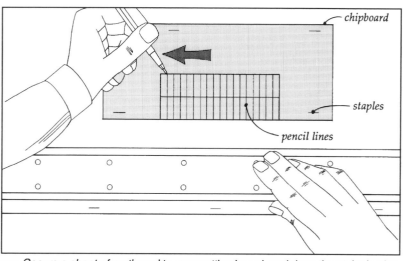

2 Secure a sheet of matboard to your cutting board and draw the stairs in plan twice.

Step 3 *Cut out the treads.*

Next, cut out the treads at every other cut line so that you have **18** pieces with two treads on each. Perform all of the vertical cuts first and then make the two continuous horizontal cuts. Flatten down the flaired edges and they are ready to be glued together.

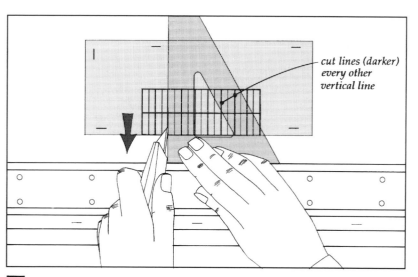

3 With the use of a utility knife cut along every other vertical line.

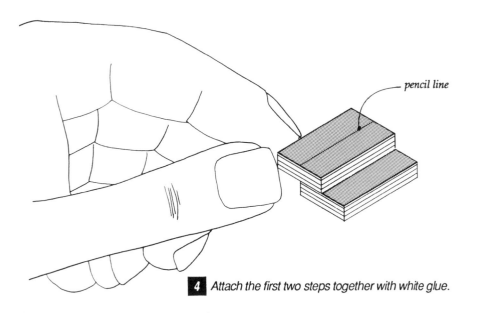

pencil line

4 Attach the first two steps together with white glue.

Step 4 *Attach first two steps.*

Apply a thin line of white glue to the back tread of your first step and attach it to the underside of your second step as illustrated. Squeeze the two together for one minute and then apply the third step in the same manner. As you can see the steps are attached together by lap joints, this is why you needed to draw the stairs twice.

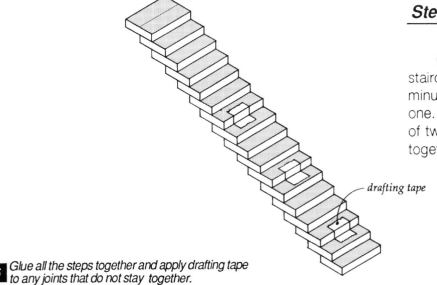

drafting tape

5 Glue all the steps together and apply drafting tape to any joints that do not stay together.

Step 5 *Attach the remaining steps.*

Continue this procedure for all 18 risers until the staircase is completed. You may need to allow 5 or 10 minutes for each joint to dry before attaching the next one. If so, go ahead and attach the treads in groups of two or three at a time, and then attach them all together.

Step 6 *Attach staircase to model.*

To attach the staircase at the base and upper level, simply apply a thin layer of white glue to the underside of the bottom tread and the topside of the top tread and hold each joint between your fingers for a few minutes. If the top connection does not hold by itself a strip of drafting tape can be applied to secure it until the glue dries. Remove the tape and your staircase is complete.

Follow the same procedures for constructing 1/4" scale steps with 1/8" thick Foamcore board. More time must be allowed for the glue to dry in-between attaching each step.

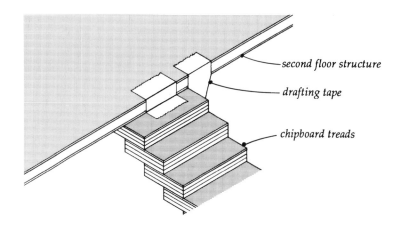

second floor structure

drafting tape

chipboard treads

6 *Attach staircase to underside of second floor structure with white glue.*

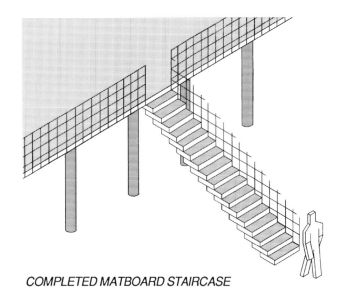

COMPLETED MATBOARD STAIRCASE

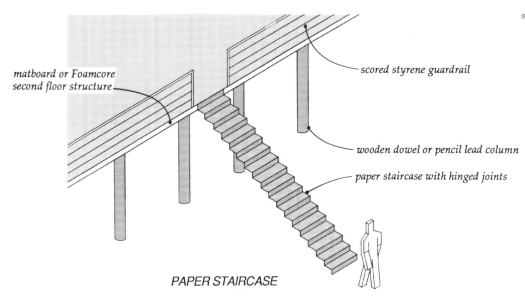

matboard or Foamcore second floor structure

scored styrene guardrail

wooden dowel or pencil lead column

paper staircase with hinged joints

PAPER STAIRCASE

Straight Stair: Paper Construction

Another method for constructing stairs is to score the steps into a sheet of heavyweight paper creating a series of hinged joints. This is a fast and easy method for constructing stairs on 1/8" and 1/4" scale models. Let's look at this procedure:

Step 1 *Attach paper to cutting board and draw stairs.*

Secure a sheet of heavyweight paper, such as Canson paper, to your cutting board with drafting tape and draw the stairs in plan with the risers between the treads. Notice that the top tread needs an extra riser length adjacent to it to attach to the second floor.

pencil lines

11" 6"

tread
riser

drafting tape

Canson paper

1 Secure a sheet of Canson paper to your cutting board and draw the stair treads and risers in plan.

Step 2 *Score the stair nosing lines.*

Now, with the use of an Xacto knife and triangle score the tread nosing lines half-way into the paper. (The other lines will be scored on the backside in step 5). If any score lines cut through the paper, they can be repaired with transparent tape on the back.

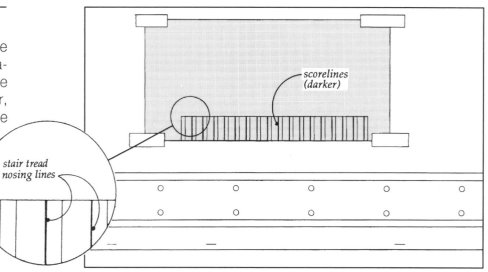

2 | With the use of an Xacto knife and triangle score the stair nosing lines.

Step 3 *Pierce ends of tread lines.*

With the tip of your Xacto knife penetrate the paper at each end of the remaining tread lines. These will be your guidelines when scoring the backside of the paper.

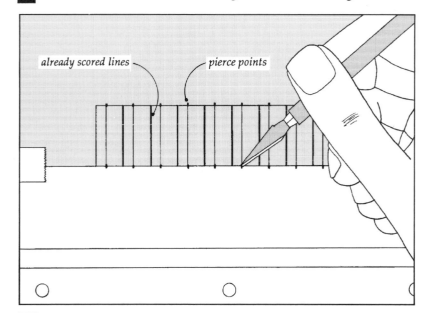

3 | With an Xacto knife pierce both ends of each remaining tread line.

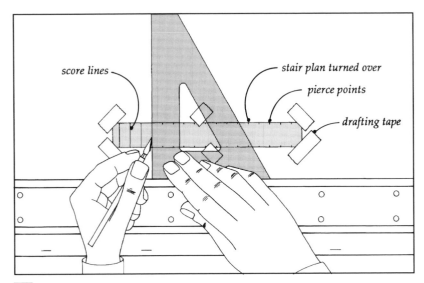

score lines

stair plan turned over

pierce points

drafting tape

4 *Cut out, turn the paper over, and make score cuts at the pierce points.*

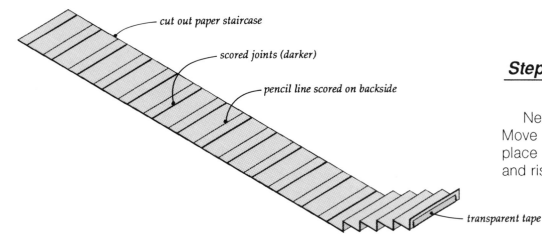

cut out paper staircase

scored joints (darker)

pencil line scored on backside

transparent tape

5 *Bend the paper at the score lines. Joints cut all the way through can be mended on the backside with adhesive tape.*

Step 4 *Cut out and score the remaining joints.*

Cut out the outline of the steps at the perimeter and turn it over. Secure it to your cutting board with drafting tape. Now, with your Xacto knife and triangle score the remaining joints utilizing the pierce marks as guide points. Score only half-way through the paper.

Once all the scores are made, erase any pencil marks with a white plastic eraser.

Step 5 *Bend at the scorelines.*

Next, bend the paper at all of the scorelines. Move the joints back and forth until they stay in place with 90 degree angles between the treads and risers.

Step 6 *Cut out and attach stringer to stairs.*

- First, draw a stair stringer in elevation onto a piece of matboard and cut it out with a triangle and utility knife. (II. 6a)

- Then, apply a thin line of white glue to the edge of the stringer and attach the stringer in the middle of the staircase.

- Check the angle of each tread and riser with a small triangle to make sure they are all 90 degrees. (II. 6b)

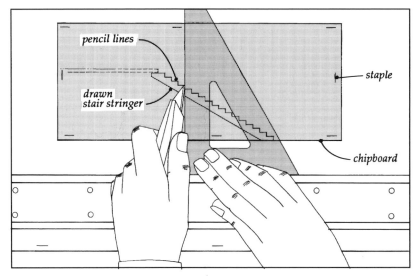

6a *Draw and cut out a stair stringer to attach your stairs to.*

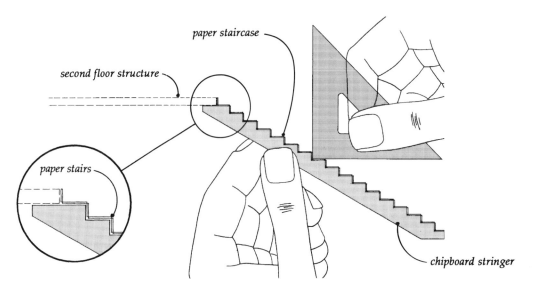

6b *Apply glue to the stringer and attach it to the staircase. Push each riser into position with a small triangle.*

drafting tape

second floor structure

7 Apply glue to the vertical edge of the second floor structure and attach the top riser to it.

top paper riser

chipboard stringer (dotted)

paper staircase

glue

8 Apply glue to the bottom of the stringer and set the stairs in place.

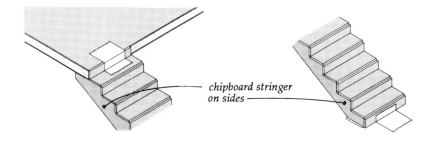

chipboard stringer on sides

Another stair construction method is to cut out two stringers and attach them along both sides of the stairs.

Step 7 Attach staircase to upper level.

To attach the top riser of the staircase to your upper level matboard or Foamcore, glue it to the vertical edge of the level as illustrated.

Apply a thin coat of white glue to the vertical edge of the matboard or Foamcore and attach the top riser to it. Make sure the edges are level and hold the riser in place for a few minutes. If the glue does not hold, apply a strip of drafting tape to the joint. (Additional support can be added by applying glue between the stringer and second floor structure).

Step 8 Attach staircase to floor plan.

To attach the base of the staircase to your floor plan simply apply a line of white glue to the bottom of the stringer, and set it in place. Apply a strip of drafting tape to the joint if necessary. After the glue is dry remove the tape and your staircase is complete.

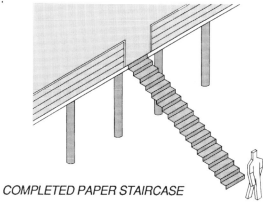

COMPLETED PAPER STAIRCASE

Curved Stairs

A curved staircase can be constructed in the same manner as straight stairs out of chipboard or Foamcore, but not out of hinged paper.

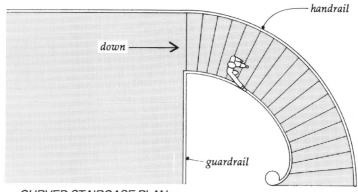

down →

handrail

guardrail

CURVED STAIRCASE PLAN

Spiral Stairs

A spiral staircase is a difficult building component to construct and is best to buy at an architectural model supply store. But, if you must construct your own I recommend using a 1/16" thick Strathmore board for a 1/8" scale staircase, and 1/8" thick Foamcore for 1/4" or larger scale stairs. Since the construction procedures are the same for either material we will illustrate only the Foamcore method.

Spiral Stair: Foamcore Construction

To construct the spiral stairs we will use a 1/8" thick Foamcore for the treads and a 1/16" diameter pencil lead for the pipe column. (Use the strongest weight lead you have). The treads will be attached to each other with lap joints in the same manner as the straight stair construction.

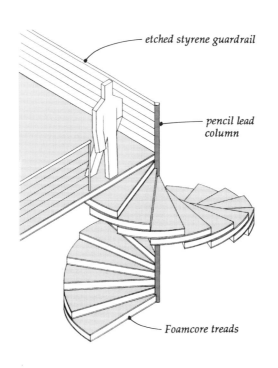

etched styrene guardrail

pencil lead column

Foamcore treads

FOAMCORE SPIRAL STAIRCASE

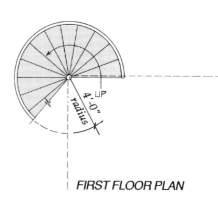

4'-0" radius

FIRST FLOOR PLAN

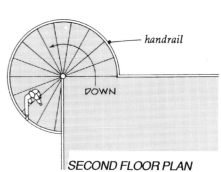

handrail

DOWN

SECOND FLOOR PLAN

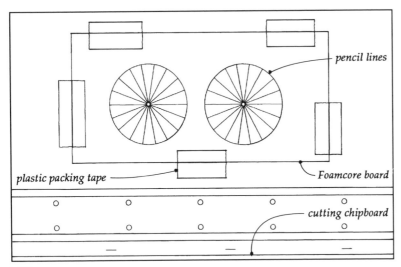

1 Secure a sheet of Foamcore to the cutting board and draw the staircase twice.

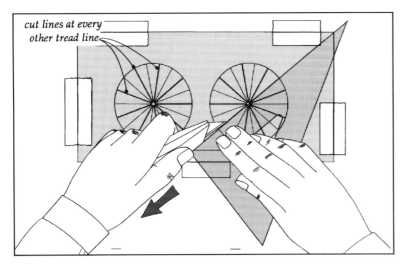

2 Cut out the treads at every other line.

Step 1 Draw staircase plan on Foamcore.

First, secure a sheet of Foamcore to your cutting board with strong adhesive tape such as packing or duct tape, and draw the staircase twice in plan at 1/4" scale. As with the straight stairs you will be cutting every other riser, so you'll need to draw the plan twice to cut out enough treads. For a 9'-0" floor-to-floor distance you will need 18 risers and 17 treads.

Step 2 Cut out the treads.

Using an Xacto knife and triangle, cut out the treads at every other tread line so that you have 18 pieces with two treads on each. Flatten down the flaired edges and they are ready to be attached to each other.

Step 3 Cut the pencil lead to its desired length.

Cut the pencil lead with an Xacto knife to the desired length. If you would like the column to extend above the top floor add 3'-6" to the 9'-0" floor to floor height, making the column 12'-6" long at 1/4" scale. Cut the lead by setting it on top of your cutting board and rolling your Xacto blade over it.

Step 4 *Glue the steps together.*

Apply a thin layer of white glue to the back tread of your first step and attach it to the underside of your second step as illustrated. Squeeze the two together for a moment and apply a piece of drafting tape across the joint to hold it while you attach the remaining treads.

Repeat this procedure for all of the steps until they are all attached.

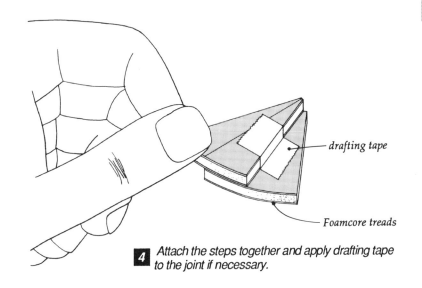

drafting tape

Foamcore treads

4 *Attach the steps together and apply drafting tape to the joint if necessary.*

Step 5 *Attach column to treads.*

Insert the pencil lead down the center of the stairs. Glue the lead to the treads at the bottom, middle, and top, and let the staircase set for one hour before attaching it to the model.

Step 6 *Attach staircase to model.*

Attach the staircase to the bottom and upper floors as described in step 6 of the straight stair construction and your staircase is complete.

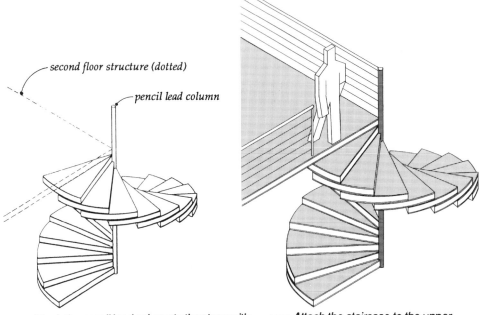

second floor structure (dotted)

pencil lead column

5 *Attach the pencil lead column to the steps with white glue at the top, middle and bottom.*

6 *Attach the staircase to the upper and bottom floors.*

This chapter has just dealt with some of the many building components that can be built or bought by the model maker. Others can be found in architectural model supply catalogs and in your own imagination. Visualize how a component can be simulated on a model and then build it. Coming up with a very realistic simulation can be as gratifying as developing a design concept.

Let's move on to the next chapter to look at methods of constructing scaled landscape components.

CHAPTER 7

Constructing Scaled Landscape Components

Landscape components, when applied to a model, give it a human scale that the viewer can associate with. The viewer subconsciously knows the dimensions of a person, or a car, and can instantly relate, from the model scale, to the size of the building and its components.

In this chapter we will look at the construction techniques of the most common types of landscape components: outdoor decks and patios, fences, trees, bodies of water, ground covers and parking lots. We will also look at constructing people, automobiles, boats and planes.

TREE
- store bought deciduous

PEOPLE
- matboard figures

GRASS- green flocking

SHRUBS- store bought

SIDEWALK- white bond paper
with inked scorelines

PRESENTATION MODEL

AUTOMOBILE
- hinged paper

TREE- frayed wire

BRICK
- pattern photocopied
onto colored paper

BRICK PAVING

Outdoor Decks and Patios

Outdoor decks and patios are best represented on a model by drawing or photocopying a pattern onto a colored paper or plastic film. Material patterns such as brick paving, wood strips, ceramic tile and flagstone can be bought at graphic arts supply stores in 1/8" or 1/4" scales. The most common types of decks and patios are brick pavers, ceramic tile, granite pavers, wood decking, and scored concrete. Let's look at methods for simulating each of these materials.

Brick Paving

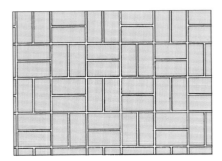

BRICK PAVING

Brick paving is best simulated by photocopying a brick pattern onto a sheet of colored Canson paper. The color of the paper should be as close as possible to the color of your bricks, and the pattern can be drawn in pencil or selected from a catalog at your graphic arts supply store. Since it would be a copyright infringement to photocopy the pattern of a manufacturers' product I recommend buying the patterned decals and laminating them to your colored paper, or photocopying the patterns depicted on these pages.

Once you have the pattern on the paper you are ready to attach it to the model. It is best to apply the paper to your floor plan before the walls are constructed, but if that is not possible the paper can be cut to fit into its location on the model. Let's look at the procedures for applying a brick pattern into an area of a model with existing walls. We will use the patio illustrated at the left:

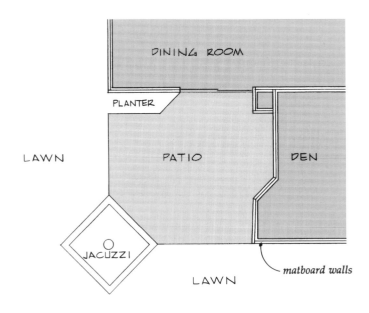

PATIO FLOOR PLAN

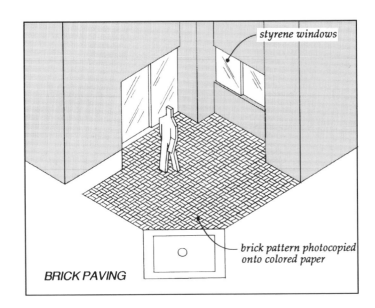

BRICK PAVING

Step 1 *Attach pattern to cutting board.*

First, attach the patterned paper to your cutting board with drafting tape making sure the pattern is parallel with your parallel bar.

Step 2 *Measure and draw outline on pattern.*

Now, utilizing the 'thin strip of matboard' method measure each dimension of where the pattern will be placed on the model and draw the outline with light guidelines onto the paper. You will notice that not all of the walls are straight and perpendicular to each other with 90 degree angles. This must be taken into account when drawing the plan.

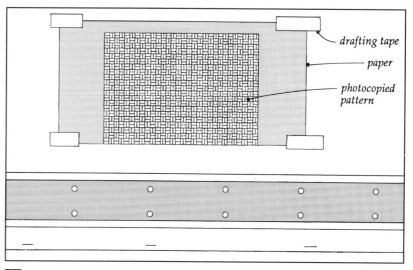

drafting tape

paper

photocopied pattern

1 *Attach patterned paper to your cutting board.*

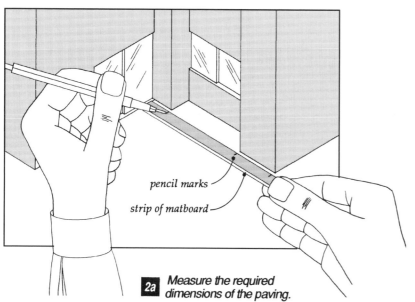

pencil marks

strip of matboard

2a **Measure the required dimensions of the paving.**

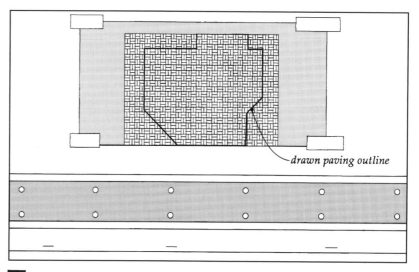

drawn paving outline

2b *Draw the paving outline on the pattern.*

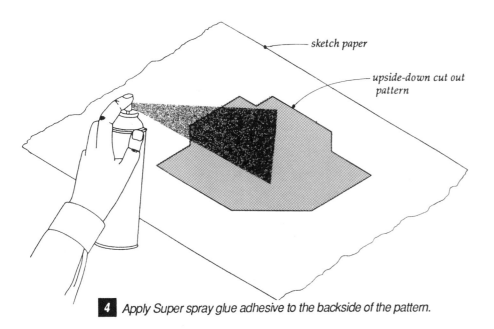

trim these two edges
to make it fit properly

pattern is too short here

cut out pattern in place

3 Cut out the pattern, and set it in place without glue to check the fit.

sketch paper

upside-down cut out
pattern

4 Apply Super spray glue adhesive to the backside of the pattern.

Step 3 *Cut out pattern along outline and set in place.*

Once you have the paving layout drawn onto the paper the next step is to cut out the paving with an Xacto knife and triangle along the guidelines, and set the pattern in place on the model without glue on and trim any edges that do not fit. Don't trim too much off at a time or it could end up too small.

Step 4 *Adhere pattern in place.*

Next, apply a light coat of Super spray adhesive to the backside of the pattern. Set the pattern in place on the model. If it adheres to the floor plan before you have a chance to position it lift it out and start again. Smooth the paving out and your brick paving is complete.

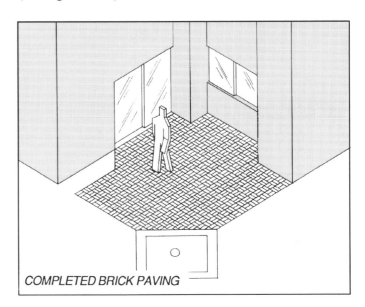

COMPLETED BRICK PAVING

Ceramic Tile

Ceramic tile is best simulated by photocopying a grid pattern onto a sheet of paper or plastic film. The film will give you a more realistic appearance since it has a glossy finish, but is difficult to achieve a consistent color due to the air bubbles that are created when the film is laminated. Smooth out the film with a straightedge to eliminate most of the bubbles.

As with brick paving, the color of paper or film should be as close as possible to the actual ceramic color and the pattern can be selected out of a catalog at your graphic arts supply store. Many different types of patterns are available on plastic decals, such as square, rectangular, octagonal, and honeycomb patterns. If the lines are not too close together the pattern can also be drawn directly onto the colored paper or film with pencil or ink.

Once you have the pattern drawn or photocopied onto the paper or film it is ready to be attached to the model. Follow the same procedures described for attaching the brick paving pattern.

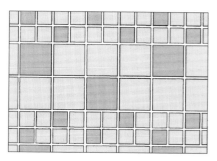

CERAMIC TILE IN PLAN

Granite Pavers

Granite paving is created by drawing or photocopying a grid pattern onto a colored paper. Some colors of Canson paper have a speckled finish that is excellent for simulating granite at 1/4" scale. You must remember to 'think-to-scale' when selecting the paper to simulate granite, most likely it would look like a very fine, speckled finish. Since plastic film is a solid color it is not recommended for simulating granite at 1/4" scale, but is excellent for a 1/8" scale interior granite floor.

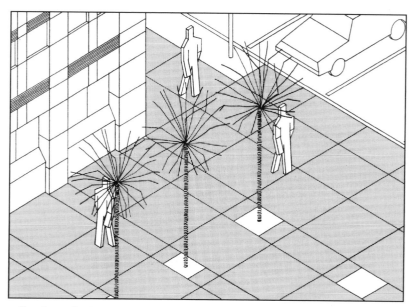

Granite paving is best simulated by inking lines onto a speckled colored Canson paper.

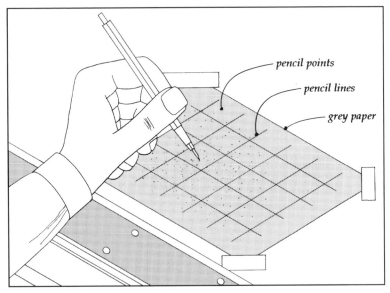

Concrete is best simulated on a model by stippling a pencil point on a grey colored paper.

pencil points

pencil lines

grey paper

Scored Concrete

For scored concrete decks, draw scorelines onto grey or white colored paper. Control joints are usually spaced a minimum of 5' on center in concrete slabs, so at 1/8" or 1/4" scale the number of lines would be few enough to draw instead of photocopying from a preprinted pattern.

Exposed concrete is best represented with 'stippled' light grey paper or board. Stippling is a procedure where you lightly tap a sharp pencil point to create a dotted pattern. It can be done to paper already in place on the model, or on your drawing board. Since it only takes a few stipples to create the effect, do not spend more than a few minutes on any area.

Wood Decking

Draw or photocopy parallel lines onto a colored paper or film to create wood decking. Lined patterns of many different widths are available on plastic film at your graphic arts supply store. The paper color should match as closely as possible the painted or stained wood.

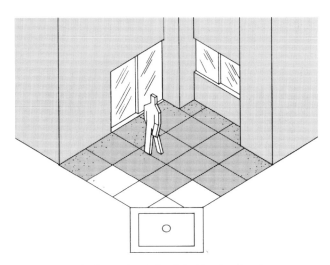

Scored concrete decks are best simulated by drawing lines onto white or grey paper.

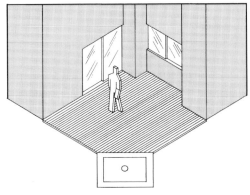

WOOD DECKING

FENCES

Fencing is an interesting material to simulate on a model since it is usually constructed of many small size members. Various types of fencing can be bought, pre-made, at architectural model supply stores, or built by the model maker utilizing various screens and plastic extrusions. Let's look at the three most common types of fencing: chain link, picket, and wrought iron.

Chain Link

Chain link is best simulated on a 1/8" or 1/4" scale model with one of many types of screens available at hardware stores or building supply outlets. Metal and plastic screens are available in many different sizes. The smallest size used for covering windows in a house, can be cut with scissors and attached to matboard with white glue. The metal type is more rigid than the plastic and therefore easier to work with on 1/8" and 1/4" scale models.

Picket Fence

Picket fencing, usually constructed of 1"x4" vertical wood slats attached to 2"x2" horizontal members, is difficult to construct at 1/8" or 1/4" scales due to the number of small members that have to be attached to each other.

The easiest method for simulating a professional-looking fence at this scale is to buy it at an architectural model supply store. But, if you do decide to build the fencing refer to page 167 for constructing a trellis. The construction procedures would be the same as that for building a trellis with thin plastic strips.

CHAIN LINK IN ELEVATION

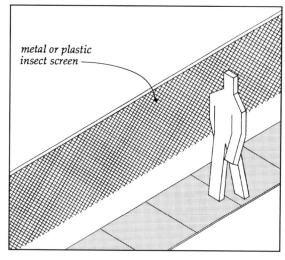

A chain link fence is best simulated at 1/4" or 1/8" scale with a window screen.

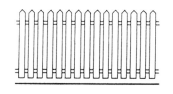

PICKET FENCE IN ELEVATION

A picket fence at 1/4" or 1/8" scale is best simulated with a store bought fence.

Wrought iron fencing is best simulated on a 1/8" or 1/4" scale model with store bought fencing.

WROUGHT IRON IN ELEVATION

Wrought Iron

Wrought iron fencing is also difficult to construct at 1/8" or 1/4" scale and is best to buy at an architectural model supply store. It is also attached to the model baseboard with white glue.

TREES

Trees can either be constructed by the model maker or bought at an architectural model supply store in various species and scales. Store-bought trees are excellent for final presentation models while hand-made trees are fine for schematic models. The most common types of materials used for tree construction on schematic models are twisted wire, Styrofoam balls, and dried flowers.

Store Bought Trees

Trees bought at architectural model supply stores are the most realistic looking type of tree the builder can use, and also the most expensive. Because of this, store-bought trees should only be used on final presentation models. They are available in many different species, colors and sizes and can be selected out of a catalog at the store.

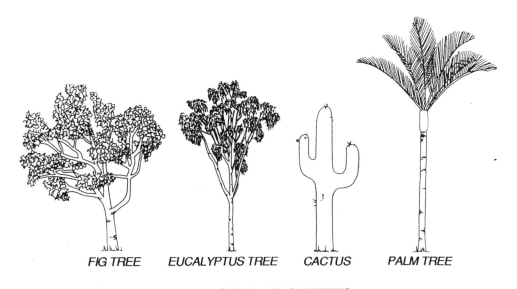

FIG TREE   **EUCALYPTUS TREE**   **CACTUS**   **PALM TREE**

STORE BOUGHT TREES

Twisted Wire Tree

Trees constructed of twisted wire can be built quickly and are excellent for schematic study models since they are very inexpensive. They can be constructed of any type of electrical wire that has a multi-stranded core wrapped with a plastic coating. The wire can be bought at building supply outlets or hardware stores. Keep in mind, though, when selecting the wire that its diameter should equal the scaled tree trunk diameter. Let's look at constructing this type of tree:

TWISTED WIRE TREE

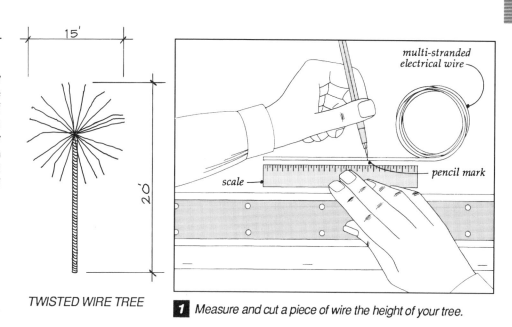

1 Measure and cut a piece of wire the height of your tree.

Step 1 *Cut wire to desired length.*

Once you have selected your wire cut it to the required height of the tree. For our example we will make the tree 20' high with a 15' diameter ball and a 6" diameter trunk at 1/8" scale.

First, measure the wire length with a scale and make a pencil mark at the 20' length. Then, with wire cutters or scissors cut the wire at the mark.

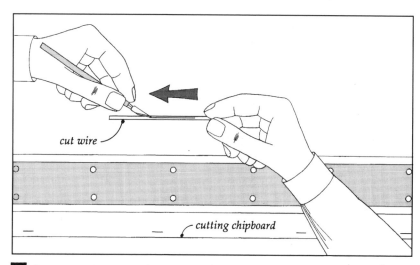

2 Cut away a portion of the outer plastic coating.

Step 2 *Strip off plastic coating.*

With the use of an Xacto knife cut a slice through the outer plastic coating along the length of the wire, stopping 1/4" from the end. Strip the plastic away.

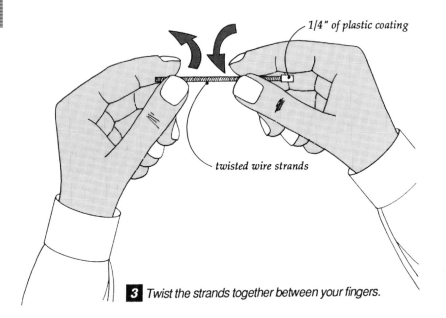

1/4" of plastic coating

twisted wire strands

3 Twist the strands together between your fingers.

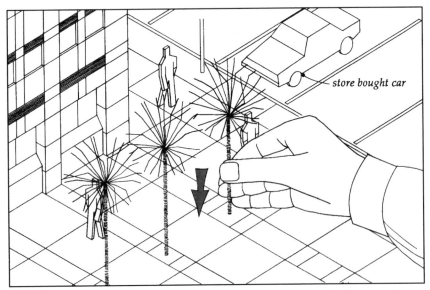

store bought car

4b Peel the strands away to create a ball of branches, and attach the tree to the model base.

Step 3 Twist the strands together.

Now, with the strands exposed twist the wire between your fingers the entire length until the strands are strongly held together.

Step 4 Create a ball of branches.

Now, begin peeling each strand away from the trunk at whatever length you would like. Pull as many out as it takes to create a ball of branches approximately 15' in diameter. Shape the strands into a spherical shape and trim them with scissors if necessary.

4a Shape the strands into a spherical shape.

Your tree is now complete and can be attached to the model base as described on page 64 . Remove the remaining plastic covering at the base of the tree and twist the wires together. Stick the bottom of the tree trunk far enough into the model base so that the tree supports itself.

Styrofoam Ball Trees

Trees constructed of Styrofoam balls and pencil leads are fine for schematic models but not suggested for final presentation models unless they are representing trees on a conceptual basis. Styrofoam balls can be bought at craft supply stores in many different diameters and basically two colors, white and green. For color variety, they can be spray painted with a special paint available at the craft stores. Be sure to choose a ball diameter equal in scale to the tree diameter.

The trunk can be constructed with any type of stick that can be cut to the required length and is the proper scaled tree trunk diameter. Pencil leads, toothpicks, wood pencils, wire, nails, machine screws, straws, for example, can be cut and inserted into the Styrofoam balls to simulate the trunk.

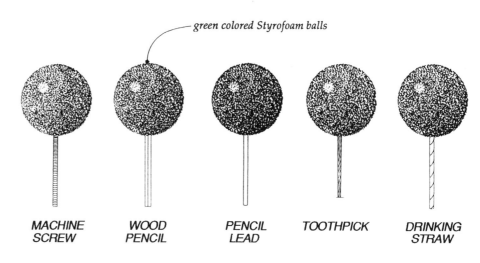

green colored Styrofoam balls

| MACHINE SCREW | WOOD PENCIL | PENCIL LEAD | TOOTHPICK | DRINKING STRAW |

TREE TRUNK TYPES

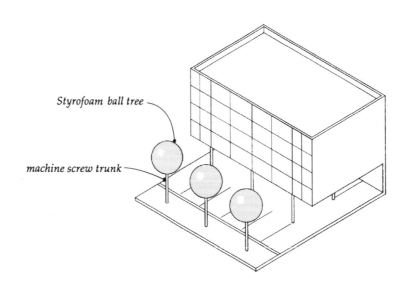

Styrofoam ball tree

machine screw trunk

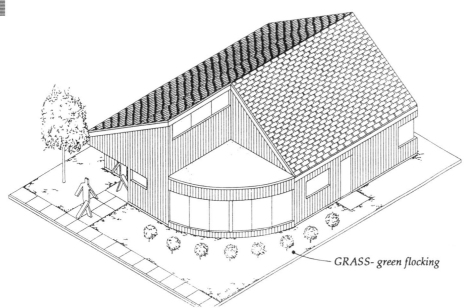

GRASS- green flocking

Ground cover can be simulated on a final presentation model with green flocking.

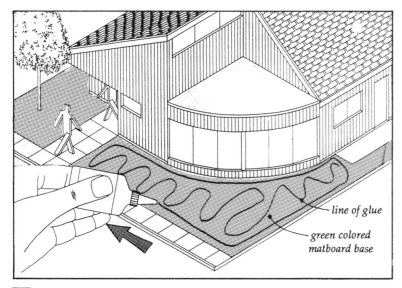

line of glue

green colored matboard base

1 *Squeeze out a thick line of glue where the grass is to be.*

Ground Covers

Ground covers such as grass, ivy, and flowers are difficult to simulate on a model due to their scaled size. Flowers and ivy will be very small at 1/8" scale yet are required on presentation models in order to obtain the most realistic results. On schematic models, ground cover can be simulated with a green colored matboard base, or green colored paper applied to the baseboard.

Grass

Grass can be simulated with either green matboard or paper, or green colored flocking available at architectural model supply stores and hobby stores.

The flocking is made of granulated foam rubber in various colors and textures. It provides the most professional results but is very messy to work with. Because it has such a fine consistency it floats in the air onto other parts of the model. The color and texture selected must properly relate with the model scale. For example, a lawn of grass at 1/4" scale is best represented with a light green colored fine flocking. You must 'think-to-scale' to select the best color and consistency. Let's look at how to apply the flocking to the model base:

Step 1 *Apply glue to baseboard.*

First, squeeze out a thick line of white glue around the perimeter of the grass area and then into the center.

Step 2   Trowel out the glue.

Next, smooth out the glue with a 2"x3" piece of matboard until it has a consistent thickness of approximately 1/32" thick. Be careful not to get the glue onto other parts of the model.

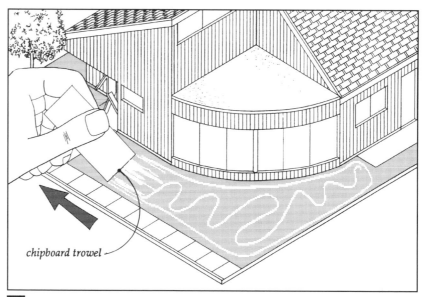

2 Smooth out the glue with a matboard trowel.

Step 3   Apply flocking to baseboard.

With the use of a 1"x3" piece of matboard apply the flocking on top of the glue until it is about 1/4" thick. Pat it down with your fingers to get the flocking embedded into the glue. Let the glue dry for about one hour.

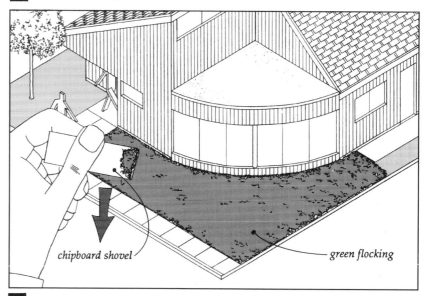

3 Apply flocking on top of the glue and pat it down with your fingertips.

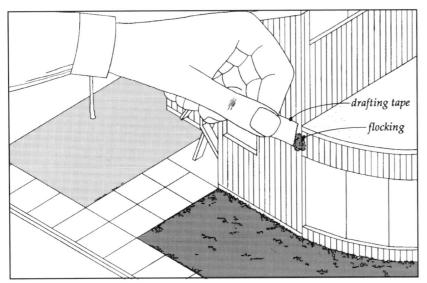

3 *Clean the flocking off the building by lifting it off with a piece of drafting tape.*

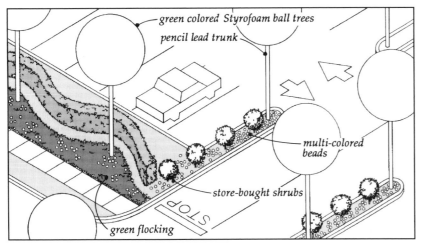

Flowers are best represented on 1/8" and 1/4" scale models with multicolored beads, while shrubs are best store bought.

Step 4 *Blow off flocking.*

Take the model outdoors and blow the extra flocking off with short breaths. It will fly all over the rest of the model so be prepared to clean off the building with drafting tape. Or, you can cover it with sketch paper before blowing it off.

After you have removed the excess flocking the ground cover is complete. Flowers can now be sprinkled on if desired.

Flowers

Flowers add color to the landscaping but can also distract from the design intent of the building. But, if flowers are part of the design concept they can be applied to both schematic and final presentation models. They are best applied when mixed in with a ground cover flocking and thus in contact with the glue. Their size must relate to the models' scale.

At 1/4" and 1/8" scale, flowers are best represented with multicolored beads available at architectural model supply stores, or with colored sand, available at craft stores that can be sprinkled on.

Shrubs

Shrubs are best represented on a final presentation model with those available at architectural model supply stores. They come in various sizes and colors, and can be attached to the model baseboard with white glue. Shrubs are usually not necessary on schematic study models.

BODIES OF WATER

Lakes, ponds, streams, oceans, and other pools of water are best represented with a glossy type of plastic sheet. The type used depends on the scale of the model and whether the water is to be simulated as moving or still.

Lakes, Ponds, and Pools

Generally, ponds, lakes, and pools (fountains and swimming pools) are simulated as still, and are constructed of a solid flat plane of colored Plexiglass or clear styrene with colored paper behind it. The color can be any that you desire, but it should simulate the depth of the water, dark for deep or light for shallow. Below are listed bodies of water and the color most commonly associated with them:

LAKES- dark blue
POOLS and FOUNTAINS- light blue
PONDS- blue-green
STREAMS- medium blue
OCEANS- dark blue-green

Waterfalls

Vertical planes of water, such as a sheet of water flowing over a raised edge on a fountain, can be represented by drawing strokes of blue ink with a design sketch marker onto a sheet of clear styrene and attaching it to the fountain edge.

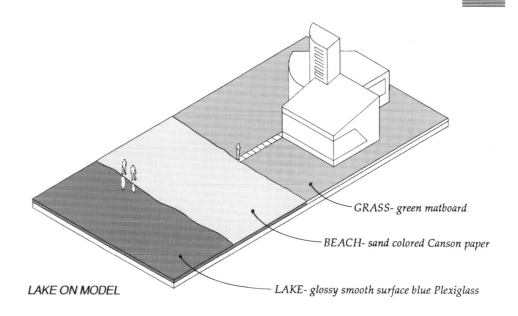

GRASS- green matboard

BEACH- sand colored Canson paper

LAKE ON MODEL

LAKE- glossy smooth surface blue Plexiglass

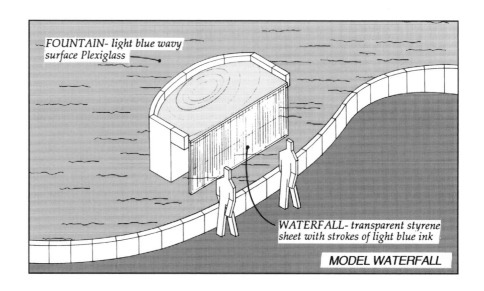

FOUNTAIN- light blue wavy surface Plexiglass

WATERFALL- transparent styrene sheet with strokes of light blue ink

MODEL WATERFALL

Oceans and Streams

Oceans and streams are generally considered as moving water and can be simulated with a solid, wavy plane of colored Plexiglass, available in many colors excellent for representing moving bodies of water at any scale.

A stream of water can be simulated by gluing a crumpled piece of plastic wrap to a sheet of colored paper or plastic film. The paper or film is cut in the shape of the stream in plan and the wrap is glued to it with spray glue.

ROCKS- *pea gravel bought at aquarium supply store*

STREAM ON MODEL

wavy plastic wrap

BOULDERS—
- *aquarium rocks*

WATER —
- *wavy blue Plexiglass*

BOATS —
- *white plastic store bought*

MARINA MODEL

AUTOMOBILES

Automobiles are an excellent means of adding scale to a model. The viewer immediately associates the size of the car to the scale of the model. They can be attached to the baseboard by applying white glue to the tires and setting them on a street or driveway. They can be built by the model maker out of paper or matboard, or bought at model and hobby supply stores.

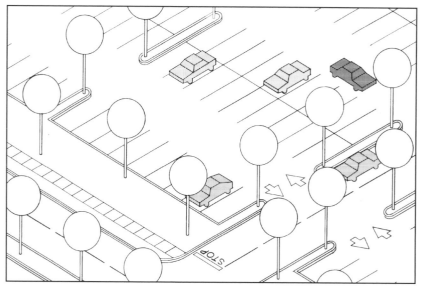

Automobiles are an excellent means of adding scale to a model.

Store-Bought Cars

Autos are best represented on a model with the store bought type which are available at architectural model supply stores and hobby stores. The cars are exact replicas and add a professional appearance to the model. It is very important that you select a car that is exactly the scale of the model. If it is too large or too small it will appear obviously out of scale and distract from the design intent. Take your architectural scale with you to the store and measure the car before you buy it to make sure it is the correct size. Some of the cars are constructed in metric scale so try to come as close as possible to your model scale. The cars can be removed from one model and used on another, saving you time and money.

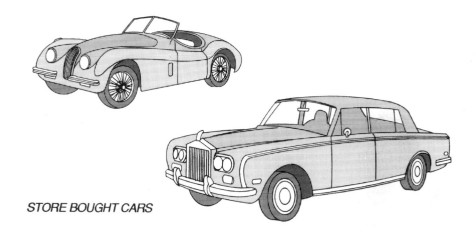

STORE BOUGHT CARS

hinged joints

HINGED MATBOARD CAR

HINGED PAPER CAR

headlights and
steering wheel
drawn in pencil

FRONT   SIDE   REAR

CAR ELEVATIONS

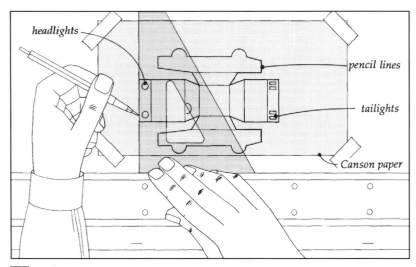

headlights

pencil lines

tailights

Canson paper

1a *Attach a sheet of Canson paper to your cutting board and draw the car pattern.*

Automobiles: *Paper Construction*

Autos can also be constructed with paper or matboard. These types are excellent for schematic models and student final presentation models. Various parts of the car (headlights, tail lights, steering wheel, etc.) can be drawn on in pencil or ink, and they can be painted any color you desire. Utilizing the 'hinged joint' construction technique a car can be built with Canson paper or any heavyweight paper at 1/8" or 1/4" scale. Let's look at how to construct a paper car:

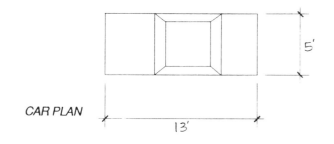

CAR PLAN

5'

13'

Step 1 Draw car pattern onto paper.

With the sheet of Canson paper, any color you wish the car to be, already attached to your cutting board with drafting tape, you are ready to draw the car pattern. Using your pencil and triangle, draw the car in plan at the model scale with its elevations adjacent as illustrated. (The car illustrated on this page is drawn at 1/8" scale if you would like to trace or photocopy it). We will be cutting out the car pattern and creating hinged joints wherever possible. Take note that the sloped glass dimensions need to be measured from the elevations as illustrated, and used on the actual roof plan. (Il. 1b)

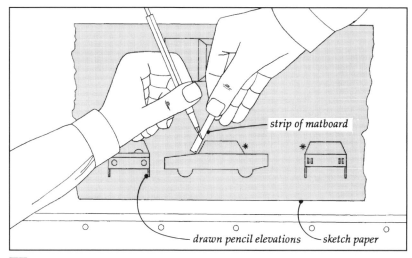

1b *Measure your sloping lines from the elevations when drawing the pattern in plan.*

Step 2 *Perform scoreline cuts.*

With the use of your Xacto knife and triangle perform your scoreline cuts as illustrated. Cut only half-way through the paper. The scorelines with an * adjacent to them indicates scores that must be performed on the backside of the pattern. Perform these after you have the pattern cut out. Once the score lines are completed use your Xacto knife and triangle to cut out the pattern along the outside perimeter line.

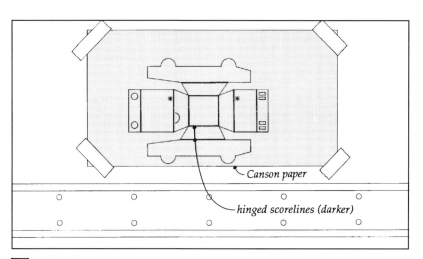

2 *Perform the score cuts on this side of the pattern.*

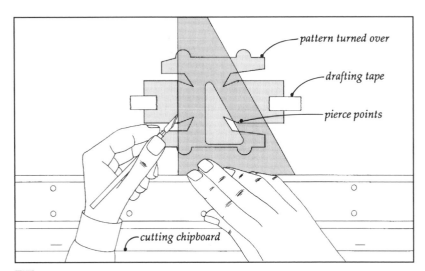

3 | Turn the pattern over and perform the score cuts on that side.

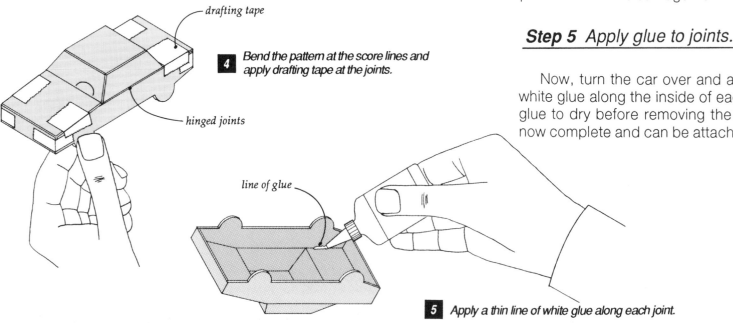

4 | Bend the pattern at the score lines and apply drafting tape at the joints.

5 | Apply a thin line of white glue along each joint.

Step 3 *Perform scoreline cuts on the back.*

With the pattern separated from the taped down sheet, turn it over and perform the remaining scorelines. Since the guidelines are drawn on the front side make a pierce point with an Xacto knife at each end of the scoreline on the backside to see where to set your triangle.

Step 4 *Bend at scorelines and apply tape to joints.*

Smooth down the flaired edges with your fingernail and bend the paper at each scoreline. Bend the hinged joints until the car can stand by itself. Apply small strips of drafting tape at the intersecting planes to hold the car together while glue is applied.

Step 5 *Apply glue to joints.*

Now, turn the car over and apply a thin line of white glue along the inside of each joint. Allow the glue to dry before removing the tape. Your car is now complete and can be attached to your model.

PARKING LOTS

Parking lots and driveways are best simulated with colored paper or matboard, and are appropriate for both schematic and final presentation models. The color selected should depend on whether the paving is concrete or asphalt. Parking lot graphics (striping, arrows, and handicapped symbols, etc.) can be drawn on the paving with colored pencils providing a very realistic appearance. Let's look at some paving materials and how to simulate them.

Concrete and Asphalt

Concrete is best simulated with white or light grey paper or matboard. The paper can be laminated to your baseboard with spray adhesive and is best applied before your building is attached. If matboard is used as the top layer of your baseboard then you don't have to laminate paper to it, your building and parking lot graphics are applied on top of it. If the scale of the model is 1/8" or larger, a pencil stippling can be added to the concrete finish to give it a more realistic appearance.

Asphalt is best represented with dark grey or black paper or matboard. Parking lot graphics contrast very well with these darker tones.

Parking Lot Graphics

Parking lot and street graphics add scale and a more realistic appearance to a model. Striping, directional arrows, and handicapped symbols can be drawn onto the paving with a white or yellow pencil and straightedge. Since it is difficult to erase the colored pencil marks from the paving if you make a mistake, I recommend drawing light guidelines first with your drafting pencil. Sharpen the colored pencils frequently to get sharp clean lines. The directional arrows can be drawn with a template available at graphic arts supply stores.

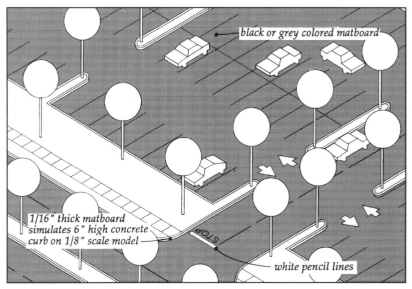

black or grey colored matboard

1/16" thick matboard simulates 6" high concrete curb on 1/8" scale model

white pencil lines

Parking lots can be simulated with either colored paper or matboard.

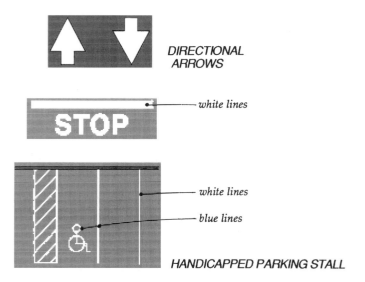

DIRECTIONAL ARROWS

white lines

STOP

white lines

blue lines

HANDICAPPED PARKING STALL

Parking lot graphics are best simulated by drawing them with a white or yellow pencil.

HUMAN FIGURES

Human figures can be constructed out of matboard or Foamcore, or can be bought at hobby and architectural model supply stores in many different scales. Let's look more closely at the various methods of construction.

Foamcore Construction

Human figures constructed of Foamcore are best used on schematic models 1/4" scale and larger. Due to their crude nature they are also not recommended on final presentations. They are constructed in the same manner as matboard. Also, note that to bend the arms and legs in opposite directions one side of the Foamcore must be scored, as is also the case with matboard construction.

Paper Construction

Figures constructed of a heavyweight paper, such as Canson paper, are best used on schematic and final presentation models 1/16" scale and smaller. Since they are so small the viewer cannot see the cutting flaws, making them appropriate for final presentations. They are also constructed in the same manner as matboard, but the arm and leg joints do not need to be scored to be bent.

Store Bought Figures

Human figures can be bought at architectural model and hobby stores in many different scales. They are excellent for schematic and final presentation models since they have actual human features. They can be attached to the model baseboard with white glue.

Perform the cuts in the numbered sequence.

—Foamcore board

1/4" SCALE FOAMCORE FIGURE

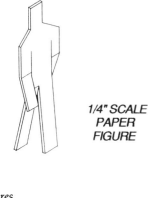

1/4" SCALE PAPER FIGURE

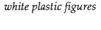

white plastic figures

STORE BOUGHT PLASTIC HUMAN FIGURE

plastic flange is provided to insert into baseboard

Photograph Construction

Human figures can also be cut out of photographs to realistically simulate people on schematic and final presentation models of any scale. The photographs can be cut out of a magazine or 'staged' by the model maker.

Staged photographs can be taken of people standing or walking on the sidewalk. If taken with an instant camera the size of the figures can be measured right away to make sure they are the correct size for the scale of the model. Otherwise you must wait for the pictures to be developed to see if you have the right size figures. Its a fun method for the model maker and his friends to get into the finished model. If the photographs are too flimsy to stand up by themselves they can be laminated to matboard before the figures are cut out.

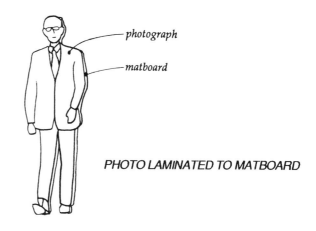

— *photograph*

— *matboard*

PHOTO LAMINATED TO MATBOARD

BOATS AND PLANES

Boats and planes may be necessary for an airport or marina model and are best simulated with plastic store bought components. They can be bought at architectural model supply stores and are available in various scales. They are attached to the model with white glue.

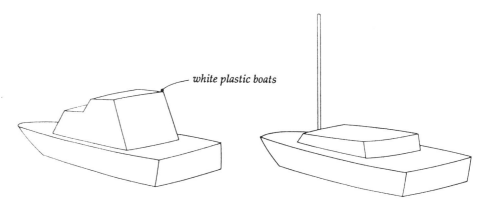

white plastic boats

STORE BOUGHT PLASTIC BOATS

As you can see, there are many ways to simulate landscaped components on a model. As with building components, many more can be found in catalogs and by simply browsing around craft stores. Use your imagination to come up with more.

AFTERWORD

I wrote this book in order to share my knowledge and experience of model making with every individual who wants to express their ideas in a three-dimensional form. I have not held back any secrets. Please help me improve the book for future editions by sending me your comments on ways to make it better. What techniques can be explained in a better way? What other methods of construction can be used to construct a component? What interior, building, or land-scaping components that were not addressed in this book would you like to see in the next book? Each and every one of your comments will be personally reviewed by me and in appreciation for taking the time to help make the next book better, your name will appear in the next editions' acknowledgements.

Hopefully, after reading and working with this book you have gained the self confidence necessary to construct models you will be proud to show your instructor and classmates. There is no better means of expressing a design concept than through a three-dimensional object that you can literally touch and shape into any form you desire. The model, or the building that it represents, is a sculpture that you create. So go now and create your dreams, and have fun doing it.

Thank You,
G. Matthew Buckles

Index